Python Debugging

RL Zimmerman

Look Inside

Learn the difference between data structures and explore range and generator objects. Chapter 3 looks at lists, tuples, strings, dictionaries, zips, maps, sets, and filters.

- Add
- Update
- Remove or replace characters with slicing and functions
- Delete
- Sort (with multiple values)
- Copy objects & remove duplicate objects with "sets"
- Split & combine objects
- Change type
- Search objects
- Comparisons

Save time and simplify your code. Learn about time-saving functions like namedtuples, Counters, and defaultdicts. We'll also look at zip, map, and filter functions, as well as lambda expressions and comprehensions. Because comprehensions are powerful, I've included several detailed examples.

- A simple lambda expression
- A lambda expression with map()
- A dictionary comprehension
- Zip and unzip using zip() and unpacking with zip
- Two list comprehension examples

Lab Experiments. In Chapter 6, you'll work with objects in the interactive Console, Debug Mode, Variable Explorer, and Editor. Here you'll also see the specific indexing syntax, which varies between strings, lists, tuples, or dictionaries. We'll also dig into how you can find critical information about any function.

- What is the object value or type?
- Use len() to find how many items are in non-scalar object.
- What arguments does a function expect?
- What are unpacking operators?

- What does the function do?
- What does the function return?

Compound objects are more complex to index and copy. Work along with the step-by-step examples to build the "Elements in a Dictionary" example. The multi-level lists and tuples use indexing to walk through items. The topic, "Indexing Elements in Nested Lists" has five pages of charts and detailed examples. We'll also explore shallow and deep copy behavior of multi-dimensional compound objects.

Review scope diagrams for recursive function calls and walk through five memory stacks analyzing values within each scope. Use the locals() and globals() functions with Variable Explorer to watch local, global, and enclosing scope change with three nested functions and a global variable.

Table of Contents

3. Python Basics

4. Debugging Tools

1. Introduction

The primary goal of this book is to learn the simple basics of debugging a Python script. Debugging is the process of finding and removing "bugs" or defects in a program. Debugging is also useful in quickly getting your code to run in the first place! Chapter 3 presents "Python Basics" because a big part of debugging is knowing the correct syntax for a particular object and task. This book doesn't try to cover all the nuances of Python but does cover the terms and syntax you're likely to encounter in your first few weeks or months of programming. The overhead and clutter are gone, leaving behind clear and simple instructions.

Code examples are self-contained, so you can copy and paste them into your IDE and run the program. There are certainly more elegant ways to do many of these tasks, but I wanted to demonstrate each concept with a working piece of code limited to a few lines. In Chapter 3, we'll look at the following topics and more.

- Functions, Lists, Dictionaries, Tuples, Ranges, Comprehensions
- Indexing, Slicing, Comparison Operators, Control Statements

When looking at concepts such as indexing, slicing, scope, or recursive functions, I've included lots of diagrams. We'll look at syntax relevant to each type of object. For example, to add to a "list," you could use 'append,' 'join' or 'extend' methods. While adding a new key:value pair to a dictionary is straightforward, adding to an existing dictionary is not. In this scenario, it's not about the value of the object in the key:value pair, but more about the "type" of object in the key:value pair. Once you know the type of the dictionary object, you'll use the corresponding methods to add or change values, whether it's a "list," "string," "tuple," or even another dictionary.

There are dozens of code examples, and I tried to use real-world examples. Between the detailed Table of Contents and extensive Index, I hope you can quickly find what you're looking for. The Index includes common phrases for those times when you don't know the technical term. For example, to find a string in Python, you could use the "in" comparison operator. Whether you look for "find," "search" or "locate," the Index refers you to the "in" comparison operator. The examples are varied so you can work with different types of data, such as:

XML

HTML

matplotlib (plots/charts/graphs)

OS (files/directories)

*.txt, *.csv

user input

URL

datetime

To help my daughter with her first Python class, I looked around for debugging information that I could share with her. I wanted a simple guide with everything in one place and suggestions for how to go about the process of debugging. Initially, my research focused on gathering examples of common issues, but I knew something was missing. After all, what happens if there is no example of the "bug" that you're experiencing?

I knew I needed to provide a debugging "foundation." Not just how to use debugging tools, but when to take action and why. With that goal in mind, Chapters 1 through 6 build a debugging arsenal, so you're ready to tackle the examples in Chapter 7. Each example has "References" to the related topics covered in earlier chapters. So theoretically, you could jump right into the examples in Chapter 7.

I also made a point to cross-reference topics so you can easily locate whatever you're interested in from any point in the material. This approach means you can pick up the book at any time and quickly jump back in where you left off. Or, if you prefer, you can hop around from topic to topic with as much detail as you want.

Hopefully, after reading this book, you won't feel like this man who posted a plea for help on a chat board. His frustration show's through in his comment, "For the love of God, how is this done?" Instead, you'll know exactly how it's done and have fun doing it!

1.1 Overview

How you may ask, are we going to build your debugging arsenal? Let's begin with these topics.

- How to use the debug environment.
- The Python Error Codes and specific examples of how they happen.
- Step-by-step instructions on the process of debugging code.
- Finding the information you need to **modify your program**: help on Syntax, Functions, Classes, and more.

The goal of debugging is a working program, and debugging is just part of writing code. When I realize I have a "bug," I'll experiment and try a few things to find a clue where the issue is. You'll see this process in the examples in Chapter 7, where I use different approaches from my "debugging toolbox" to isolate an issue. You might take a different approach to the sample problem, and there is no wrong approach. The idea is to try a few things and see what works.

In this book, I demonstrate Python using the open-source "Anaconda Data Science Distribution" that includes Python version 3.7. Spyder, the Scientific Python Development Environment, comes with Anaconda. The Spyder IDE, or Integrated Design Environment, includes an Editor, Console, and debugging tools. You may notice slight differences in screenshots, depending on whether I am using Spyder on my Windows or Mac computer.

1.2 What This Book is About

My intent in writing this book is to provide a guide to debugging Python with Anaconda's Spyder application and IDE. Python debugging concepts apply equally to other IDEs, but the screens and debugging tools may vary slightly. I found it difficult to explain an IndexError without first explaining data structures and their indexes. Similarly, a Dictionary KeyError doesn't mean much without an understanding of a Dictionary. Syntax errors are fairly obvious in Spyder, but it doesn't hurt to have a brief explanation of the syntax the parser expects. Chapter 3 has many examples and details of the basic Python language, and is a wonderful reference.

Finally, Chapter 6 demonstrates how to view values, types, and the length of objects. Since the syntax varies by the type of object, I wanted to provide a reference with the exact syntax for each object type.

1.3 What's Next?

The next chapter walks you through installing Anaconda and the basic Spyder environment. We'll also look at an overall plan for debugging code. You can download sample code at:

https://github.com/cryoung6/Python_Coding_One_Year_Later

2. Debugging Overview

In this chapter, we discuss

Writing code begins with your vision of what the program should do. You write code, see what happens, and make changes along the way. When the code doesn't do what you want, debugging helps you zero in on what's happening while the code runs. In essence, you can pause program execution and "freeze" your program at that point in time, looking at variable and object values at that moment.

This chapter outlines a few suggestions to approach programming and debugging. The Examples in Chapter 7 follow a similar methodology.

Intended Outcome: What I wanted the program to do.

Actual Result: What the program did.

Incorrect Code: A look at the code before any changes.

Debugging Experiment: What I suspect is wrong with the program and the steps I tried to "debug" what the program is doing.

How to Resolve the Issue: A brief description of the change to the code to achieve my "Intended Outcome."

Correct Code: The finished code that works as I intended.

2.1 Plan for Debugging

Programming is not my primary job. Instead, programming is a tool I use for data mining or organizing projects. A day in my programming life includes lots of interruptions. It may be weeks or months before I pick up a project and continue coding. For this reason, I've adopted a few suggestions from programming friends to make my life easier.

1. Work on small chunks of code, test, and then move on to the next piece.
2. Keep multiple backup versions of your files.
3. Have a clear idea of what you want your program to do.
4. Use small data file samples that you know have clean data to develop your code. When you've tested your code and are confident there are no bugs, use live data connections or real data files.
5. Keep notes of where you stopped programming and the next steps.

Start Small

Write small chunks of code. Test and validate that piece of code, then move on. This "**Correct Code**" is also a good baseline for backups.

Keep Multiple Versions of Your Code

Keep multiple backup versions of your files. My backup files often include the date and time in the filename. That way, if I really mess up the code, I can easily go back to the "**Correct Code**" that worked earlier today or last month. The Chapter 4 topic, "Backups," has a sample Python script to backup files every five minutes.

Intended Outcome

While I'm not suggesting you have a vision statement for your program, it doesn't hurt to have an "**Intended Outcome**" of what you're trying to accomplish. This synopsis is beneficial in several ways:

- Pair programming or asking for another opinion.
- When you check-in your code to a source control program.
- During peer review.
- In a Sprint Review, where you demonstrate your program to others.

In case you reach out to another programmer for assistance, share as much information as possible.

1. The incorrect code. If you have the last working version of your code, that might also be helpful.
2. Your **Debugging Experiment** methodology and what you've already tried.
3. The "Actual Result." What happens when you run the program?

Computational Complexity

While writing code, strive for efficient programs. Sometimes my program runs as expected, except that it takes too long to complete because it's inefficient. Chapter 4 looks at several ways to identify timing bottlenecks. Let's look at three simple ways to improve run time.

- Working with a *.txt file, I could import the file each time, which is straightforward, but it's more efficient to import the file into a dictionary and reuse the dictionary.
- It's more efficient to "update" a list than make a copy of a list or use a "generator" to retrieve list data; this is especially true if you have a large list of potentially millions of elements.
- When looking up data in a list several times, use a sorted list. However, if I only use the data one time, the cost of sorting the list just adds overhead to my program.

When discussing the relationship of running time to the size of data, programmers use asymptotic notation. "Big O" is a common form of asymptotic notation to refer to algorithmic complexity. Evaluate programs looking at these scenarios.

- Best-case
- Expected-case
- Worst-case

Count each "operation," taking into account loops and nested loops.

- Comparisons
- Mathematical operations
- Assignments
- Accessing objects in memory

Constant running time, **O(1)**, is more efficient than other operations and does not change based on the size of data input. One example of constant complexity is a simple mathematical operation like **2.02 * 3.03**. There may be loops or recursive calls in the code, but the data input size does not affect constant running time.

Logarithmic running time, **O(log n)**, increases based on the size of the data. A bisection search that divides itself in half is an example of logarithmic complexity.

Linear complexity, **O(n)**, is based on each element "n." For example, printing a list is based on the length of the list.

With this brief introduction to computational complexity, you may decide to pursue an in-depth exploration of the subject.

Testing

To simplify testing, I'll often break my functions into external *.py files and later combine them as needed. I write a small "test script" that creates variables and invokes the function. For example, a function **menu()** takes **mydictionary** as an argument - or menu(**mydictionary**).

For testing purposes, I only need a **mydictionary** object with a few elements. To create a dictionary for testing purposes, first, I run the main program that creates **mydictionary**. Then, in the Console, I type **mydictionary**. The Console prints out all the values so I can copy a smaller subset of data for a test version of **mydictionary**. In my test script, I use the data in an assignment statement for the "test" dictionary.

In Chapter 4, the topic "Test Objects" demonstrates this concept and code to create a dictionary with many elements.

Test Data Files

Web scraping and external data files can be messy and huge. Take a moment to familiarize yourself with samples of the live data or data dumps. Make small "test data files" or mock-ups of the data. Scrub the data to ensure it's clean.

If you plan to code for blank data, hidden characters, or type conversions, set aside a version of the data for that purpose. Initially, keep the test data as simple as possible. Use these test data files to save time iterating through thousands (or millions) of rows of data.

Look for hidden characters and blank cells or data elements. Make notes of data types and other issues as a reminder. Later you can add logic to your code to handle the data correctly.

Often, when you dump database data to a CSV or Excel file, there is an error when you try to open the file. For example, as you open an Excel file, the app prompts you to "fix" data. I always open my data files at least once and "clear" all rows that appear empty to avoid hidden characters.

Chapter 4 has an example of a mock-up HTML data file in the topic "Create Test Data."

Plan for Tomorrow

When you're done for the day or decide to take a break, leave a note for yourself of where you stopped. Include what is or is not working and what you want to do next.

Review your pseudocode and **Intended Outcome** to be sure you're on the right track. Pseudocode is an outline of your program design in simple terms, often written in plain English. Pseudocode notes remind me of where I left off programming and what I need to work on next.

2.2 Debugging Steps

In some ways, debugging is more of an art than science. Since I'm analytical, I am more inclined to use the scientific method for my debugging. It's really up to you to decide on your debugging style and if you'll use any of these suggestions.

1. When debugging, keep a **logbook** of your experiments, so you know what you've already tried.
2. Divide and conquer. Divide the code in half and test each half to see which part has the error. Repeat these steps to drill down to the location with the error.
3. Make a backup of your files before starting your experiments.
4. Start with a clear **Problem Statement** of the defect.
5. Don't believe everything you hear. If the initial defect is that the program works with Oracle data and not Cassandra data, verify that is really the case.
6. Examine the environment.
7. Create a list of possible suspects.
8. If you're out of ideas and haven't found the defect, take a break. Work on something else, go for a walk, or come back to the problem tomorrow.

Logbook

Keep a logbook of your debugging experiments. Write down the steps and outcome for each task. Writing down my issues frees my mind from worrying about the problem and allows me to brainstorm at my leisure.

Divide and Conquer

When debugging, pick a logical point to divide the code in half. Use a process of elimination to drill down to the error in the code.

1. Divide the program into **Part 1 Code** and **Part 2 Code**.
2. Run **Part 1 Code**. If there are no errors, you know that Part 1 is working. If you have errors, divide **Part 1 Code** again. Repeat the process until you drill down to the root cause.
3. If **Part 1 Code** ran without errors, run **Part 2 Code**. If you find an error, divide **Part 2 Code** and repeat the steps.

Wherever possible, eliminate the code that is unrelated to the error. Chapter 4 has an example of skipping unrelated code in the topic "Focused Testing."

Backup Files Before Debugging

Create a backup of your files before you change anything.

Problem Statement

Develop a clear problem statement with as much detail as possible. Who can you contact for more details? When determining how critical the issue is, consider the impact on business and if there is a workaround.

Doubt Everything

Verify the accuracy of the original defect report by recreating the issue yourself.

Look Around Your Environment

Before creating a list of possible causes, gather background on the environment.

1. Has the program ever worked?
2. When was the last time the program ran successfully?
   - Did it work last month?
   - Is this the first time it ran on a Monday or the first day of the month?
   - Is there a heavy load on the environment because it's the end of the month or quarter?
3. Can you connect to devices outside of the program successfully? Can you query the Cassandra database outside of your program? Is the webserver responding to requests? Is one of the integrated systems down?
4. If the program is OK on your machine, and doesn't work on a user's machine, look at what is different. Could it be a timing error caused by the user's slower machine? Is the user working remotely or running other conflicting applications?
5. Did the program encounter an Out of Memory error?

Create a List of Suspects

As a starting point for your experiments, make a list of components that could be causing the defect.

- Your app
- The last few lines of code you changed, or the line(s) just before the code causing an "exception"
- Reset memory and run your code again to ensure your variables are correct
- Python language
- OS
- Connection to a web page
- The format of a database table or web page changed
- Is there a scope issue? Draw a diagram of the scope and namespace variables as outlined in Chapter 3.
- Does the program produce the desired outcome?
- Does the program work except on the first day of the month?
- Does the program take too long to run? (Look at the algorithmic complexity of your code).
- Are there two libraries with the same name in different directories? Does one of your script files have the same name as a library or module?

What Do You Think is the Cause?

Chances are, at this point, you have some idea where you want to start your investigation. Make a list of your ideas or hypothesis of what might be wrong.

Refine Your Experiment

As you refine your **Debugging Experiment**, you'll probably notice parts of the code you don't need to test. Your goal is to narrow the search by removing things that don't contribute to your hypothesis. Chapter 4 has an example that narrows your search in the topic "Focused Testing." Modify your program to eliminate these items temporarily from your experiment. Consider hard coding values or using temporary mock-ups of data.

Experiment

Change one thing at a time, and observe what happens. Please, write everything down in your logbook, noting each step and the outcome. The simple act of writing down my experiment forces me to pause and consider what happened and why.

- What steps did you take?
- What did you expect to happen?
- What actually happened?

Review the experiment and see if you can develop a theory about the cause of the defect.

- Is there something you should not see?
- Do you need to refine your experiment further?
- Do you have a theory about what might be causing the defect?
- Do all your test results fit in with your theory, or is there one result that doesn't quite fit? Don't ignore the evidence that contradicts your theory. If you aren't sure how that piece of code works, dig into the code because that might be where the problem lies.

Keep a log of the things you've tried as you debug your program to avoid repeating the same tests.

Success at Last

The last experiment you conduct that unequivocally works is the fix. The program does what you want, and you reach your "**Intended Outcome**."

2.3 The Debugging Environment

For this book, I am using the Anaconda Distribution that includes the Spyder application. My Anaconda programs support Python 3.7.

Python

Python is an open-source (free) programming language for Web Development, GUI development, Scientific and Numeric data science, Software

Development, and System Administration. The examples use the open-source Anaconda Data Science Distribution that includes Python version 3.7.

Spyder, the Scientific Python Development Environment, comes with Anaconda, and I run Python scripts in Spyder primarily on a Windows machine. For variety, I've also included several examples on a MAC computer.

In this chapter, we'll install Anaconda and set up your environment. If you are familiar with Python and want to jump into debugging, feel free to skip ahead to Chapter 4.

Anaconda

Download the Anaconda Distribution that includes Python version 3.7. Other Python versions may vary slightly compared to the examples in this manual. When prompted, update your path settings. The install takes a while, so you might want to grab a cup of coffee or something.

Spyder

Spyder is an Integrated Desktop Environment or IDE. Spyder includes an Editor, Console or Spyder Shell, Variable Explorer, Help module, and other tools. These modules are displayed in "Panes" in Spyder.

On a Windows machine, launch Spyder from the Start Menu in the Anaconda folder. On a MAC computer, open the Anaconda Navigator and launch "Spyder."

A Spyder layout with three panes is shown below. You can return to the default layout at any time from the View menu under Windows - Layouts. You can close or open other panes to suit your preferences.

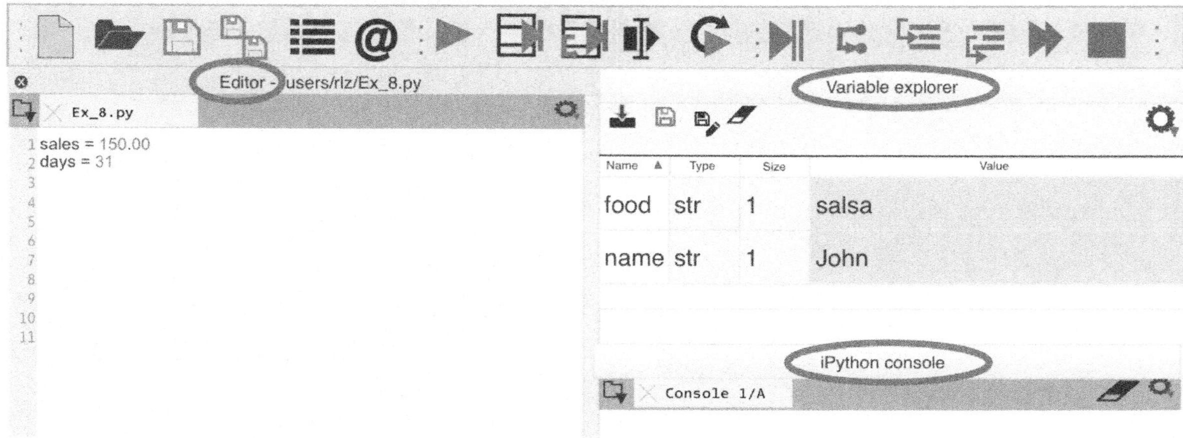

Figure 2.1 Spyder

1. The **Editor** pane is where you type your code and create your script files.
2. The **Variable Explorer** pane lists variables in the current program scope after you run the code.
3. The iPython **Console** or Python shell is located in the lower right panel by default. When you start Spyder, the Console prompt is **In[1]:**.
4. When you click "Run," ▶ the results are output to the Console. When you type a command in the Console, Python immediately runs the command. The Console is useful when debugging or experimenting with different statements for your code.
5. Results displayed in the Console include code output and error messages. For example, if you use the print() method, the results are output to the Console window. In the example below, the **Console** displays "**Welcome to Project1.1.py**."

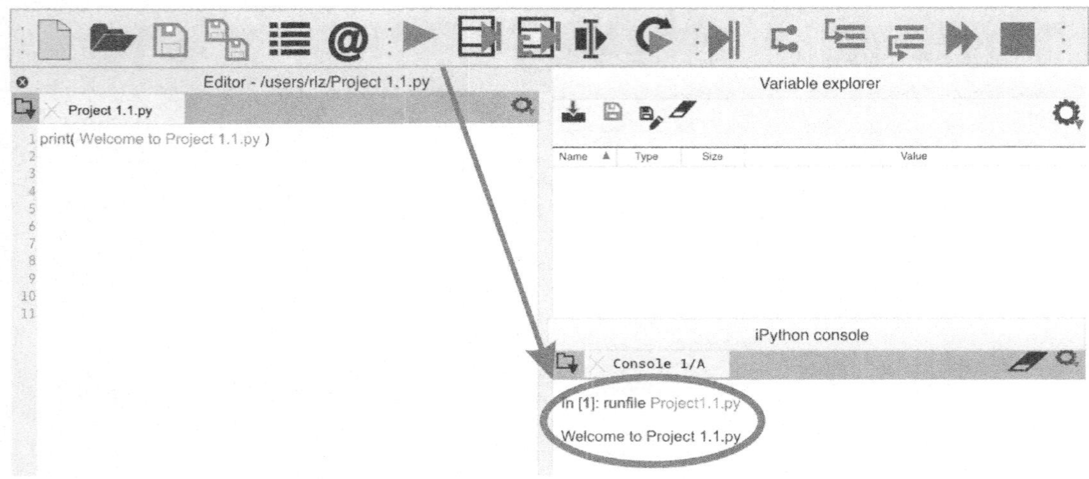

Figure 2.2 The iPython Console

6. The Help pane displays syntax, function help, and more.

Run a Script or Program

With Spyder open, click on the File menu to "Open" or create a "new" script file. In the next example, the "*Ex_8.py*" file is open in the Editor.

Click on the green arrow ▶ or use the **Run** menu, as shown below.

Figure 2.3 Run the Program

In the Run menu, select "Run selection or current line" to run only the selected lines of code.

In the next figure, I have three panes open. The Editor is on the left, and the **Console** window is on the right. Initially, the **Console** window displays the prompt **In [1]:**. After I click "**Run**," the Console window changes, as shown below. The first output line displays the name of the program file and the working directory.

'/Users/hlz/Python_Coding/CODE/Ex_1.py',

```
In [1]:   runfile('/users/hlz/Python_Coding/CODE/Ex_1.py',
wdir='C:/Python_lab1/Project1')
150.00 31

In [2]:
```

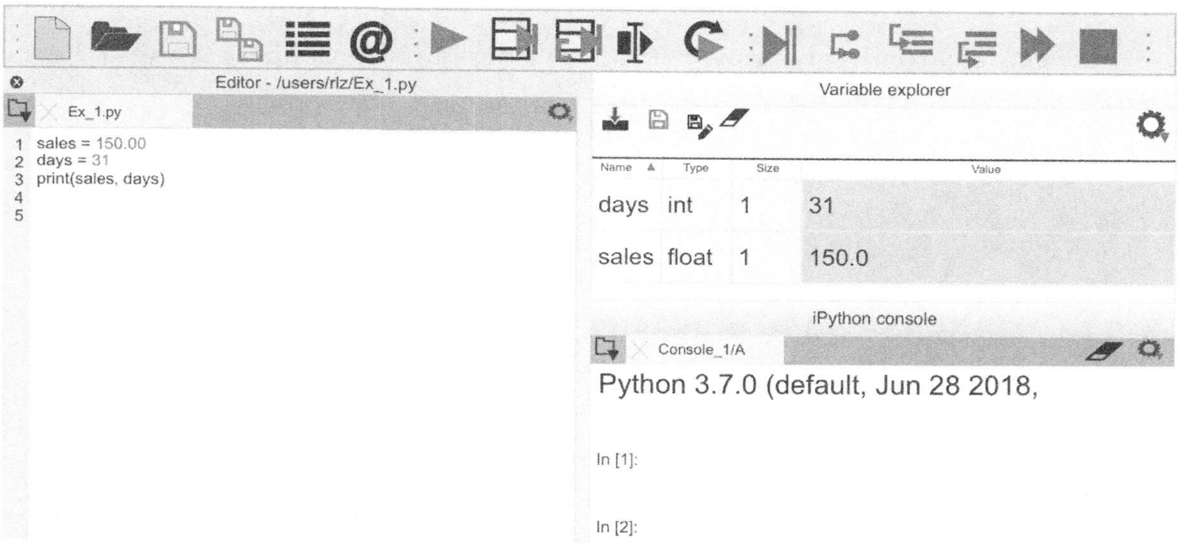

Figure 2.4 The Console

Stop a Program or Restart the Kernel

Click within the Console window and *press any key* followed by "Cntrl C" to stop program execution with a keyboard interrupt. You can also select "Restart kernel" from the "**Consoles**" menu.

Adding a "**break**" statement to your code causes program execution within that code block to stop. For example, if you are inside a loop, the "break" statement halts the loop, exits the loop, and continues running the next code block.

2.4 Help

In Spyder, click on the **View** menu and click "Panes" to open the "Help" pane. Now, click on the **Help** menu and click on "Spyder Tutorial." The tutorial opens in the Help pane. The topic "Recommended first steps for Python beginners" is an excellent resource for new programmers.

Chapter 4 demonstrates Debug Mode, Interactive Mode, and Variable Explorer. These tools look at your code while it's running, in effect, "debugging."

To open Help for an object, place the cursor on an object name in the **Editor**, press Ctrl-I or Command-I on a MAC. Help inspects the object and gathers docstring information.

2.5 What's Next?

Your Lab environment is now setup. Let's move on to Chapter 3 and review a few basic Python language guidelines.

3. Python Basics

In this Chapterwe discuss

Python Syntax
Objects
Immutable Objects
Variables
Expressions
Types of Data
Numbers
Data Structures
Strings
Lists
Methods for Lists
Tuple
Dictionary
Range
Generators
Set
collections
Indexes
Slicing
Operators
Identifiers
Compound Statements

Indented Code (a Suite)

Functions & Methods

Classes

Modules & Libraries

Attributes

Scope, Namespace & Memory

Now that your environment is set up, we'll take a brief look at a few basic Python concepts. Syntax and runtime errors often involve incorrect syntax, indentation errors, or a mismatch in object types. This chapter is by no means a complete Python language guide; instead, think of it as an abbreviated part of the Python language documentation. I need this small subset of information to demonstrate how you will refer back to the Python documentation as you debug your program. The "Appendix - References" at the end of this book has links to the Python documentation related to these topics.

3.1 Python Syntax

The Spyder Integrated Development Environment (IDE) includes an **Editor** that warns you when you have a syntax error in your script. A yellow triangle on the left side of the Editor pane next to the line number indicates an error. Next, we'll look at a few common causes of syntax errors. The python.org site has the **PEP** documents, or Python Enhancement Proposals.

- Valid characters for variable names or identifiers vary between Python 2.x and Python 3.x. Python 3 added support for Unicode characters in PEP 3131 to accommodate programmers who are unfamiliar with the English language. To avoid errors, I adhere to these guidelines.
    - Identifiers begin with a letter.
    - Numbers are allowed in object names, except as the first character. Object names are also known as identifiers.
    - In Python 2.x, the only special character allowed in an identifier name is an underscore. Instead of spaces in identifier names, try an underscore. Illegal spaces or characters like $, #, and @ will cause a syntax error, as shown in Example 7.12 in Chapter 7.
- The PEP 8 Style Guide suggests lowercase characters for identifier names and functions. A PEP is a design document providing information to the

Python community. Classes begin with an uppercase letter. For example, variables and list names are lowercase.

- Python is case sensitive. There is a difference between "myString" and "mystring." The Python Interpreter displays a NameError when there is a misspelled identifier, as shown in Example 7.10 in Chapter 7.
- When defining a function or control statement, the line should always end with a colon.
- Text to the right of the # hash character is a comment. You can add comments anywhere in the line.
- A data structure name should be plural, and items in the data set should be singular. For example, a **List** named "vacations" with List items: vacation[0], vacation[1], etc.
- Do not use reserved keywords as identifiers. Example 7.16 in Chapter 7 has a misspelled keyword. Example 7.43 uses the reserved keyword "str" incorrectly. A missing keyword in a function call also causes a SyntaxError, as shown in Example 7.37. Functions also have keyword arguments.
- An empty Suite (indented block of code) is illegal. See "Indented Code (Suite)" or Example 7.7 for more information.

Python has reserved **keywords** like "global" or "try." When you use a keyword as a variable name, it causes a syntax error. To see keywords, in the Console type **help("keywords")**.

These Chapter 7 examples illustrate a few syntax errors: Example 7.7, 7.8, 7.9, 7.10, 7.11, 7.12, and 7.16.

Referencing Object Values

To begin you may ask, "How do I get the value inside a variable." At any time, you can type the object name in the Console, and the Python Interpreter will display the value at that moment. Here my variable "mystr" has a value of "apple."

In [**1**]: mystr

Out[1]: apple

Chapters 3 and 6 walk you through examples with the syntax for the various objects, including items inside data structures or objects from imported modules or libraries.

Variables in Imported Modules

To reference a class attribute or a variable inside another module, use dotted notation. In this script, I import a module "mymodule2" that has the variable "mystr2." The expression **module2.mystr2** returns the value of **mystr2**.

```
import mymodule2
print(mymodule2.mystr2)
```

3.2 Objects

The building blocks of Python are objects. Objects have an identity, type, and value and are Python's abstraction for data.

- Data with state
- Defined behavior (methods)

State refers to the properties of an object, the attributes or value of the object. The object's behavior is how the Python Interpreter interacts with that type of object.

The "identifier" or "identity" of the object is the "name" of the object. With the library "**openpyxl**," you assign **objects** to both the workbook and worksheet, and then you use those **objects** with **methods** to read or update values (the data). In this example "wb2" is the name of the workbook. There is also a unique "identifier" associated with the object "wb2." In the next topic we'll look at a variable "bfr" and bfr's identifier.

```
from openpyxl import load_workbook
wb2 = load_workbook('myfile.xlsx', data_only = True)
ws2 = wb2["ExportedData"]
```

3.3 Immutable Objects

In Python strings, numbers, and "tuple" types are immutable, meaning the values are fixed and can't change. While you can **not** change existing strings, numbers (integers or floats) or tuples, you can create new objects with changed data to replace objects.

If you're new to programming, this concept may seem strange. Take the case of a Python object of the type "**int**." The code statement **bfr = bfr + 1** seems to change the value of **bfr**. In reality, this statement creates a new object. The new object has a new identifier and a different location in memory. To see this in action, run this code in the **Console** to see the identifiers for the **bfr** objects.

```
In [1]: bfr = 'Hello'
In [2]: print(id(bfr))
Out [2]: 12345678
In [3]: bfr = bfr + 1
In [4]: print(id(bfr))
Out [4]: 9876543210
```

The comparison operator "is" returns "True" when two variables point to the same object in memory, as shown later in the topic "Operators."

Immutable objects are quicker to access and hashable, and this improves code performance. Another advantage of immutable objects is understandability, and knowing the object will never change.

The Python definition of "hashable" is an object that "has a hash value which never changes during its lifetime (it needs a __hash__() method), and can be compared to other objects (it needs an __eq__() method)." We'll look at these special methods at the end of this chapter.

__hash__()

__eq__()

3.4 Variables

In Python, a variable name refers to an object. An object is a place in memory that has a **value** such as a letter or number. An **assignment statement** or "binding" creates a variable and binds or associates the name with an object. The object is a place in memory. *You must have an equal number of variables and values on the left and right side of the assignment statement*. Chapter 7 examples 7.4, 7.41, and 7.50 demonstrate assignment statements.

Python is case sensitive, and mixing case can cause a **NameError** as shown in Example 7.10 in Chapter 7. Special characters like $, #, and @ are not allowed for variable names, and will cause an error as shown in Example 7.12. The left side of an assignment statement must be a variable name, and the right side is a value. The assignment operator is the equals = sign.

mynumber = 2000000

The Python style guide suggests that variable names begin with a letter.

Indirection is using a name to refer to an object. When you add "mynumber" to a list named "mylist," there are two levels of indirection. When a program runs, the **variable** might be assigned a different value; meaning the variable name might be assigned to a different object in memory, or the object itself might be updated.

Global Variables

When you have a variable with a different value than you expected, it may be due to scope. When you run the program, the Python Interpreter creates variables and adds them to the "global scope" or the first memory "stack." While the program execution remains in this suite of code, the objects are also in the "local scope." In Python, you can read, but not change, the value of a global variable at any point in your program or from within functions, as long as everything is within the **same *.py file**.

Each time the code moves into a "function," a new "local" scope is created. Within the local scope of a function, you can't **change** the values of objects in the outer global scope or enclosing scopes. *At any time, you can only change values within the local scope.* When you create objects inside a function or method, those objects or variables are typically not available outside the scope of that function. To change a global variable within a function, use the keyword "global" to make the global variable part of the "local" scope.

We look at scope in detail at the end of this chapter in the topic, "Scope, Namespace, and Memory."

A word of warning about global variables, they are dangerous! It's easy to lose track of which function is updating a global variable. To avoid global variables, try a recursive function and pass the data through an optional function parameter.

> In a bit, we'll look at using a function argument with a default value as another way to implement the concept of a "global variable." There is an example of this process in the "Function" topic "optional arguments" later in this chapter, as well as the topic recursive functions.

In the next diagram, the program has "var1" in the main body of the program (lines 5-7) and "var2" (on line 2) within myfunction().

To explore global variables, run this code in debug mode and step through the code, running one line at a time.

1. The Python Interpreter evaluates the **function definition** on line 1 and quickly moves to line 5. If myfunction() had optional arguments with default values, they are assigned using the "scope" that exists at line 1 (the global scope.)

   If there had been an error within the **function definition**, the interpreter would stop and raise the error.

2. The Python Interpreter then runs line 6.

3. If you choose to "**step into**" myfunction() on line 6, the code moves up to line 1.

4. Next, the code moves inside the function, to lines 2 and 3. At this point, you'll see Variable Explorer displays both var1 and var2.

5. The program then moves back to line 7. At this point, var2 disappears from Variable Explorer, and that "scope" is gone.

```
1  def myfunction():
2      var2 = 4
3      print(var2)
4
5  var1 = 7
6  myfunction()
7  print(var1)
```

In the next block of code, let's explore using "var1" inside of "myfunction." This code runs as expected and prints "var1" on line 2 because I'm not trying to change the value of var1.

```
1 def myfunction():
2     print(var1)
3     var2 = 4
4     print(var2)
5
6
7 var1 = 7
8 myfunction()
9 print(var1)
```

However, it's a different story if I attempt to change "var1" within myfunction(). This next code causes an error and the **Console** displays the UnboundLocalError shown below. The **UnboundLocalError** is raised because "var1" does not exist within the local scope of "myfunction()."

"**UnboundLocalError**" local variable 'var1' referenced before assignment.

```
1 def myfunction():
2     print(var1)
3     var2 = 4
4     var1 = 9
5
6
7 var1 = 7
8 myfunction()
9 print(var1)
```

To prevent the UnboundLocalError use the keyword "global" to declare "var1" a global variable on line 2 inside myfunction(). Notice in the next example there is no "**assignment**" value on line 2. When line 3 prints "var1," it has a value of "7" from the assignment statement for "var1" on line 7 in the main program. Line 5 assigns "9" to the global variable "var1" within the local scope of myfunction(). When line 9 prints "var1," the value is now 9.

You can read more about scope and namespace at the end of this chapter.

```
def myfunction():
        global var1
        print(var1)
        var2 = 4
        var1 = 9


var1 = 7
myfunction()
print(var1)
```

Unpacking

When you **unpack** a tuple or list you assign individual elements to new variables. We'll look at unpacking later in this chapter in the topic, "Functions, Unpacking Operator. In the next example, **mytuple** has four elements. On the second line, I unpack the four tuple elements and assign them to four variables.

```
In [1]: mytuple = (1, 2, 3, 4)
In [2]: myvar1, myvar2, myvar3, myvar4 = mytuple
```

Ignore or Throw Away Variables

Sometimes you'll see code where the underscore character is used when a programmer wants to ignore an element in a tuple or list. These are often called "throw away" variables. In the second statement below, the "2" element is assigned to the underscore _. In the third statement I use the variable "dummy" as a "throw away" variable, which may provide more clarity.

```
a, b, c, d = (1, 2, 3, 4)
a, _, c, d = (1, 2, 3, 4)
a, dummy, c, d = (1, 2, 3, 4)
```

The PEP 3132 "Extended Iterable Unpacking" specifies a "catch-all" name which is assigned to a list of all items not assigned to a "regular" name.

```
a, *b = (1, 2, 3, 4)

a = 1
b = (2, 3, 4)
```

3.5 Expressions

An expression is a piece of syntax that evaluates to some value. The actions that a program takes are referred to as "expressions" or statements. A simple statement is comprised in a single logical line. A compound statement contains groups of other statements; for example: for, with, or while. Objects, literals, names, function calls and operators are combined to form expressions.

<object><operator><object>

myvar = 7

We'll look at comparison operators, compound control statements, and loops later in this Chapter.

Comments

Code comments begin with the hash # symbol.

Joining Lines

Python uses explicit line joining. Expressions that span more than one physical line are joined into logical lines with a backslash.

```
print('the swift fox jumped over the \
lazy dog and then ran into the briar patch.'
```

Python also implements implicit line joining. Expressions in parentheses, square brackets, or curly braces can be split over more than one physical line without using backslashes.

Escape Sequence

Special characters in strings are identified with an "escape sequence" or backslash. For example, the line feed character is '\n' within a string. The Python Interpreter ignores the escape sequence when you add the 'r' prefix, so that the backslash is simply a backslash character.

```
r'c:\users'
```

In the previous example, if you omit the prefix 'r,' a SyntaxError is raised.

SyntaxError: (unicode error) 'unicodeescape' codec can't decode bytes in position 2-3: truncated \uXXXX escape

Apostrophes in strings also use escape sequences, with a backslash as shown below.

mystr = '\''

> In the Editor, when you hover your mouse over a parenthesis, the paired parenthesis is highlighted in green. If a parentheses is missing, the starting parenthesis is highlighted in orange. In Chapter 7, Example 7.8 demonstrates this behavior.

3.6 Types of Data

Python has several types of data. Numeric primitives such as "floats" and "ints" are scalar objects, in that there is no internal structure. A 'bool' and the "None" type are also primitive scalar objects. A string is a non-scalar primitive object, and you use an index to indicate the position within the string. Moving through items using an index is referred to as iteration.

Containers are non-scalar objects with internal structures. Examples of container objects are a list, tuple, dictionary, or range. A range was introduced with Python v3. We'll look at these data structures in-depth in later topics. For now, a few of the basic data types are shown in the next table.

Type	Description	Assignment	Value(s)
int	integer	my_var = 3	3
float	floating-point number	my_var = 3.85	3.85
bool	boolean (true/false)	my_var4 = False	False
NoneType	Function with no return value	myfunction()	None
str	string of characters	my_var2 = 'Hi'	Hi
tuple	any type of data - immutable	mytuple = ('Hi', 4)	Hi, 4
list	any type of data - mutable	mylist = [4, 9, 'hi']	4, 9, hi
range	integers - immutable	range(4, 9)	4, 5, 6, 7, 8

Table 3.1 Data Types

When my_var = 3, the statement **float(my_var+5)** returns **8.0**.

When my_var = 3, the statement **print(34//my_var)** returns **11**.

In the case of the statement **3 == 3**, the Python Interpreter returns "True."

Boolean Values

A boolean value is either "False" or "True" and behaves like the integers 0 and 1 respectively. Therefore, the statement "not 0" is True. In Chapter 7, Example 7.53 encounters a bool error.

```
In [1]: not 0
Out[1]: True
```

The next example uses the "**modulo**" operator "**%**" that returns the remainder when dividing two numbers. This expression returns "0" indicating there is no remainder. In simple terms I am asking, "does x % 7 have a remainder?" and the answer is "no" or "0."

```
In [1]: x = 21
In [2]: x % 7
Out[2]: 0
```

When combined with the boolean "not" operator the expression is "True."I n this example I am asking, "is it true that x % 7 does not have a remainder?" and the answer is "yes that is True."

```
In [3]: x = 21
In [4]: not x % 7
Out[4]: True
```

What is the Data Type?

If you're unsure of an object's type, the **type()** function displays the type of data. The second statement below uses the "isinstance()" function that returns "True" when an object is the specified type. In this example, I am testing if the "mystr" is a "str" type. To see this in action, type the code in the Editor and click "run."

```
print(type(mystr))
print(isinstance(mystr, str))
```

Later in this chapter, we'll look at identifying types of objects in dictionaries in the topic, "Find the Type of a Dictionary Element." In Chapter 7, Example 7.21 looks at a function with the wrong argument type.

Converting Data Types

When working with data, you may need to change or convert the data type. In other programming languages this is called casting. For example, during a calculation, you may want to convert between a **float** and an **int** to remove decimal places.

```
int(my_var)
str(my_var)
float(my_var)
bool(my_var)
```

Converting Floats to Ints

Notice in this example the value "45.9" is converted to "45."

```
myfloat = 45.9
int(myfloat)
```

The next statement rounds the float number up to the whole number "46."

```
myfloat = 45.9
round(myfloat, 0)
```

Converting Strings to Ints

When concatenating numeric values and strings, the statement str(**my_int**) converts the string to an integer. While I can't convert the string '1.25' into a whole number **int**, it is legal to first convert the string to a float, and then convert the float to an int, as shown in Example 7.49 in Chapter 7.

NoneType or None

In Python, the absence of a value is called "None," which is capitalized. The type is "NoneType" and the value is "None." In other languages, this would be a null value. A function with no return statement returns the value "None." When working with external data sources, you may have to account for this type of value, as shown in Chapter 7 in Example 7.17. An "if statement" that tests for a value of "None" is shown below. Example 7.27 demonstrates matching strings and taking into account a NoneType value. The Chapter 6 topic, Does the Object have a Value of None or Whitespace? looks at NoneType and whiteSpace.

```
if myvar is not None:
    pass
```

While I could compare the type of "mystr" on line 2 to **type(None)**, the preferred expression is to use "isinstance," as shown on line 5. The expression on line 2 would return "**True**."

```
1  mystr = None
2  if type(mystr) is type(None):
3      print('the type of mystr is None')
4
5  print(isinstance(mystr, str))
```

3.7 Numbers

Floats and integer types represent numbers in Python and are scalar objects that have no internal data structure. When assigning integer values to variables, do not use commas. Python interprets 2,000,000 as three integers separated by commas.

mynumber = 2000000

In the previous example, I assign 2000000 to the integer variable "**mynumber**." For readability, in Python 3.6 and later, you can add underscores as a separator.

mynumber = 2_000_000

Floating Point Numbers

Non-integer numbers or floats are stored in computer memory as a binary representation of 0's and 1's. Calculations can introduce subtle differences where you may think both float values are 1.08, but the actual binary representation is slightly different.

The function **repr()** displays a printable representation of a float, and is useful in troubleshooting rounding errors.

> Example 7.45 in chpater 7 demonstrates float comparisons, and the "comparison" topic later in this chapter has details on comparing 'floating point' numbers.

NAN

A NAN is a special floating-point value that can't be converted. NAN stands for "not a number." The "math" function math.**isnan(x)** returns True if "x" isn't a number.

3.8 Data Structures

Python has several built-in compound data structures or sequence types for non-scalar objects. Non-scalar objects have an internal structure. A list, tuple, or range is a sequence type. A string is a **text sequence type**. Objects that contain references to other objects are "containers." These data structures have an ordered sequence of **elements** or items. That is not to say the items are arranged in a particular order, but rather that Python assigns a sequence of indexes to the items.

The **docs.python.org** site refers to containers or sequence objects as "iterables." Iterables are objects with a sequence of elements referenced by an index. You use an index to iterate through these containers to access the value of a particular element in the container.

- Lists
- Tuples
- Strings
- Range

We'll look at iterables later in this chapter in the topic, "Control Statements - Iterables."

While there are other data structures in Python, the last common one we'll look at in-depth is a dictionary. A dictionary is a "mapping type" of data. Later in this chapter we'll briefly look at set, zip, map, and filter data structures.

- Dictionary
- Set
- Zip
- Map
- Filter

Python uses the operations listed below for all of these data structures. Later in this chapter, we'll look at these common operations, and you'll see the syntax is the same regardless of whether you're working with a list, tuple, string, or dictionary. For example, the function len() tells you how many objects are in the data structure. In the case of a string, len() tells you how many characters are in the string. For a list, len() tells you how many elements are in the list.

- len()
- Comparison operators "in" and "not in"
- Control loops like "for"

A list, tuple, or string also uses these operations, which we'll look at in detail later in this chapter.

- Indexing
- Slicing

With the exception of a range, you can use concatenation and multiplication on data structures. For example, to concatenate two lists using the plus "+" symbol, use the expression **mylist1 + mylist2**.

- Concatenation
- Multiplication

Tuples also support concatenation, as shown below and in Chapter 7, Example 7.44.

```
In [1]: mytuple = (1,'two', 3)
In [2]: mytuple
Out [2]: (1, 'two', 3)
```

```
In [3]: mytuple + ('H', 2, 'O')
In [4]: mytuple
Out [4]: (1,'two', 3, 'H', 2, 'O')
```

3.9 Strings

A **string** is a sequence of characters. These non-scalar objects have an internal data structure accessed through indexes. To assign a value to a string variable, use single quotation mark '' or double quotation "" marks, as shown below.

```
b = 'bookstore'
```

If you forget the closing apostrophe in your assignment statement, a SyntaxError is raised for "EOL while scanning string literal." Strings can be concatenated, indexed, and sliced. In the previous example, the index for the letter 's' is b[4] because Python starts counting at 0. String indices **must be integers**. We'll look at string indices and slicing in later topics.

Strings are immutable and can not be changed. Later in this chapter, in the topic "Append to Dictionary," we look at an AttributeError caused by trying to change a string value in a dictionary. To assign a value to a string, use the same syntax and, in effect, create a new string variable with the same name. The new string has a different "identifier" and location in memory, as discussed earlier in the topic "Immutable." Strings support **concatenation**; for example, 'hello' + 'world.' In Chapter 7, Example 7.32 concatenates two strings.

Before comparing string values, you may want to ensure both objects are of type "string," and account for uppercase and lowercase letters. The string methods **.upper()** and **.lower()** convert a string. The example below converts a variable to a string with all uppercase letters and is also shown in Example 7.27.

```
str(my_var).upper()
```

Occasionally, you may run across whitespace or a special character with an escape sequence, like the line feed '**\n**' character. The "string module" also has a function to create a list of whitespace characters. The function **repr()** displays a printable representation of a string including whitespace and is demonstrated in Chapter 7 in Example 7.28.

> To see the methods available to a string variable, in the Console type **dir(my_str_var)**. Or, type **help(str)** for more detailed information.

String Methods

Let's take a moment to look at some of the common string methods. In a bit we'll also look at the "String Module." To see all the string methods available for your version of Python, checkout the web site docs.python.org. In the top left corner of the web site you can select your language and version, and then on the right side of the page under "Text Sequence Type -- String, click on "String Methods." After creating a string variable "mystr," in the **Console**, type "dir(mystr)" to see additional information.

Syntax	Comments
mystr.isalpha()	Returns True if all characters in the string are alphabetic (a-z) and there is at least one character.
mystr.capitalize()	Converts to Camel Case
mystr.count('39')	How often is '39' in "mystr"
mystr.find('39')	Index of first occurrence of '39'
mystr.index('9')	Returns the index for '9', or returns error if not found
mystr.isnumeric()	Returns True if all characters are number (0-9) and there is at least one character.
mystr.join(mytuple)	Creates a new string by joining an iterable (tuple, list, set, dictionary.) Elements are separated by the "mystr" value.
mystr.lower()	Change to lowercase
mystr.lstrip()	Remove whitespace on the left
mystr.rindex('9')	Same as index but counting from right
mystr.replace(old, new)	Return a copy of the string with old substring replaced by new.
mystr.rpartition(',')	Spiti or tokenize string into a tuple based on the separator ','
mylist.rsplit(**sep='a'**)	Returns list of words in the string, using **sep** as the delimiter string. Similar to the idea of tokens in C programming.
mylist.rstrip()	Remove whitespace on the right
mylist.split(**sep='a'**)	Returns a list of words in the string, using **sep** as the delimiter string.
mystr.strip()	Return a copy of the string with the leading and trailing characters removed.
mystr.swapcase()	Return a copy of the string with uppercase characters converted to lowercase and vice versa.
mystr.upper()	Change to uppercase
mystr.zfill(**width**)	Return a copy of the string left filled with '0' digits to make the string length **width**. Think of zfill as padding numbers.

Table 3.2 String Methods

In Chapter 4, the topic "Test Objects" demonstrates removing characters at the end of a string using the **.rstrip()** method.

> An example using the find() method with a string is shown in the "Find a Substring" topic that follows. The topic "Slicing" also demonstrates retrieving part of a string.

Split String

The split() function is useful for splitting strings into a "list." If no argument is given, split() assumes a space.

```
mystr = 'hello world'
mystr.split()
```

After I run the program the Console shows the value of "mystr" is a list.

```
In [2]: mystr
['hello', 'world']
```

The String Module

In addition to the built-in string methods we just looked at, there is a "string" module with several invaluable methods. The string module is useful to create strings of ASCII characters.

The next chart shows a few of the functions in the "**string**" module. In the Console, after importing the string module, you could also type "**help(string)**" to see more information.

Syntax	Comments
.ascii_letters	Both lower and uppercase letters
.ascii_lowercase	abcdefghijklmnopqrstuvwxyz
.ascii_uppercase	ABCDEFGHIJKLMNOPQRSTUVWXYZ
.digits	'012345689'
.punctuation	!"#$%&'()*+,-./:;<=>?@[\]^_`{|}~

Syntax	Comments
.whitespace	‘ \t\n\r\x0b\x0c’
.printable	all printable characters

Table 3.3 Some String Module Methods

The **string.ascii_letters()** method is a simple way to build a list of letters. On line 1 I import the string module. The list() function converts the string to a list, as shown below.

```
1 import string
2
3 alphabet_string = string.ascii_letters
4 alphabet_list = list(alphabet_string)
5 print(alphabet_list)
```

Create a String of Lowercase letters

To create a string of lowercase letters use the syntax shown below. Notice in line 4 I convert the new string into a list.

```
1 import string
2 all_ltrs = string.ascii_lowercase
3 print(all_ltrs)
4 all_ltrs_list = list(all_ltrs)
5 print(all_ltrs_list)
```

After I run the program the Console shows:

```
In [2]:
abcdefghijklmnopqrstuvwxyz
['a', 'b', 'c', 'd', 'e', 'f', 'g', 'h', 'i', 'j', 'k', 'l', 'm', 'n', 'o', 'p', 'q', 'r', 's', 't', 'u', 'v', 'w', 'x',
'y', 'z']
```

Create a String of Numbers 0-9

To create a string of numbers 0-9 use the syntax shown below.

```
import string
str_Numbers = string.digits
print(str_Numbers)
```

After I run the program the Console shows:

In [3]:
0123456789

Whitespace Characters

To see "whitespace" characters use the **repr()** function, as shown below. On line 3, I use the repr() function to display the printable representation of the whitespace characters.

```
1 import string
2 all_ltrs = string.whitespace
3 print(repr(all_ltrs))
```

After I run the program the Console shows:

In [3]:
\t\n\r\x0b\x0c

In the Chapter 6 topic, "Does the Object have a Value of None or Whitespace?" we look at functions to remove whitespace. Example 7.29 in Chapter 7 demonstrates whitespace errors.

Iterate (Loop) Through Strings

String indices must be integers. The next example of a "for" loop is perfectly legal for the loop expression, and prints the message, 'abc'

```
mystr = 'abc'
for i in mystr:
    print(mystr)
```

What happens if you want to print the string values using the index notation? The "print" statement shown below uses "i" as the index. An **error** is raised because the respective "i" values are "a", "b," and "c," and are not integers.

```
mystr = 'abc'
for i in mystr:
    print('mystr char is:', mystr[i])
```

The **Console** displays a traceback message with a "**TypeError.**" I've abbreviated the traceback message below for readability.

In [**2**]:
Traceback (most recent call last):

TypeError: string indices must be integers

A slight modification in the code would prevent the error. In the example below, I am using the "range()" function combined with the length function "len()" to get the length of the list. The range() function returns a data structure of integers. We'll look at "range" in detail later in this chapter.

```
mystr = 'abc'
for i in range(len(mystr)):
    print('mystr char is:', mystr[i])
```

3.10 Lists

A **list** is a collection of objects. Lists are usually of the same type but can be a combination of types. A list is similar to an array in other languages and contains a sequence of elements. A unique index refers to each list item, and the index is an **integer**. When creating Lists, use square brackets **[ ]**. An index is used when updating a particular list item.

mylist = ['a', 'b', 'c']
mylist[2]

List values are mutable which means the values **can** change. Because lists are mutable, they cannot be used as dictionary **keys**. Lists can be used as dictionary "**values**" as demonstrated later in the topic, "Append to a Dictionary." A list can grow or shrink as needed.

> Python starts counting at **0**. The first item in a list has an index of **0**, and the second item has an index of **1**. Examples 7.1 and 7.2 demonstrate an **IndexError** when the list index is out of range.

When creating a List, use square brackets **[]**. A list will usually have homogeneous data but can mix different data types - commas separate items.

Description	Syntax	Comments
Create a List and assign values	mylist = ['a', 'b', 'c']	
Create a List and assign number values	mylist2=[1,2,3,4]	
Assign a value to the first item in the List	mylist2[0] = 8	

Description	Syntax	Comments
Access the value of the List item	mylist2[1]	Returns the value of the second item in the List
Access the value of the last List item	mylist2[-1]	Use negative index numbers when counting from the right
Return all items in a List	mylist	

Table 3.4 List Objects

Update an Element in a List

Use the index to update a particular element in a list. This example updates the second element in the list. See the topic that follows, "Index: Location of a List Element," to locate a particular index.

mylist2[1] = 8

Iterate Through Items in a List

A "for loop" is one option to iterate through items in a list, as shown below.

```
myList = [0, 1, 2]
for j in myList:
    print('mylist item is:', myList[j])
```

These Chapter 7 examples illustrate a few list errors: Example 7.1, 7.2, and 7.3.

Copy Lists

List copies have different behavior depending on how you make a copy of the list, as outlined in the python.org docs.

- Create a reference (same values, different identifiers)
- A shallow copy with one level
- A shallow copy with compound objects
- A deep copy

Create a Reference or Alias

The statement **mylist1** = **mylist2** creates a reference or alias. This behavior is referred to as "**indirection**." With an alias, regardless of the object name, you are actually using "mylist1." If **mylist1** has values [1, 2, 3, 4], **mylist2** references the same exact values [1, 2, 3, 4]. A change to any of the values in mylist1 is seen in mylist2, and vice versa.

Copy a Simple List

To make a copy of a list, add **[:]** at the end of the expression, as shown below. This creates a shallow copy that is one level deep. A shallow copy creates **mylist2** and inserts references to objects found in **mylist1**. You can also use the second expression to copy a list. If you leave off the **[:]** Python creates an "alias" or "reference," so that "mylist2" points to the "mylist1" object in memory.

```
mylist2 = mylist1[:]
mylist2 = list(mylist1)
```

In the case of a simple list object that is one level deep, this type of copy behaves the way you would expect. Changes at the first level are independent between the parent and copied lists, and vice versa. If you add objects to the second list, there is no change in the original list.

```
In [1]:  mylist1 = [0, 1, 2]
In [2]:  mylist2 = mylist1[:]
In [3]: mylist2[0] = 8
In [4]: mylist1
Out[4]: [0, 1, 2]
In [5]: mylist1
Out[5]: [8, 1, 2]
```

Copy a List with Compound Objects

The same copy syntax behaves differently with compound objects. Compound objects contain other compound objects. In this next example, "mylist3" has two lists, and is two levels deep. These internal lists are shown below:

```
mylist3[0] = [1, 2, 3, 4]
mylist3[1] = ['a', 'b', 'c', 'd' ]
```

Here I create a shallow copy of **mylist3** called **mylist4**.

```
mylist3 = [[1, 2, 3, 4], ['a', 'b', 'c', 'd' ]]
mylist4 = mylist3[:]
```

The first level of mylist3 is the combined list:

```
[[1, 2, 3, 4], ['a', 'b', 'c', 'd' ]]
```

Changes made at the first level are independent between mylist3 and mylist4. When I replace the first level compound list mylist3[0] with a string, it has no impact on "mylist4," and vice versa.

```
In [6]:  mylist3[0] = 'hello'
In [7]:  mylist3
Out [7]: ['hello', ['a', 'b', 'c', 'd' ]]
In [8]:  mylist4
Out [8]: [[1, 2, 3, 4], ['a', 'b', 'c', 'd' ]]
```

Let's start over with mylist3 and mylist4 just after the copy that creates mylist4.

```
In [9]:  mylist3
Out [9]: [[1, 2, 3, 4], ['a', 'b', 'c', 'd' ]]
In [10]:  mylist4
Out [10]: [[1, 2, 3, 4], ['a', 'b', 'c', 'd' ]]
```

The first list object in both mylist3[0][0] and mylist4[0][0] is **[**1, 2, 3, 4**]**.

The second list object in mylist3[0][1] and mylist4[0][1] is **[**'a', 'b', 'c', 'd' **]**.

Now I'm going to change an object at the second level. A simple copy is only one level deep, which means changes at the second level effect both the original list **mylist3** and the copied list **mylist4**. As expected, a change to mylist4[0][2] changes mylist3[0][2], and vice versa.

```
In [11]:  mylist4[0][2] = 'z'
In [12]:  mylist4
Out [12]: [[1, 2, 'z', 4], ['a', 'b', 'c', 'd' ]]
In [13]:  mylist3
Out [13]: [[1, 2, 'z', 4], ['a', 'b', 'c', 'd' ]]
```

To avoid this shallow copy behavior with compound objects, import the "copy" library to use **copy.deepcopy()** to create a new list and insert copies of all objects in the original list. The new list is completely independent of the original list.

List Comprehension

A List comprehension is an elegant way to create a new list from a comprehension. A comprehension consists of a single expression followed by at least one for clause and zero or more for or if clauses. The only difference between a list comprehension and map() is Python returns a list instead of a map object.

The comprehension is an "**expression**" followed by "**for**" loop(s) to iterate over elements. The comprehension may also include conditional "**if**" statement(s).

newList = **[expression or variable** - **for item in iterable**- **if]**

The code below has three statements that I want to combine in a "list comprehension." The list comprehension will compute sales tax for "sales_list" elements of type "float."

expression or variable	round(i * 1.065, 2)
for item in iterable	for i in sales_list
if	if type(i) == float

```
for i in sales_list
    if type(i) == float:
        round(i * 1.065, 2)
```

1. In the example below, the slash **** at the end of line 2 below means the list comprehension continues onto line 3. The Python Interpreter considers lines 2 and 3 one statement.

   On line 2, the first part of the list comprehension computes the price of items with sales tax, and rounds the result to two decimal places.

2. The second statement loops over items in the "sales_list".

3. Finally, the third statement on line 3 checks that elements are a float, skipping over strings and integers in the sales_list. The result is assigned to a new "receipt_list."

```
1 sales_list = [1, 'iPad', 399.99, 2, 'charging cable', 29.99]
2 receipt_list = [round(i * 1.065, 2) for i in sales_list \
3     if type(i) == float]
4 print(receipt_list)
```

After I run the program the Console shows the output below. Note that the first element in **sales_list** is a whole integer and not a float, so "1" is not included in the rounding calculation.

```
In [2]:  receipt_list
Out [2]:  [425.99, 31.94]
```

This comprehension creates a list of vowels from a string.

```
mystr = 'charging cable'
newList = [v for v in mystr if v in 'aeiou']
```

After I run the program the Console shows:

```
In [2]:  newList
Out [2]: ['a', 'i', 'a', 'e']
```

Remove Characters When Converting

In the previous example, the console printed the brackets, apostrophes, and commas as part of newlist. When you convert a list to a string, the square brackets around the original list, the apostrophes, and the commas between list elements become part of the new string, as shown in the next topic, "Change a List to a String."

When converting objects, you might want to remove those extra characters. Example 7.27 in Chapter 7 demonstrates slicing to remove square brackets and apostrophes. With strings, you can use the **.replace()** function to remove square brackets or commas. In Chapter 4, the topic "Test Objects" demonstrates removing characters at the end of a string.

The same principle applies when you convert a string object to a list. A string object begins with an apostrophe and ends with an apostrophe. The apostrophes become part of the new list element.

Delete an Item from a List

This expression uses the del() function to delete the second item in "mylist."

```
del(mylist[1])
```

In the example below, the statement "**del(mylist[4])**" deletes element 'o' from your original "mylist" object.

```
mylist = ['h', 'e', 'l', 'l', 'o']
del(mylist[4])
print(mylist)
```

After I run the program the Console shows:

```
In [2]:
['h', 'e', 'l', 'l']
```

Change a List to a String

In case you have a "list" object and need a "string" type instead, convert the list to a string using "**str(**myList**)**." In this example, I convert a list element to a string.

```
myList = [‘hi’]
mynewvar = str(myList)
```

After I run the program the Console shows:

In [2]: mynewvar

"[‘h’, ‘i’]"

In the Console, type "mynewvar." The object has **double quotes** around the output, indicating the object is now a string. The **square brackets** that were around the original list object, as well as the **quotes** and **commas** that separated the original list elements are part of the value of the new string object "mynewvar." Example 7.27 in Chapter 7 demonstrates slicing to remove unwanted characters.

Change a String to a List

You can convert a string to a list using "**list(**mystring**)**." You might need to convert a string to a list to change data with a "list" method, since a list is mutable and can be changed.

```
myList = [‘hello’]
str(mysList)
```

After I run the program the Console shows:

In [2]: myStr

‘hello’

3.11 Methods for Lists

In this topic, we'll look at several handy list methods. To see common sequence operations available for your version of Python, check out the **docs.python.org**. In the top left corner, you can select your language and version, and then on the left side of the page under "Sequence Types -- **list, tuple, range**, click on Mutable Sequence Types.

Syntax	Comments
mylist.append('there')	Adds an element to the end of the list
mylist.clear()	Removes all items from mylist
mylist.copy()	Creates a shallow copy of mylist (same as **newlist = mylist[:]**)
mylist.count('l')	Count occurences of 'l'
mylist.extend('you')	Add 1 element to end of list
mylist.index[1]	Returns 2nd element
mylist.insert(2, 'a')	Insert item at index location
mystring = '_'.join(mylist)	Joins list elements into a new string
mylist.pop(2)	Deletes element '2' and returns '2'
mylist.remove(2)	Removes element '2' from mylist
mylist.reverse()	Reverses the items of mylist in place
mylist.sort()	Sorts the original list & returns nothing

Table 3.5 List Methods

Append an Item to a List

The function "**append()**" adds a single element to the end of your list. Append changes your original list.

```
mylist = ['h', 'e', 'l', 'l', 'o']
mylist.append('there')
```

When I run the program the Console shows:

```
In [2]:
['h', 'e', 'l', 'l', 'o', 'there']
```

Extend a List, or Combine 2 Lists

The function "extend()" adds each element in the second string as a separate element to the end of the first list. In this example, when I extend the list with 'you,' it separates the letters in 'you' into three elements.

```
mylist = ['h', 'e', 'l', 'l', 'o']
mylist.extend('you')
```

When I run the program the Console shows:

In [2]:
['h', 'e', 'l', 'l', 'o', 'y', 'o', 'u']

Index: Location of a List Element

To find the index for the element 'e,' use the .index method. In this example, .index returns "1" which is the index for the letter 'e.' Python begins counting at "**0**," so the second element 'e' has an index of "1." Once you know the index for an element, you can change that element.

```
mylist = ['h', 'e', 'l', 'l', 'o']
mylist.index('e')
```

After I run the program the Console shows "1," indicating "e" is the second element in "**mylist**."

In [2]:
1

Insert an Item to a List

To add an item "a" at index position '2' in a list, use the following expression.

```
mylist = ['h', 'e', 'l', 'l', 'o']
mylist.insert(2, 'a')
```

After I run the program the Console shows:

In [2]:
['h', 'e', 'a', 'l', 'l', 'o']

Join List Elements into a String

The join() function is useful for joining elements in an iterable such as a list, tuple, dictionary, or set. In this example, I am creating a **new string** from the elements in "**mylist**." The "_" underline character is used as an argument so that the new string "**mylist2**" has "_" between each letter.

```
mylist = [‘h’, ‘e’, ‘l’, ‘l’, ‘o’]
mystring = ‘_’.join(mylist)
```

After I run the program the Console shows:

```
In [2]: mystring
h_e_l_l_o
```

In the next example, I join "**mylist**" elements into a string, and nothing is added between the elements.

```
mylist = [‘h’, ‘e’, ‘l’, ‘l’, ‘o’]
mystring = ‘’.join(mylist)
```

After I run the program the Console shows:

```
In [2]: mystring
‘hello’
```

> Instead of ‘_’, you could use ‘\n’ to add a line feed between elements.

Add Character When Joining Strings

In the next example, I use the "map" function to change elements to a string with the str() function. Then, I join the elements together with a comma as the separator. The output to the Console when I run the program is **hi, stranger**.

```
mylist = [‘hi’, ‘ stranger’]
mystr = ‘,’.join(map(str, mylist))
print(myStr)
```

Pop (Remove) an Element from a List

The function "**mylist.pop()**" removes the last item in the list or the item where you provide the index. The function "pop()" also returns the item you remove.

```
mylist = [‘h’, ‘e’, ‘l’, ‘l’, ‘o’]
pop_item = mylist.pop(4)
print(pop_item)
```

After I run the program the Console shows:

```
In [2]:
o
```

Remove an Element from a List

The function **mylist.remove(‘o’)** removes the argument in parentheses from a list, but does not return the object. In this example, I remove **‘o’** from “**mylist**.”

```
mylist = [‘h’, ‘e’, ‘l’, ‘l’, ‘o’]
mylist.remove(‘o’)
print(mylist)
```

After I run the program the Console shows:

```
In [2]:
[‘h’, ‘e’, ‘l’, ‘l’]
```

Remove Duplicate Elements from a List

To quickly remove duplicate elements in a list, convert the list into a **Set**, as explained in the topic, “Set” later in this chapter.

The sort() Method

There are several ways to sort list items. The mylist**.sort**() method changes the original “mylist” into a sorted list and returns nothing.

```
mylist = [‘h’, ‘e’, ‘l’, ‘l’, ‘o’]
mylist.sort()
```

After I run the program the Console shows:

In [2]:
['e', 'h', 'l', 'l', 'o']

The sort() method also has two keyword arguments: **key** and **reverse**. The following shows two possible keyword arguments for the list.sort() method.

key=str.lower

reverse=True (reverse sort)

The sorted() Function

The "**sorted**()" function returns a new, sorted version of your list (or any iterable.) In this example, mylist2 is a new sorted list.

```
mylist = ['h', 'e', 'l', 'l', 'o']
mylist2 =sorted(mylist)
```

After I run the program the Console shows:

In [2]: mylist2
['e', 'h', 'l', 'l', 'o']

Sort Order and the Key Parameter

The sorted() function also has the **key** and **reverse** keyword arguments. The **reverse** keyword allows you to sort in "descending" or "ascending" order. In the next example, "reverse" is a keyword argument of the sorted() function. The **key** argument specifies a function to be called on each list element prior to making comparisons. In this example, I use the **str.lower** method to change strings to lowercase before the **sort** comparison.

```
mylist = ['red', 'Red', 'blue']
mylist2 = sorted(mylist, key=str.lower, reverse=True)
```

Sorting by the Second Element in the List

The "operator" library includes the "itemgetter()" function which allows you to choose which element in the list you want to sort. In this example, on line 4 I am sorting by the second element and then the first element.

```
1 from operator import itemgetter
```

```

mylist = [(‘red’, 3), (‘Red’, 1), (‘blue’, 2)]
mylist2 = sorted(mylist, key=itemgetter(1, 0))
```

3.12 Tuple

A **tuple** is similar to a list in that it is an ordered sequence of elements. That is not to say the items are arranged in a particular order, but rather that Python assigns a sequence of indexes to the items. The first item in a tuple has an index of “0.” Tuples are enclosed in parentheses **( )** and **commas** separate items. Tuples are immutable, which means they cannot be changed, as demonstrated in Chapter 7 in Example 7.42.

Tuple Assignment

Tuples can also contain other tuples. In this next example, when I create “mytuple2,” the fourth element [3] is “mytuple1.” Notice mytuple2 includes numbers, strings, and a tuple. Tuples can have heterogeneous data, meaning tuples can have different data types.

```
In [1]: mytuple1 = (1,’two’, 3)
In [2]: mytuple2 = (‘H’, 2, ‘O’, mytuple1, 4)
In [3]: mytuple2
Out [3]:(‘H’, 2, ‘O’, (1, ‘two’, 3), 4)
```

Using the **mytuple** object we just created, when you type this expression in the Console to test the value, the Python Interpreter returns “True.”

```
In [4]: mytuple2[2] == ‘O’
Out [4]:True
```

When working with functions, you’ll notice they often return a tuple. An alternate expression for **tuple assignment** follows.

```
def myfunction():
    return 1, 2

myvar1, myvar2 = myfunction()
```

After the program runs, myvar1 = 1 and myvar2 = 2.

Tuples are Immutable

If you try to assign a new value to an item in a tuple, a TypeError is raised. Tuples are immutable, and the value can not be changed. In Chapter 7, Example 7.42 looks at this error.

In [3]: mytuple[1] = 'three'
Traceback (most recent call last):

File "<ipython-input-3-db66c3391d15>", line 1, in <module> mytuple[1] = 'three'

TypeError: 'tuple' object does not support item assignment

Elements are separated by commas. Dictionary **keys** are always immutable elements so you can use tuples as dictionary keys. Lists are mutable and therefore can't be dictionary keys.

> Tuple indices must be integers not **strings**.

Description	Syntax	Comments
Create a Tuple and assign values to 4 items	mytuple = ('a', 'b', 'c', 'd')	
Create an empty Tuple	mytuple = tuple()	
Create a Tuple with one item	mytuple2 = ('fruit',)	Notice the comma at the end to instruct Python this is a Tuple and not a String.
Assign number values to several Tuple items	mytuple3 = (1, 2, 3)	
View the value of the 2nd Tuple item	**In [1]:** mytuple4[1] **Out [1]**: Orange	The Python Interpreter returns the value Orange.
one-line swap	a, b = b, a	swap values

Table 3.6 Tuple Objects

Tuple Indexes

Earlier, I created mytuple2 and assigned these values: **('H', 2, 'O', (1, 'two', 3), 4).** When I use indexing with my tuple, I can retrieve the value of the **fourth** item, as shown below. The index for the fourth item is "**3**" because Python starts counting at zero.

In [4]**:** mytuple2[**3**]
Out [4]:(1, 'two', 3)

Looking at this same example, **('H', 2, 'O', (1, 'two', 3), 4)**, what index would I use to retrieve the 2nd element "two" inside of mytuple1, which is inside mytuple2? Hint: because Python starts counting at zero, the index of the second element is [**1**].

mytuple2[**3**][**1**]

Let's say I wanted to use the last element in **mytuple2** for addition. Because "4" is inside of tuple2, I use this expression.

10 + mytuple2[**4**]

This expression evaluates to "14."

Iterate Through Items in a Tuple

A "while loop" is one option to iterate through items in a tuple, as shown below.

```
mytuple4 = ('Apple', 'Orange', 'Watermelon')
j = 0
while j < 3:
        print('my fruit is:', mytuple4[j])
j += 1
```

A "for loop" is another option to iterate through items in a tuple. Indices must be valid integers. The two samples below are valid and do the same thing.

```
mytuple4 = (0, 1, 2)
for k in mytuple4:
        print('my number is:', k)
```

```
mytuple4 = (0, 1, 2)
```

```
for k in mytuple4:
    print(‘my number is:’, mytuple4[k])
```

The sample code below is invalid and causes an "**IndexError**," because there are only three objects in the tuple with values 1, 2, 3. Python starts counting at 0. The print statement is using "**mytuple4[k]**" or mytuple[1], mytuple[2], and mytuple[3]. When you run the program, the Python Interpreter warns that "**3**" is not a valid index because '**3**' is beyond the limits of the tuple.

```
mytuple4 = (1, 2, 3)
for k in mytuple4:
    print(‘my number is:’, mytuple4[k])
```

Example 7.52 in Chapter 7 looks at a tuple index error.

Tuples and Function Return Objects

By definition, a function can only return one object. One way around this is to return a tuple of more than one object. Sometimes you'll see return values "swapped," as shown below. We look at these "unpacking" statements later in this Chapter in the topic, "Functions." Also, the function in Chapter 7 in Example 7.33 returns a tuple.

myvar1, myvar2 = myvar2, myvar1

The example below is a function that returns one tuple with two objects in the tuple. The first few lines create the function. Line 7 invokes the function and assigns "myint1" and "myint2" to the function's return objects. Because the function returns "var1" and "var2," the result is the same as the expressions that assign **myint1, myint2 = ("var1, "var2").**

```
1 def myfunction():
2     var1 = 3
3     var2 = 4
4     return var1, var2
5
6
7 myvar1, myvar2 = myfunction()
8 print(‘myvar1 is:’, str(myvar1) + ‘; myvar2 is:’, str(myvar2)
```

Example 7.52 in Chapter 7 looks at a tuple index error.

Repetition and Concatenation

Tuples support both concatenation and repetition. In the examples that follow, I am using repetition and concatenation for tuples. Because tuples are immutable and can't be changed, this concatenation does not change the value stored in "mytuple." The Console output shows the result of the concatenation, but the result is not assigned to an object. This behavior is illustrated in the expressions I typed in my **Console**, as shown below.

In [**1**]**:** mytuple = (1, 'two', 3)

In [**2**]**:** mytuple
Out [**2**]: (1, 'two', 3)

In [**3**]**:** mytuple + ('H', 2, 'O')

In [**4**]**:** mytuple
Out [**4**]: (1, 'two', 3, 'H', 2, 'O')

Example 7.44 in Chapter 7 concatenates a tuple to a tuple. You can't concatenate a tuple with a string object.

	Expression	Returns:
Repetition	2 * ('H', 2, 'O')	('H', 2, 'O', 'H', 2, 'O')
Addition	mytuple + ('H', 2, 'O')	(1,'two', 3, 'H', 2, 'O')

Table 3.7 Tuple Expressions

Related Tuples

Often, the relationship between elements in two or more tuples is dependent on the "order" of the elements. In this section, we use multidimensional data in simple tuples. For additional examples of multidimensional data, check out **numpy.py** which is specifically for arrays.

roster1 = **(**('Joan', **[**'art', 'pc'**]**, **[**60, 59**]**), ('Henry', **[**'math'**]**, **[**96**]**),
('John', **[**'english', 'SS'**]**, **[**80, 87**]**)**)**

- The first element in the tuple is the **student name**.
- The second element in the tuple is a list of **courses**.
- The third element in the tuple is a list with the **grades** for the corresponding course.

Henry data in roster1			
	Name	Course	Grade
index	roster1[1][0]	roster1[1][1][0]	roster1[1][2][0]
value	Henry	math	96

Table 3.8 Index Values for Henry in Roster1

The roster1 tuples
('Joan', ['art', 'pc'], [60, 59])
('Henry', ['math'], [96])
('John', ['english', 'SS'], [80, 87])

Table 3.9 Class Roster

You may decide that you want to add a third list for the school term to each student's tuple. In the next example, I create a new tuple "roster2" with each student's data in their own tuple, as shown below.

- The first element in the tuple is the **student name**.
- The **second** element in the tuple is a list of **courses**.
- The **third** element in the tuple is a new list with the course **term** for the corresponding course.
- The **fourth** element in the tuple is a list of **grades** for the corresponding courses.

```
roster2 = (( 'Joan', ['art', 'pc'], ['spr', 'spr'], [60, 59] ),
( 'Henry', ['math'], ['fall'], [96]),
( 'John', ['english', 'SS'], ['fall', 'fall'], [80, 87]))
```

The new roster2 tuples
('Joan', ['art', 'pc'], ['spr', 'spr'], [60, 59])
('Henry', ['math'], ['fall'], [96])

The new roster2 tuples
('John', ['english', 'SS'], ['fall', 'fall'], [80, 87])

Henry data in roster2				
	Name	Course	Term	Grade
index	roster2[1][0]	roster2[1][1][0]	roster2[1][2][0]	roster2[1][3][0]
value	Henry	math	fall	96

Table 3.10 Class Roster2

Because you changed the elements in the tuple, the code needs to be "**refactored**" to account for this change. In this example, we need to refactor or change the internal code so it behaves the same way with the course and grade elements.

Henry's grade initially: roster1[1][2][0]

Henry's grade after the change: roster2[1][3][0]

NamedTuple

To avoid having to refactor code, the "collections" library includes a "**namedtuple**" which makes these types of tasks very simple. In the example below, I create a new **namedtuple** "Roster" on line 3. On lines 5-7, I assign values to "Roster3."

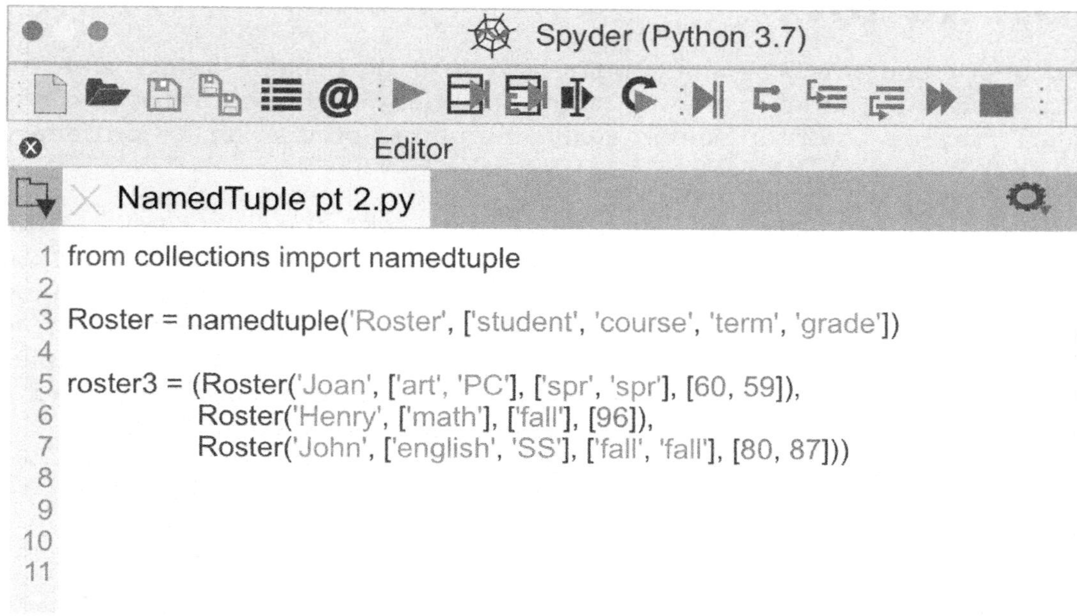

Figure 3.1 Create a namedtuple

Now that we are using a "namedtuple" called Roster3, the syntax to access the data is a little different. First, let's look at Henry's data.

Henry's data in roster3			
Name	Course	Term	Grade
roster3[1]. student	roster3[1]. course[0]	roster3[1]. term[0]	roster3[1].grade[0]
Henry	math	fall	96

Table 3.11 New Class Roster3 data for Henry

Joan is the first tuple in Roster3. Here we look at her second course, term and grade, which is index [1].

Joan's data in roster3			
Name	Course	Term	Grade
roster3[0]. student	roster3[0]. course[1]	roster3[0]. term[1]	roster3[0].grade[1]
Joan	PC	spr	59

Table 3.12 New Class Roster3 data for Joan

3.13 Dictionary

A dictionary contains key:value pairs and is a non-scalar object with an internal data structure. The key:value pairs are not in any particular order, and any type of object may be used for values. Only immutable objcts can be dictionary "keys."

Dictionaries are often depicted as two columns, with the list of keys in the first column and values in the second column. Dictionaries are mutable and you can change or add key:value pairs. Values can be duplicated, but keys must be unique and hashable. You can only use immutable elements such as integers or strings as dictionary keys, as shown in Chapter 7 in examples 7.39 and 7.46. While tuples can be used as dictionary keys, mutable lists can not be used as dictionary keys. I would avoid floats as keys, given the way floats are actually stored in memory.

Keys (Immutable Objects)	Values (may be any object type)
Name	John
Grade	A
Course	Python Programming

Table 3.13 Sample Dictionary

A dictionary has unsorted elements that can grow and shrink as needed. When creating dictionaries, use curly braces **{}**. In the assignment statement, the key is followed by a colon **:** and a value.

myDict = **{**key:value, key:value, key:value**}**

The syntax for changing dictionary objects depends on the type of object in the dictionary "value." If the value is a list, you can use list methods to change data. If the value is a string, you can't change the string because strings are immutable; however, you can replace the value in the key:pair with a new object of any type.

In this section we'll explore these topics.

- Elements in a Dictionary
- Create a Dictionary
- Append to a Dictionary
- Copy a Dictionary
- How Many Elements are in a Dictionary List?
- Assign a Dictionary Value Using the Key Name

- Update a "List" Value in a Dictionary
- Find the Value of a Dictionary Item
- Find the Type of a Dictionary Element
- Add a New Key to an Existing Dictionary
- Delete a Key in an Existing Dictionary
- Iterate Through Dictionary Key-Pairs
- Iterate Through Keys in a Dictionary
- Retrieve Keys
- Search for a Key Name
- Title and Value Methods
- Combine Dictionaries

Earlier I said adding a new key:value pair to a dictionary is straightforward, but adding to an existing dictionary is not. When changing dictionary elements the important aspect is the "type" of object in the key:value pair. As you'll see in the next topic, you must know the type of the value so that you can use the corresponding methods to add or change values.

Elements in a Dictionary

This topic explores the relationship between elements in a dictionary. A dictionary is a set of key:value pairs that are not in any particular order. The keys are immutable objects like strings or integers. The values in the key:value pair can be any type of object. Often you'll see nested lists, tuples, or dictionaries in a dictionary **key:value** pair.

In the following example, we combine two lists into one "combined" list. The "combined" list will be the dictionary value. The order of elements in the two lists establishes the relationship between the two lists. The keys are student names, and the value for each student is a "combined" list that contains two lists. Recall that a dictionary is not in any kind of order, so there is no guarantee that the key "Joan" will be the first in the dictionary.

Key	Value
Joan	[['art', 'social studies'], ['A', 'D']]
Henry	[['math, 'english', 'science'], ['A', 'B', 'C']]
John	[['english', 'history', 'algebra'], ['B', 'B+', 'C']]

Table 3.14 Student Dictionary

Because dictionaries don't store data in the same order you input the data, the actual data can end up looking like the next example.

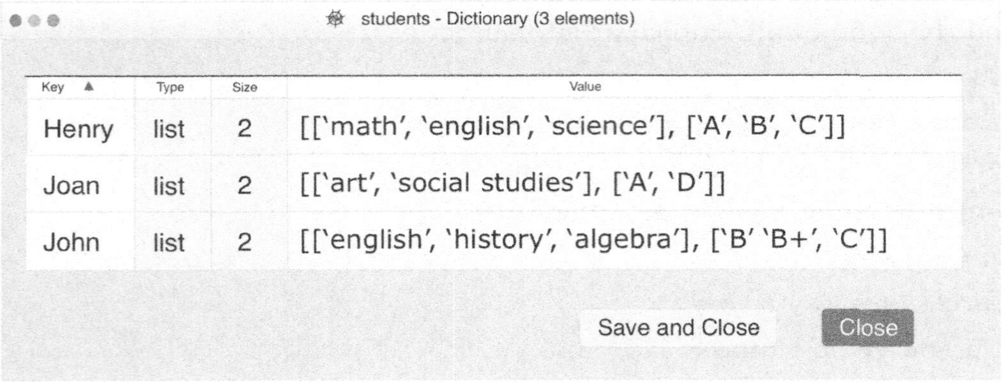

students - Dictionary (3 elements)

Key ▲	Type	Size	Value
Henry	list	2	[[‘math’, ‘english’, ‘science’], [‘A’, ‘B’, ‘C’]]
Joan	list	2	[[‘art’, ‘social studies’], [‘A’, ‘D’]]
John	list	2	[[‘english’, ‘history’, ‘algebra’], [‘B’ ‘B+’, ‘C’]]

Save and Close   Close

Figure 3.2 Variable Explorer Showing Dictionary

When looking at Joan’s data, you can see two lists. The first course list has two elements. The second grade list also has two elements. If Joan is taking four classes, each list would have four elements.

```
[‘art’, ‘social studies’]
[‘A’, ‘D’]
```

The “combined” list represents the “value” for the key “Joan.”

```
[[‘art’, ‘social studies’], [‘A’, ‘D’]]
```

When looking at this combined list, the first element in the “combined” list is a list of classes. The second element is a list of grades.

[0] -> class_list

[1] - > grade_list

We’re going to create a dictionary with three students, and each student is taking several classes. Notice that we assign the list data when we create the dictionary. We don’t have a separate statement to create the two lists, although we could add an additional statement for clarity.

Joan is taking art and social studies. Joan’s respective grades are A and D.

```
['art', 'social studies']
['A', 'D']
```

John is taking English, history, and algebra. John's respective grades are B, B+, and C. When we create the dictionary, our class list will look like this example.

```
['english', 'history', 'algebra']
```

The grade list will look like this example.

```
['B', 'B+', 'C']
```

Henry is taking math, English, and science. Henry's respective grades are A, B, and C.

```
['math', 'english', 'science']
['A', 'B', 'C']
```

Now let's create the "students" dictionary with one student.

```
students = {'John': [['english', 'history', 'algebra'], ['B', 'B+', 'C']]}
```

At this point, let's say I want to display John's grade in his history class. I will use indexing to look at the data in this dictionary key:value pair. You can follow along with this code in your iPython Console to see the data returned. To see all of John's classes type the statement below. In this example, the first list is element [0].

```
students['John'][0]
```

To see all of John's grades type this statement. In this example, the second list is element [1].

```
students['John'][1]
```

Because dictionaries don't store data in the same order you input the data, the actual data can end up looking like the next example.

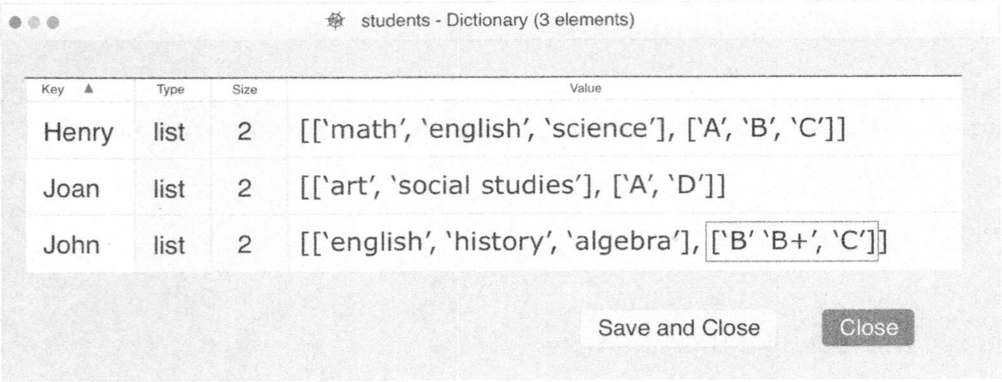

students - Dictionary (3 elements)

Key ▲	Type	Size	Value
Henry	list	2	[['math', 'english', 'science'], ['A', 'B', 'C']]
Joan	list	2	[['art', 'social studies'], ['A', 'D']]
John	list	2	[['english', 'history', 'algebra'], ['B' 'B+', 'C']]

Save and Close Close

Figure 3.3 John's Grades

To see the class name 'history' type this statement. In this example, you want to see the second element [1] in the first list [0].

```
students['John'][0][1]
```

Finally, to see the class name **algebra** with John's grade, type this statement. Here we are using the third element in the first list [0][2], along with the third element in the second list [1][2].

```
print(students['John'][0][2], students['John'][1][2])
```

Recall that a dictionary assignment statement follows this syntax.

```
myDict = {key:value, key:value, key:value}
```

To create a dictionary with all students use this expression.

```
students = {'John': [['english', 'history', 'algebra'], ['B', 'B+', 'C']],
            'Henry': [['math', 'english', 'science'], ['A', 'B', 'C']],
            'Joan':[['art', 'social studies'], ['A', 'D']]}
```

To view Joan's grade in social studies, use this statement. In this example, we're looking at the second element [1] in the first list [0], and the second element[1] in the second list [1].

```
print(students['Joan'][0][1], students['Joan'][1][1])
```

students - Dictionary (3 elements)

Key	Type	Size	Value
Henry	list	2	[['math', 'english', 'science'], ['A', 'B', 'C']]
Joan	list	2	[['art', 'social studies'], ['A', 'D']]
John	list	2	[['english', 'history', 'algebra'], ['B' 'B+', 'C']]

Save and Close Close

Figure 3.4 Joan's Grade in Social Studies

Create a Dictionary

To create an empty dictionary use the following expression.

```
mydictionary = { }
```

To create a dictionary with three key:pairs, use the following syntax. In the example below, the first key is 'Name,' and the value is '**Zimmerman**.' The second key is 'Grade,' and the value is '**A**.' A comma "**,**" separates the key:pairs. For readability, the key:pairs are usually written in this format. To create a dictionary with "string" values use the following syntax.

```
mydictionary = {'Name': 'Zimmerman'
                'Grade': 'A',
                'Course': 'Python Programming'}
```

In the following example, I am creating a dictionary with "list" values. Inside the "list' is a string value. Because it is a "list" there are square brackets around the string values.

```
mmydictionary2 = {'Name': ['Young']
                  'Grade': ['B'],
                  'Course': ['Excel Fundamentals']}
```

Because a dictionary can have any type of object, you must know the object's type in order to work with the data. Strings are contained in **quotes** (single or double), tuples use **parentheses()**, and lists use **square brackets [ ]**.

Append to a Dictionary List Value

Append adds elements to an existing key that contains a "list." For example, if you have a key "Name" with a "list" value, you can use append to add additional strings 'Smith' and 'Jones' to the "list."

Why should you care about the object type of elements in your dictionary? If you try to **add** elements to a "string" using the "append" method, the Python Interpreter raises an AttributeError, as shown below.

```
In [4]: mydictionary['Name'].append('Smith')
AttributeError: 'str' object has no attribute 'append'
```

The same syntax for "**mydictionary2**" is successful, because the value in the key:pair "Name" is of type "list."

```
In [5]: mydictionary2['Name'] = ['Zimmerman']
In [6]: mydictionary2['Name'].append('Smith')
```

To see the new dictionary values, in the Console, I type "mydictionary2." Notice the output shows the key "Name" now has two values. The square brackets indicate **[**'Zimmerman', 'Smith'**]** is a "list."

```
In [6]: mydictionary2
Out [3]: {'Name': ['Zimmerman', 'Smith'],
'Grade': ['A'],
'Course': ['Python Programming']}
```

Copy a Dictionary

Use the **.copy()** method to make a shallow copy of a dictionary.

```
thisdict1 = {3: 'k'}
thisdict2 = dict1.copy()
```

Import the "copy" library and use **copy.deepcopy()** if the dictionary contains mutable objects that can be changed.

How Many Elements are in the Dictionary List?

Continuing with the earlier example, I can count the number of values associated with the key "Name" by using the len() method to retrieve the length of the list.

In [**6**]: len(mydictionary['Name'])
Out [**3**]: 2

Assign a Dictionary Value Using the Key Name

To update a dictionary value use the following syntax.

mydictionary['Name'] = 'Smith'

Update a "List" Value in a Dictionary

There will be times when you want to "update" the value for a key in your dictionary. In this example, the key:value pair has a value that is a "list." First, I check if the key already exists in the dictionary. If the key is there, I append "myvar2" to the "list." If the key is new, I add the key and "list" value to the dictionary.

```
1 mydict = {}
2 mykey = 'phrase'
3 myvar2 = 'hello'
4 if mykey not in mydict:
5       mydict[mykey] = [myvar2]
6 else:
7       mydict[mykey].append(myvar2)
```

Next I'll use .setdefault() for the same task on line 4.

```
1 mydict = {}
2 mykey = 'phrase'
3 myvar2 = 'hello'
4 mydict.setdefault(mykey, []).append(myvar2)
```

The .get() method is another way to avoid an error if a key is not in the dictionary. Later in this chapter we'll look at the "defaultdict" object in the collections library.

The .get() method

The collections library "defaultdict"

The .setdefault() method

> Examples 7.20 and 7.31 in Chapter 7 demonstrate an error when a key is not in a dictionary.

Find the Value of a Dictionary Item

This example uses the **Console** to display the value of the key "Name." Compared to a list where I need to know the correct list index, with a dictionary, I simply provide the name of the "key." The Python Interpreter returns the value "Zimmerman" to the Console pane.

In [**3**]: mydictionary['Name']
'Zimmerman'

Keep in mind that a dictionary key:pair might contain anything. For example, the key:pair value could contain a tuple with several lists, and each list could have multiple elements. In that case, you use indexes to locate the elements that may be nested several layers into the dictionary key:pair.

To test if a particular key is in a dictionary, you could use the "in" operator. Continuing with our previous dictionary example, I might look for the keys "DoB" or "Course" with these expressions.

In [**4**]: **"DoB"** in mydictionary
Out [**4**]: False

In [**5**]: **"Course"** in mydictionary
Out [**5**]: True

Find the Type of a Dictionary Element

In case you've run across a dictionary and are wondering about the type of an object, let's look at how to find the object type. In the Editor, I've created "mydictionary2." Notice the values are in square brackets, indicating they are "lists."

```
mydictionary2 = {'Name': ['Young']
                 'Grade': ['B'],
                 'Course': ['Excel Fundamentals']}
```

After running this code in the Editor, I want to look at the type of the value in the key:pair. As shown below, in the **Console**, I use the type() function to determine the type of the value where the key is '**Name**.' The Python Interpreter returns "list."

```
In [2]: type(mydictionary2['Name'])
Out [2]: list
```

Now let's revisit the first dictionary and look at the type of the values.

```
mydictionary = {'Name': 'Zimmerman'
               'Grade': 'A',
               'Course': 'Python Programming'}
```

After running this code in the Editor, I want to look at the type of the value in the key:pair. As shown below, in the **Console**, I use the type function to determine the type of the value where the key is '**Name**.' The Python Interpreter returns "string."

```
In [3]: type(mydictionary['Name'])
Out [3]: str
```

Add a New Key:pair to an Existing Dictionary

To add a new key 'Credits' to an existing dictionary, use this syntax. Recall that you can only use immutable elements such as integers or strings as dictionary keys.

```
mydictionary['Credits'] = '3'
```

Delete a Key in an Existing Dictionary

To remove the key:value pair ['Credits']:'3' from the dictionary, use "del."

```
del(mydictionary['Credits'])
```

Iterate Through Dictionary Key:pair Values

This "for loop" returns the key:pairs in the dictionary. Line 4 in this example creates two variables, "mykey" and "myvalue," that will represent the key:value pairs. The method **items()** returns a list of the key-value pairs.

```
for mykey, myvalue in mydictionary.items():
    print("\pKey: ", mykey, "\tValue: ", myvalue )
```

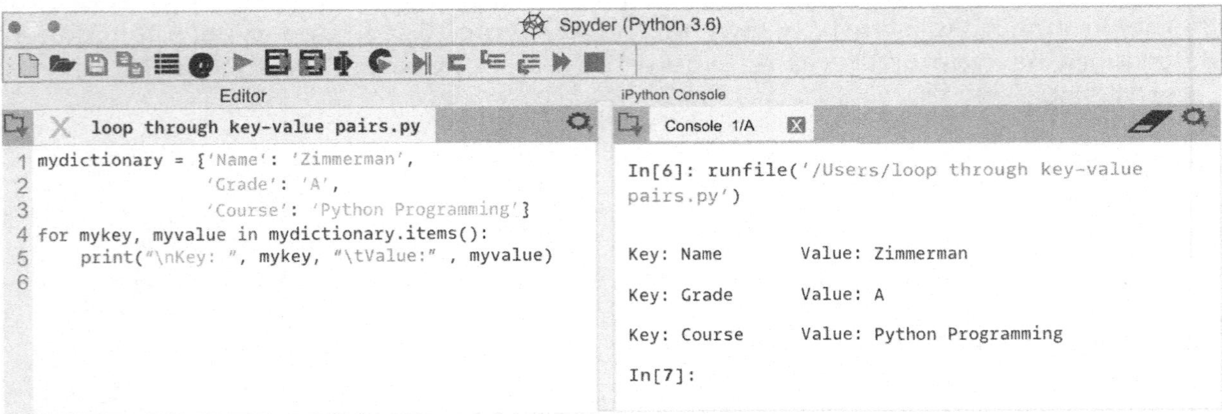

Figure 3.5 Print Key-Value Pairs

Iterate Through Keys in a Dictionary

This "for loop" returns the keys in the dictionary. To make your code easier to read, add the keys() method to the same statement.

```
for mykey in mydictionary:
    print("\pKey: ", mykey )
```

The next example is the same statement with the **.keys()** method.

```
for mykey in mydictionary.keys():
    print("\pKey: ", mykey )
```

Retrieve Keys

To retrieve the dictionary keys use the "**.keys()**" method.

In [**6**]: mydictionary**.keys()**
Out [**6**]: dict_keys(['Name','Grade', 'Course'])

Search for a Key Name

To test if a particular key is in a dictionary, you can use the "in" operator. Continuing with our previous dictionary example, I might look for the keys **"Grades"** or **"Course"** with these expressions. In this example, I am typing in the Console, and the expression returns either False or True.

In [**4**]: **"Grades"** in mydictionary
Out [**4**]: False

In [**5**]: **"Course"** in mydictionary
Out [**5**]: True

Test if Key is in the Dictionary

In another example, let's say you have a dictionary called 'mydictionary' for student IDs, where the **key** name is the student ID number. This expression that uses the "in" operator to find a student ID "12345" returns "**True**." Note I am searching for the **key** name, not the value in the key:pair.

In [**6**]: if '12345' in mydictionary:
Out [**6**]: True

Value Method

In this next example, I modified the previous code that returned the keys in the dictionary. Here I use the **value()** method to access the dictionary values. The first expression returns all values in the dictionary, while the second expression entered in the **Editor** iterates through each item.

In [**7**]: mydictionary.values()
Out [**7**]: dict_keys(['Name', 'Grade', 'Course'])

```
for myvalue in mydictionary.values():
     print(myvalue)
```

In [8]:

Combine Dictionaries

The **update()** method combines two dictionaries. If key names are the same, the key:pair is updated with the newer value. If the key:pair doesn't exist, it is added.

```
dict1, dict2 = {key1: 'data1', key2: 3}, {key3: '4'}

dict1.update(dict2)
```

Dictionary Comprehensions

Earlier, we looked at list comprehensions. Dictionaries also support comprehensions.

{expression or variable - for item in iterable- if}

```
In [16]:    myl = [1, 2, 3, 1, 3, 4, 1]
In [17]:    dd = {num: myl.count(num) for num in myl}
In [18]:    print(dd)
            {1: 3, 2: 1, 3: 2, 4: 1}
```

expression or variable	num: myl.count(num)
for item in iterable	for num in myl

3.14 Range

The range function was introduced with Python 3 and is used to generate a range of **integers**. A range is immutable and can not be changed. When you run an expression with a range, the Python Interpreter creates the first integer in the range. The next integer is created when you ask for it, and so on. So you are not hampered waiting on Python to generate a large list of integers; it's more of a just-in-time approach. The format for a range is shown below.

```
for i in range(start: stop: step):
    print('Hello #', i)
```

If only one argument is provided, the argument becomes the 'stop' value. Start defaults to 0, and step defaults to 1. The range(0, 4) starts at index 0, and ends at index 3.

```
for i in range(1,4):
    print(i)
```

When I run this "for" loop from the Editor, it prints **1**, **2**, **3**, to the Console as shown below.

In [**43**]:
1
2
3

A range uses indexing, slicing, len(), the comparison operators "in" and "not in," and works with the "for" control loop. A range is an ideal way to iterate over a list. In the next example, the length of the list is the "stop" argument for the range() function.

```
for i in range(len(my_list)):
    print('The list item is:', my_list[i])
```

3.15 Generators

A generator expression returns a 'yield' expression and is an iterator. A generator runs up to the first 'yield' expression and returns that value. The next time the generator is invoked, it resumes execution at the point it left off and runs until the next 'yield' statement. If you have a list of a million names, you don't have to create the list in memory. Instead, the generator creates each name when needed.

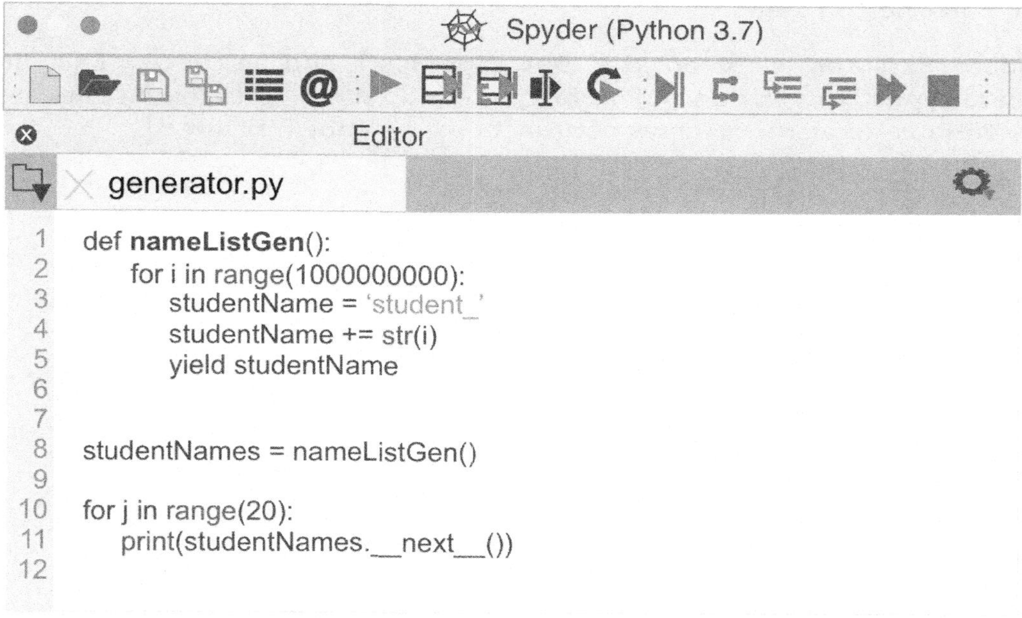

Spyder (Python 3.7)
Editor
generator.py
1 def nameListGen():
2   for i in range(1000000000):
3   studentName = 'student_'
4   studentName += str(i)
5   yield studentName
6
7
8 studentNames = nameListGen()
9
10 for j in range(20):
11   print(studentNames.__next__())
12

Figure 3.6 A Generator

Line 11 could also be rewritten with the **next()** method, as shown below.

```
print(next(studentNames))
```

3.16 Sets

A **Set** contains unordered elements with no duplicates. A Set is mutable and grows or shrinks as needed; so you can use **.add()** or **.remove()** to add or remove immutable elements like strings, tuples, or integers. However, you can't change the immutable elements in the set. Set elements can be different types.

When creating a set, use curly braces **{}** and separate items with a comma. Line 5 creates an empty set.

```
In [4]: myset = {'apple', 'orange'}
In [5]: myset = set()
```

The set**(***<iterable>***)** function creates a new set from an immutble iterable such as a list, tuple, dictionary, or string. While you can create a "set" from a list (which is mutable) using the set() function, the elements in the new "set" are immutable and can't be changed.

In Variable Explorer, click on the **Settings** icon and uncheck "Exclude unsupported data types" to view an object of type "set". When you double click on the set object, Variable Explorer displays set functions, as shown below.

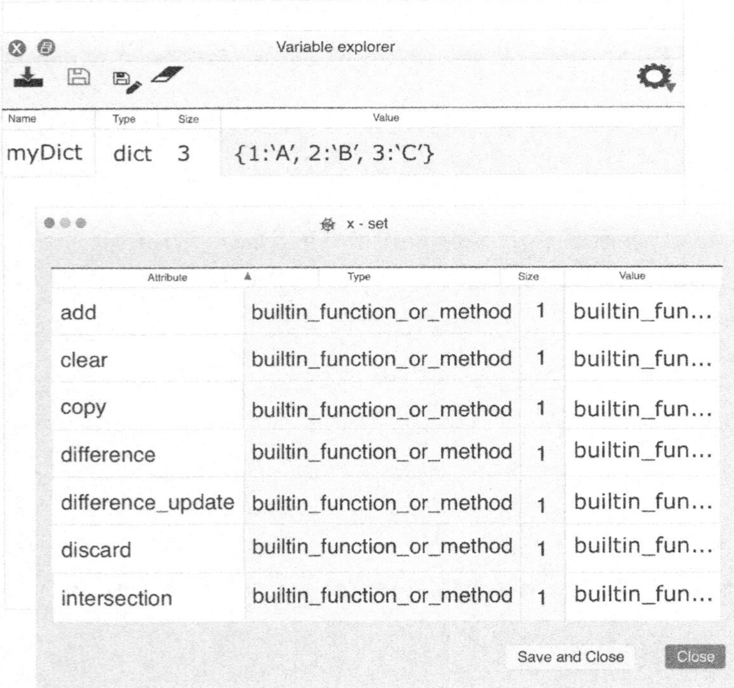

Figure 3.7 A Set in Variable Explorer

In this example, on input line 7 I enclose an immutable "string" variable in braces **{}**, creating a set.

```
In [6]: myvar = '123'
In [7]: {myvar}

In [8]: type({myvar})
Out[8]: set
```

Notice a **TypeError** is raised when I try the same syntax using a **mutable** "list" to create a set on line 10. The "Intersection" topic that follows demonstrates using the set() function to convert a list to a set.

```
In [9]: myvar = [1, 2, 3]
In [10]: {myvar}
Traceback (most recent call last):

  File "<ipython-input-20-597c80421cc7>", line 1, in <module>
    {mylist}
TypeError: unhashable type: 'list'
```

Description	Syntax
Create a Set and assign values	myset = {'a', **7**, 'c'}
Create an empty Set	myset3 = set()
Create a Set and assign values	myset3 = set('abc')

Table 3.15 Creating Sets

We'll look at these built-in functions next.

- Union
- Intersection
- Difference
- Symmetric

Union

First, let's use the "union" **|** operator to combine two sets.

```
In [12]:   myset1 = {'apples'}
In [13]:   myset2 = {'pears'}
In [14]:   myset1 | myset2
Out[14]:   {'apples', 'pears'}
```

The union() function accepts other iterator types and returns a **new** set. In the next example, I combine a set and a list into a new set.

```
In [15]:   myset1 = {'apples'}
In [16]:   mylist1 = ['oranges']
In [17]:   myset1.union(mylist1)
Out[17]:   {'apples', 'oranges'}
```

Intersection

The intersection() function finds elements in common between two sets and returns a set.

```
In [18]:   myset1 = {1, 2, 3}
In [19]:   myset2 = {3, 4, 5}
In [20]:   myset1.intersection(myset2)
Out[20]:   {3}
```

The next example uses the intersection operator **&** to create a new set with the elements in common between the two sets.

```
In [21]:   myset1 = {1, 2, 3}
In [22]:   myset2 = {3, 4, 5}
In [23]:   myset1 & myset2
Out[23]:   {3}
```

To count how many items are in common between two sets, use the len() function. This example converts two lists to sets.

```
In [21]:   myset = set([4.95, 3.20, 8.95, 5.99, 3.99])
In [22]:   sale = set([4.95, 3.99])
In [23]:   len(myset & sale)
Out[23]:   2
```

Difference

The difference() function returns a **new set** of elements in myset1 that are not in myset2.

```
In [18]:   myset1 = {1, 2, 3}
In [19]:   myset2 = {3, 4, 5}
In [20]:   myset1.difference(myset2)
Out[20]:   {1, 2}
```

The next example uses the difference operator **-** to create a new set with the elements in myset1 that are not in myset2.

```
In [21]:   myset1 = {1, 2, 3}
In [22]:   myset2 = {3, 4, 5}
In [23]:   myset1 - myset2
Out[23]:   {1, 2}
```

Symmetric Difference

The symmetric_difference() function returns a new set of elements in either set that are not in both sets.

```
In [18]:   myset1 = {1, 2, 3}
In [19]:   myset2 = {3, 4, 5}
In [20]:   myset1.symmetric_difference(myset2)
Out[20]:   {3}
```

Common Elements

The bitwise operator **&** returns a new set with the elements in common between the two sets.

```
In [21]:   myset1 = {1, 2, 3}
In [22]:   myset2 = {3, 4, 5}
In [23]:   myset1 & myset2
Out[23]:   {3}
```

Uncommon Elements

The next example uses the exclusive bitwise operator **^** to create a new set with the elements **not** in common between the two sets.

```
In [21]:   myset1 = {1, 2, 3}
In [22]:   myset2 = {3, 4, 5}
In [23]:   myset1 ^ myset2
Out[23]:   {1, 2, 4, 5}
```

Set Comprehension

This example is a set comprehension that creates a new set with unique values. A set comprehension uses this format.

newSet = {**expression or variable** - **for item in iterable**- **if**}

Let's briefly look at the original code I want to convert to a set comprehension. Line 1 creates a tuple of float "prices." Sale items end in ".99" and I'd like to create a "set" of all items on sale.

- convert "floats" to "strings"
- use slicing to find last three digits of the price
- select '.99' items

```
1 prices = (4.99, 8.75, 3.20, 1.80, 9.99)
2 for x in range(len(prices)):
3     if str(prices[x])[-3:] == '.99':
4         newSet.add(prices[x])
```

Now, let's break down each step and gradually work up to the final **set** comprehension "saleItems."

```
saleItems = {x for x in prices if str(x)[-3:] == '.99'}
```

1. The first part of the comprehensionn is simply the "variable" x.

variable	x
for item in iterable	for x in prices
if	if str(x)[-3:] == '.99'

2. Next, I add the "for" logic for each item in "prices."

for x in prices

3. The final part of the expression is the conditional "if" statement.

if str(x)[-3:] == ‘.99’

4. The original line 4 added the item to the set, and is now handled by Python because this is a "set comprehension."

saleItems = {**expression or variable** - **for item in iterable**- **if**}

variable	x
for item in iterable	for x in prices
if	if str(x)[-3:] == ‘.99’

The combined set comprehension is shown on line 2.

```
1 prices = (4.99, 8.75, 3.20, 1.80, 9.99)
2 saleItems = {x for x in prices if str(x)[-3:] == ‘.99’}
```

3.17 collections

The "collections" library has some interesting "container datatypes." Earlier in the "Tuples" topic, we looked at an example of a "**namedtuple**" from the collections library. Now we'll also look at the "Counter" and "defaultdict" functions.

Counter

The "Counter" subclass is a dict subclass and is a simple way to keep track of counts, as shown in the next example. On line 4 I create a "Counter" object. I increment a counter on line 6 to count each instance of an element in the "bills" list. On line 7 I assign "ones" to the cnt[‘one’] value.

```
1 from collections import Counter
2
3 bills = [‘one’, ‘five’, ‘ten’, ‘one’]
4 cnt = Counter()
5 for i in bills:
6     cnt.update([i])
```

```
ones = cnt['one']
print('there are %d ones' % (ones))
```

defaultdict

The "defaultdict" is a subclass of the dictionary class, and returns a dictionary-like object. Interaction with a defaultdict object is the same as a dictionary, except that a defaultdict has a **default callable object** when a key is not in the dictionary. In this example, line 4 sets the default **value** for my defaultdict "dd" to a "list." On line 7 I'm using the list "append" method to add items to the "dd" object. With this syntax, if I try to access a key that is not in "dd," the Python Interpreter returns a list object and does not raise an error.

```
1 from collections import defaultdict
2
3 mylist = [(1, 'one'), (2, 'two')]
4 dd = defaultdict(list)
5 cnt = Counter()
6 for k, v in myList:
7     dd[k].append(v)
```

In the Console, I type "dd" to see the values.

```
In [2]: dd
Out[2]: defaultdict(list, {1: ['one'], 2: ['two']})
```

3.18 Indexes

An iterable such as a string, tuple, range, or list is a non-scalar sequence object with an internal data structure. A sequence is an iterable object that supports efficient element access using **integer** indices. These objects use indexing to locate a particular element in the sequence. The format for an index is the object name with square brackets around the index. For example, in the "bookstore" example that follows, **mystr[4]** evaluates to "s" in the string "mystr."

b	**o**	**o**	**k**	**s**	**t**	**o**	**r**	**e**
0	1	2	3	4	5	6	7	8

Table 3.16 String Index Example

In Python, the sequence protocol starts an index at position 0. Indexes must be integers or a TypeError occurs. In the example below, '**bookstore**' is assigned to **mystr**, and there are nine characters. The start index is [0], and the end index is [8]. If you go beyond the end of the index, it causes an "IndexError," as shown in Example 7.1 in Chapter 7.

mystr = "**bookstore**"

0 start index

8 end index

9 length of string

To find the length of string "**mystr**" use the len() function.

In [**1**]: len(**mystr**)
Out [**1**]: 9

> len() works with many types of objects including strings, tuples, ranges, dictionaries, and lists.

Indexing is a fundamental part of Python, so we'll take a moment to look at a couple of "indexes" with data structures that have multiple levels.

Indexing Elements in Nested Lists

Earlier in the topic, "Elements in a Dictionary," we looked at how to index two lists inside of a dictionary. In this example, we'll look at three lists nested inside of the main list.

list1 = [**'apple'**, **'tangerine'**]
list2 = [**'tangy'**, **'sweet'**]
list3 = [**'red'**, **'orange'**]

mainlist = [list1, list2, list3]

The first three lists are elements [0], [1], and [2] in "mainlist." Each of the three lists has two strings, with elements [0] and [1].

To retrieve 'tangerine,' you access the second element [**1**] in "list1," and "list1" is the first element [**0**] in "mainlist."

In [**1**]: mainlist[**0**][**1**]
Out [**1**]: 'tangerine'

To view the value 'sweet,' you access the second element [**1**] in "list2," and "list2" is the second element [**1**] in "mainlist."

In [**2**]: mainlist[**1**][**1**]
Out [**1**]: 'sweet'

To view the value 'orange' you access the second element [**1**] in "list3," and "list3" is the third element [**2**] in "mainlist."

In [**2**]: mainlist[**2**][**1**]
Out [**1**]: 'orange'

Indexing Lists & Tuples in Dictionaries

These examples use strings, lists, and tuples with dictionary key:value pairs. First, I create three lists with various fruit values. The relationship between the lists is such that the first element in each list describes the "apple" - "sweet" and "red."

f1 = ['apple', 'lemon']
f2 = ['sweet', 'sour']
f3 = ['red', 'yellow']

Element	Value
f1[0]	apple
f1[1]	lemon
f2[0]	sweet
f2[1]	sour
f3[0]	red
f3[1]	yellow

Table 3.17 Fruit Lists

In the **Console**, I can type the following to see information about the "lemon." My design is such that the data about the "lemon" is the second element [1] in lists f1, f2, and f3.

In [**1**]: f1[1]
Out [**1**]: 'lemon'

In [**2**]: f2[1]

```
Out [2]: 'sour'

In [3]: f3[1]
Out [3]: 'yellow'
```

Next, I create some lists for vegetable values.

```
v1 = ['spinach', 'carrots']
v2 = ['leafy', 'crunchy']
v3 = ['green', 'orange']
```

Element	Value
v1[0]	spinach
v1[1]	carrots
v2[0]	leafy
v2[1]	crunchy
v3[0]	green
v3[1]	orange

Table 3.18 Vegetable Lists

Now I create two tuples, and each tuple consists of three lists.

```
f = (f1, f2, f3)
v = (v1, v2, v3)
```

Tuple Element	Value
f[0]	f1
f[1]	f2
f[2]	f3
v[0]	v1
v[1]	v2
v[2]	v3

Table 3.19 Two Tuples

As an example, the chart below outlines the indexes for all the values in the "**f**" tuple.

Tuple (3 list elements)	List 2 string elements	Values	Tuple "f" Index
f[0]	f1[0]	apple	f[0][0]
f[0]	f1[1]	lemon	f[0][1]
f[1]	f2[0]	sweet	f[1][0]
f[1]	f2[1]	sour	f[1][1]
f[2]	f3[0]	red	f[2][0]
f[2]	f3[1]	yellow	f[2][1]

Table 3.20 Tuple Indexes

In the Console, I can type the following to see information about "lemon" in the "**f**" tuple. The layout of data is such that the data about the "lemon" is the second element [1] in each list. Because Python starts counting at zero, the second element index is [1].

```
In [1]: f[0][1]
Out [1]: 'lemon'

In [2]: f[1][1]
Out [2]: 'sour'

In [3]: f[2][1]
Out [3]: 'yellow'
```

Finally, I create a dictionary with two key:value pairs. The values are the "**f**" and "**v**" tuples. The dictionary key names are "fruit" and "vegies."

```
d = {'fruit': f, 'vegie': v}
```

Element	Value
d['fruit']	f
d['vegie']	v

Table 3.21 Dictionary

At a glance, the dictionary might look simplistic. However, when we look inside the dictionary, you see there is quite a bit of data.

Dictionary (2 tuple elements)	"f" or "v" tuples	f1,f2, f3, v1, v2, or v3 Lists	Values (strings)
d['fruit']	f[0]	f1[0]	apple
d['fruit']	f[0]	f1[0]	lemon

Dictionary (2 tuple elements)	"f" or "v" tuples	f1,f2, f3, v1, v2, or v3 Lists	Values (strings)
d['fruit']	f[1]	f2[1]	sweet
d['fruit']	f[1]	f2[1]	sour
d['fruit']	f[2]	f3[0]	red
d['fruit']	f[2]	f3[0]	yellow
d['vegie']	v[0]	v1[1]	spinach
d['vegie']	v[0]	v1[1]	carrots
d['vegie']	v[1]	v2[0]	leafy
d['vegie']	v[1]	v2[0]	crunchy
d['vegie']	v[2]	v3[1]	green
d['vegie']	v[2]	v3[1]	orange

Table 3.22 Dictionary Elements

So far, we've looked at indexing for lists and tuples. Now, I want to look at the values in the dictionary, beginning with "apple." In the **Console**, I can access the data using the dictionary key name and indexing, as shown below and in the chart that follows.

In [1]**:** d['fruit'][0][0]
Out [**1**]: 'apple'

In [2]**:** d['fruit'][1][0]
Out [**1**]: 'sweet'

In [3]**:** d['fruit'][2][0]
Out [**3**]: 'red'

In the previous examples, the key name is "fruit." The list '**f**' is the value in d['fruit']. List '**f**' has three lists that are index [0], [1], and [2]. I'm accessing the first element [0] in all three lists.

Dictionary Key	"f" Tuple	f1, f2, or f3" List	Values	Dictionary key name and indexes
d['fruit']	f[0]	f1[0]	apple	d['fruit'][0][0]
d['fruit']	*f[0]*	*f1[1]*	*lemon*	
d['fruit']	f[1]	f2[0]	sweet	d['fruit'][1][0]
d['fruit']	*f[1]*	*f2[1]*	*sour*	
d['fruit']	f[2]	f3[0]	red	d['fruit'][2][0]
d['fruit']	*f[2]*	*f3[1]*	*yellow*	

Table 3.23 Dictionary: List Indexes

Example 7.52 in Chapter 7 looks at a tuple index error.

3.19 Slicing

Slicing is used with strings, ranges, tuples, lists and other sequence types. "**Slicing**" breaks a sequence into a substring of elements. Notice in the example below, slicing uses square brackets **[]** and takes three arguments separated by colons. The keyword argument "start" tells the function where to start slicing the string. Start defaults to 0 and "step" defaults to 1. Both start and step are optional keyword arguments. If only one argument is given, it is used as the "stop" argument.

mystr**[**start**:**stop**:**step**]**

The default for the second argument "stop" is the length of the object, in this case **len(mystr)**. Using the "bookstore" string from the previous example, follow along as we look at slicing. The function **len(bookstore)** returns **9**, so the string's length is **9** characters.

b = "**bookstore**"
b**[**4**:9:**1**]**

The Console prints: **store**.

The "stop" value "**9**" evaluates to "**9** - 1." Recall that Python starts counting at 0, so this slice **b[**4**:9:**1**]** stops at "8" and returns characters 4-8.

The previous example equates to the following, if you were to type the len() function.

b**[**4**:len(b):**1**]**

The third argument "step," tells the function which characters to return. For example, step 2 would skip every other character. "Step" can be omitted. In that case, you would type **b[**4**:len(b)]**. Here, the stop argument is the length of "bookstore."

The default slicing values are:

Argument	Description	Default Value
start	Start is the index to begin slicing	0
stop	The stop index where you want to stop. The default value len(b) evaluates to **stop value - 1**	len(bookstore)

Argument	Description	Default Value
step	Return every "**1**" character. (Step "**2**" skips every other character)	**1**

Table 3.24 Default Slicing Values

In Chapter 4, the topic "Test Objects" demonstrates removing characters at the end of a string using slicing.

Slice()

The built-in slice() function is demonstrated in the next example. I like to use slice() to assign a name to my slices. On line 1, the "**r**" preface tells the Python Interpreter the backslash "\" isn't an escape character, but rather simply a backslash.

```
1 mystr = r"c:\data\python\Example1.py"
2 path = slice(14)
3 name = slice(15, 23)
4 extension = slice(24, 26)
5 print(mystr[path])
6 print(mystr[name)
7 print(mystr[extension])
```

On line 2, there is one **slice()** argument, which is the "stop" value. On line 3 and 4, I use both the start and stop arguments. The output from lines 5-7 is shown below.

```
c:\data\python
Example1
py
```

Slicing Examples

This example b[0:4] evaluates to **book**. The Python Interpreter starts at "0" and ends at "3."

b[0:4]								
b	**o**	**o**	**k**	s	t	o	r	e
0	1	2	3	4	5	6	7	8

The next example b[4:] evaluates to **store** because only the '4' start argument is provided. If you don't provide a "stop" argument, the default of **len(bookstore)** is used.

b[4:]								
b	o	o	k	**s**	**t**	**o**	**r**	**e**
0	1	2	3	4	5	6	7	8

Don't forget the colon at the end of the start argument!

Notice the example below b[4] looks similar to the previous example but omits the colon. Now Python returns only the character "**s**" at index **4**.

b[4]								
b	o	o	k	**s**	t	o	r	e
0	1	2	3	**4**	5	6	7	8

Negative values tell Python to start counting from the right. The example below **b[::-1]** evaluates to:

erotskoob

b[:: -1]								
b	**o**	**o**	**k**	**s**	**t**	**o**	**r**	**e**
0	1	2	3	4	5	6	7	8

In this example **b[5:2:-1]**, the "-1" step argument tells the Python Interpreter to move right to left. This example starts at "5," steps right to left because of "-1", and stops before index "2" at "k":

tsk

b[**5:2: -1]**								
b	o	o	**k**	**s**	**t**	o	r	e
0	1	2	3	4	5	6	7	8

In Chapter 7, Example 7.27 uses slicing to remove square brackets and apostrophes after converting a list to a string.

In this example b[**-8**:**-3**:] a negative start argument "**-8**" counts from right to left, beginning with "**o**." There is no step argument, so the default of "**1**" is used, meaning you move left to right, from **-8** to **-7** to **-6**, and so on. The stop argument is "**-3**," telling Python to stop before it reaches **-3**. This slice evaluates to:

ookst

b**[-8:-3:]**								
b	**o**	**o**	**k**	**s**	**t**	o	r	e
-9	**-8**	**-7**	**-6**	**-5**	**-4**	-3	-2	-1

The last example, **b[-7:2:-1]** below, evaluates to an empty string because it goes beyond the end of the string. It starts at -7, moves to -8, and then -9. At that point, it has moved three indices from right to left and can't move anymore.

b**[-7:2: -1]**								
b	o	o	k	s	t	o	r	e
-9	-8	-7	-6	-5	-4	-3	-2	-1

In the topic "Find a Substring" that follows, we'll use slicing to find the word "from" in a string.

3.20 Operators

Now let's take a look at using operators for numerical operations, concatenation, and comparisons. The **docs.python.org** has a complete list of operators in the topic "Mapping Operators to Functions."

Numerical Operators

Arithmetic operators work pretty much the way you would expect in Python.

Operator	Example	Description
+	x + y	the sum
-	x - y	the difference
+=	x += 1	add 1
-=	x -= 1	minus 1
*	x * y	the product
/	x / y	division
//	x // y	floor division: **5 // 2** returns 2
%	x%y	modulo: the remainder when x is divided by y
**	i**j	i to the power of j or exponentiation

Table 3.25 Numerical Operators

These two statements both add 1 to the **mynumber** variable.

```
mynumber = mynumber + 1
mynumber += 1
```

Select Odd or Even Numbers

One way to select odd or even index numbers is to use "**+=**". Given that the first element in a tuple is mytuple1[0], I can increment a counter += 2 to iterate through all the even index elements in the tuple. The following example creates a new tuple with the first element, third element, and fifth elements from "**mytuple1**."

```
myTuple1 = (1, 2, 3, 4, 5)
myTuple2 = ()
```

```
i = 1
while i < len(myTuple1):
    myTuple2 += (myTuple1[i],)
    i += 2
print(myTuple2)
```

Modulo Operator

The "**modulo**" operator "**%**" returns the remainder when dividing two numbers. If you divide any number by 10, the modulo is the last digit in a number. This example returns '7' in the Console.

```
In [1]: n = 107
In [2]: last_digit = n % 100
In [3]: print(last_digit)
7
```

Select Odd or Even Numbers

You'll often see the remainder "%" operator used to identify odd or even numbers, as shown below.

```
for i in range(0, 20):
if i % 2 != 0:
     print("i is an odd number", i)
```

Integer Division

The '**//**' operator does integer division also known as floor division. Integer division returns the quotient and ignores the remainder. This example returns '12' in the Console, in effect reducing the original number by one digit.

```
In [1]: n = 123
In [2]: myvar = n // 10
In [3]: print(myvar)
12
```

Concatenation, Repetition and Sequence Operations

The **+** operator is used to concatenate string objects. You can also use the **+** operator to concatenate two lists and other object types. In Chapter 7, Examples 7.32, 7.34 and 7.44 demonstrate concatenation.

The * repetition operator is supported by most sequence types. An example of repetition is **3 * 'ho'**, which evaluates to "ho ho ho."

To see common sequence operations available for your version of Python, check out the **docs.python.org**. In the top left corner, you can select your language and version, and then on the left side of the page under, "Sequence Types, click on "Common Sequence Operations."

Operator	Description
len(s)	length of s
min(s)	smallest item of s
max(s)	largest item of s
s.count(x)	total number of occurances of x in s

Comparison Operators

Use Comparison Operators to compare two values. The "in" and "not in" operators are handy for searching or finding elements in a data structure.

Operator	Description
in	Test for membership in a sequence
not in	Returns True if not a member of a sequence

To test whether a **character** or **substring** is in a string, use the "in" comparison operator, as shown below. Example 7.48 in Chapter 7 illustrates comparing two strings.

```
mystr = 'apple'
if 'a' in mystr:
     print('a is in', mystr)
```

In the previous example, I searched for the string "a" in "mystr." The left operand and the right operand are both strings. A TypeError is raised if you use a "list" as the left operand and a string as the right operand. In Chapter 7, Example

7.48 illustrates this example.

> The "in" comparison operator is used with strings, tuples, ranges, and lists.

Boolean Operations

The boolean operators are "and," "or," and "not" and are sometimes referred to as short-circuit operators. The evaluation of a compound boolean expression stops when an outcome is reached. In this example, the Python Interpreter stops evaluating the expression after the argument "5 == 4" evaluates to "False."

```
if 5 == 4 and 2 != 6:
```

Identity Comparison

The "**is**" and "**is not**" operators test an object's identity. If "x" and "y" variables point to the same object identifier "x **is** y" returns True. This next statement returns "True."

5 **is not** 4

Let's say you create a variable "myvar1" and assign the value "hello." You then create a new variable, "myvar2," and assign it to "myvar1" with the statement myvar2 = myvar1. In effect, you create an "alias" from "myvar2" to "myvar1". The two statements below return "True" because the objects are the same.

```
myvar1 == myvar2

myvar1 is myvar2
```

You could also use the id() function to verify these two variables point to the same object. In this example, notice the identifier is the same.

```
In [14]: id(myvar1)
Out [14]: 140498313577904
In [15]: id(myvar2)
Out [15]: 140498313577904
```

Comparison Operators

Operator	Description
>	Greater than
<	Less than
>=	Greater than or equal to
<=	Less than or equal to
==	Equal (values)
!=	Not equal

Table 3.26 Comparison Operators

Difference Operator

Earlier, in the Sets topic, we looked at the difference operator **-** dash. This creates a new set with the elements in "myset1" that are **not** in "myset2."

```
In [21]:    myset1 = {1, 2, 3}
In [22]:    myset2 = {3, 4, 5}
In [23]:    myset1 - myset2
Out[23]:    {1, 2}
```

The Union Operator for Sets

Earlier in the "Sets" topic we looked at the "union" **|** operator to combine two sets.

Comparing Floats

Non-integer numbers, or floats, are stored in computer memory as a binary representation of 0's and 1's. Calculations can introduce subtle differences where you may think both float values are 1.08, but the actual binary representation is slightly different. Comparing two floats, as shown below, could potentially return **False**.

x == y

Instead of the == equals comparison for floats, use an arbitrarily small positive number (an epsilon) to compare two floats. In the next statement, the epsilon is .000001, and the statement returns 'True' if the float values are within .000001 of each other, which is good enough for this example. The **abs()** function converts floats to positive numbers for the comparison. Example 7.45 demonstrates float comparisons.

```
if abs(x-y) < .000001:
```

See the cmath library function **isclose()** for comparing floats.

Comparisons that Return True or False

When you compare two objects, the Python Interpreter returns "True" if the comparison is "True" or "False" if the comparison is not True. In the Console type the following statement. Python returns "True."

```
In [1]: 'apple' == 'apple'
Out [1]: True
```

The next two functions both return "True". Because the second function "**myfunction2**" is simpler, it is considered more "Pythonic."

```
def myfunction():
    if 2 == 2:
        return True


def myfunction2():
    return 2 == 2

print(myfunction())
print(myfunction2())
```

Bitwise Operators

The ampersand **&** bitwise operator copies a bit if it exists in both operands. In this example, the bitwise operator **&** returns a new set with the elements in common between the two sets. The symmetric_difference() function also returns common objects.

```
In [18]:    myset1 = {1, 2, 3}
In [19]:    myset2 = {3, 4, 5}
In [20]:    myset1 & myset2
Out[20]:    {3}
```

The next example uses the bitwise **exclusive** or **^** carat operator to create a new set with the elements **not** in common between the two sets.

```
In [21]:    myset1 = {1, 2, 3}
In [22]:    myset2 = {3, 4, 5}
In [23]:    myset1 ^ myset2
Out[23]:    {1, 2, 4, 5}
```

The bitwise **|** pipe operator returns a set of **all** objects.

```
In [21]:    myset1 = {1, 2, 3}
In [22]:    myset2 = {3, 4, 5}
In [23]:    myset1 | myset2
Out[23]:    {1, 2, 3, 4, 5}
```

Find a Substring

Earlier we looked at slicing which is a simple way to parse a string into substrings. In the next example, I use the find() method to locate all instances of the substring "**from**." I'm using a "**start**" variable for the beginning of the string and a "**stop**" variable for the end of the string.

1. As I loop through the code, each time I find a match on line 7, I print the value on line 10.
2. On line 8, I update the stop value. I am searching for "from" which has 4 characters.
3. To continue searching the remaining string, I reset the **start** value on line 12.
4. On line 11 I update "search_str" to reflect the "remaining" string.

```
1   original_str = "the apple fell far from the tree"
2   found_str = ''
3   search_str = original_str
4   start = 0
5   while start < len(original_str):
6   start = search_str.find('from')
7   if start != -1:
8   stop = start + 4
9   found_str = search_str[start:stop]
```

```
print(found_str)
search_str = search_str[stop:]
start = 0
else:
break
```

Find Last Element in a String

This next example uses the split() method to search a string for a ‘ ’ space, and then uses slicing to return the last word in the string.

In [**16**]: my_str = “the apple fell far from the tree”
In [**17**]: print(my_str.split(‘’)[-1])
Out[16]: tree

The next example uses the **.rindex()** method to return the start index of the last list element. In this example, the **stop index** in the square brackets **[ ]** is set by **[my_str.rindex(‘ ’)]**.

In [18]: print(my_str[**my_str.rindex**(‘ ’)])
Out [18]: tree

3.21 Identifiers

Classes identified by patterns of leading and trailing underscore characters have special meanings.

Interactive Interpreter

The special identifier “_” underscore is used in the interactive interpreter (or Console) to store the result of the last evaluation.

Class-Private Names

Within the context of a class definition, class-private names are often renamed to avoid clashes between “private” attributes of base and derived classes. For example, a private class variable/method/class may begin with an underscore.

System-Defined Names

Special method names refer to system-defined or “dunder” names. These "**special method names**" begin and end with two underline characters. These methods are invoked by special syntax, such as arithmetic operators or subscripting and slicing. This is Python's approach to *operator overloading*.

__add__

__enter__

__eq__

__exit__

__hash__

__init__

__len__

__lt__

__main__

__name__

__new__

__str__

__sub__

__version__

A module's **__name__** is set equal to '**__main__**' when read from standard input, a script, or from an interactive prompt. Top-level code executes at the '**__main__**' scope, as outlined at docs.python.org. A module can discover whether or not it is running in the main scope by checking its own __name__.

In the **Console**, type the module name plus **.__version__** to view the version of the module, as shown below.

openpyxl.__version__

The name of the class is found in the **.__name__** method.

openpyxl.__name__

A "**with statement**" uses the context management protocol that requires the **__enter__** and **__exit__** methods. PEP343 defines a "with statement" that wraps the execution of a block of code with methods defined by the context manager. The most common uses of a "with statement" are for file handling or network ports.

3.22 Compound & Conditional Statements

Python compound statements control the flow of the program. Compound statements begin with for, while, if, else, try, or with. Chapter 5 looks at the *try & except* statement. When the control statement is **True**, the indented lines that follow run.

- for
- while
- if
- else

The control statement always ends with a colon : and you indent the next line of code to the right. If you want to run several lines of code as part of the control statement, the lines are all indented.

The first line of the control statement, and all the indented lines that follow, are called a "Suite" in Python. Other programming languages often refer to this structure as a block of code. A statement is part of a suite (a "block" of code). A statement is either an expression or one of several constructs with a keyword, such as if, while or for. The next topic looks at suites.

> The "for" control statement is used with objects like strings, tuples, ranges, and lists.

In Chapter 7, Example 7.5 demonstrates a while loop. The tests from an "if" or "else" statement move the program into different branches depending on whether the test is "True" or "False."

Conditional Statement

A "for" or "while" loop repeats itself until a condition is met. The condition might be the end of an iterable list, or when a conditional statement is False. The

Python Interpreter evaluates the statement and continues executing that block of code if the statement is True. If the statement is False, the loop ends.

```
for i in range(0, 20):
if i % 2 != 0:
    print("i is an odd number", i)
```

For Loop

The next "for loop" iterates or moves through items in a data structure. When this program runs, each time the program loops through the code, the next item in the list is displayed.

To see a **for** loop in action, type this code in your **Editor** window, then click run.

```
fruits = ['Apple','Orange', 'Watermelon']
for fruit in fruits:
    print('my fruit is:', fruit)
```

The output of this code is shown below.

```
my fruit is:  Apple
        my fruit is:  Orange
        my fruit is:  Watermelon
```

Continue Until Break

In another example, the statement below is always **True**, so the program runs until you break out of the loop.

while **True**:

Iterables

An iteration variable can also be used to iterate through elements in a container. A container could be a list, tuple, or dictionary, As an example of an iterator, in the code that follows the variable "i" is a number with the default starting value of "0." The first time the loop runs, list[i] refers to list[0]. As the program loops, the next time the list runs, list[i] refers to list[1].

fruits = ['Apple', 'Orange', 'Watermelon']

```
for i in range(3):
    print('my fruit is:', fruits[i])
```

The output of this code is shown below.

```
my fruit is:  Apple
my fruit is:  Orange
my fruit is:  Watermelon
```

A **StopIteration** error is raised to indicate the end of an iterator, as shown in Example 7.35. In Chapter 7, Example 7.20 demonstrates a "for" control statement. Example 6 demonstrates a "while" control statement.

---

iter()

The iter() function from the itertools library has two very different behaviors. If the function call **iter(mylist)** includes one argument, like a list, the function iterates over the list. When you pass only one argument, **iter()** expects a collection object that supports the iterator protocol or sequence protocol. If a second argument, *sentinel*, is given, the object must be a callable object, like a function. Later in this chapter, in the "Function" topic, we'll look at **iter(myfunction,** ***sentinel*****)**.

The itertools library has some other interesting functions, like chain() that iterates over two containers in one function call.

3.23 Indented Code (a Suite)

In Python, the first line of a control statement, and all the indented lines that follow, are called a "Suite" of code. In the next figure, there is a red box around the code from line 28 to 48. I added a red vertical dotted line to highlight where the code is indented.

Let's look at the code on lines 29, 30, 31, 32, and 48. These lines are all indented to the same vertical level. This code Suite, or block of code, begins on line 28. The last line in this code Suite is line 48.

> **Indentation** in Python scripts defines a "Suite" or code block.

In this example, the shaded Suite (block of code) is a second "while loop" (lines 32 to 46.) This second Suite is "nested" because it is inside the first Suite. Within the nested Suite, line 38 only runs when the **if statement** on line 37 evaluates to "**True**." A nested "if statement" means there is a second "if statement" within the first "if statement."

In this example, the "**bfr**" counter on line 48 is the last line in this Suite and, in effect, moves forward in the loop to the next item.

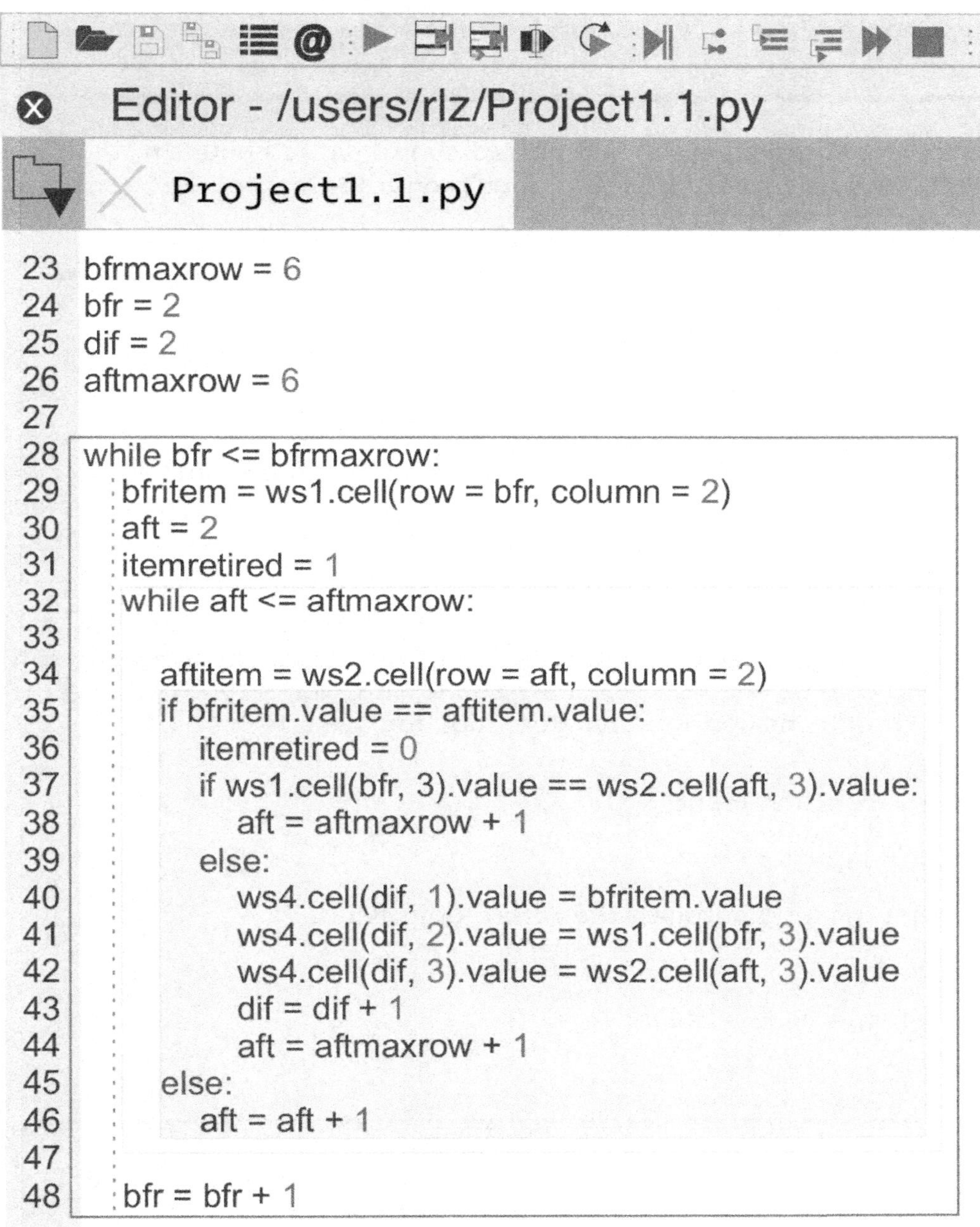

Figure 3.8 An Indented "Suite" or Block of Code

The Chapter 4 topic, "My Program Loops and Never Ends" is an example of incorrect indentation levels. In Python, an empty Suite (indented block of code) is illegal. For example, an "if statement" that does nothing is illegal. Instead, use the "pass" function when your code should take no action, as shown in Chapter 7, Example 7.7. The Chapter 7 examples 7.1 and 7.2 illustrate a few list errors.

The Outline pane is a great way to see nested control statements. In Spyder, select "Outline" from the View, Panes menu. In Chapter 7, Example 7.5 has an indentation error.

3.24 Functions and Methods

Functions are a sequence of statements. Python functions are first-class objects, which means functions are treated like any other type of object, such as integers or tuples. Functions are an example of **decomposition**, where you break a program into smaller, self-contained pieces.

First, you define a function. Once a function is defined, you can use it as many times as you like by calling or invoking the function. The term "**Abstraction"** refers to the fact you don't need to know how something works, you just need to know what it does. When considering a function, look for these features.

1. What are the function inputs?
2. What does the function do?
3. What are the function outputs (the return object?)

```
def menu(meal, special=False):
    <some code>
```

> When you define a function within a class, it is called a **method**.

Depending on whether you are defining or calling a function, you call the items in parentheses either "parameters" or "arguments." When defining a function, the items in parenthesis are **parameters**. When calling a function, the items are **arguments**.

Defining a Function

When defining a function in the **Editor**, the parameters in parentheses specify what types of arguments (objects) the function can accept. In this example, the parameter “special” assigned a default boolean value of “False.”

```
def menu(meal, special=False):
    msg = “”
    if special is True:
        msg = ‘The specials today are Mimosas. ’
    if meal == ‘breakfast’:
        msg = ‘Breakfast is eggs and toast. ’
    else:
        msg = ‘Sorry, we ran out of food. ’
    return msg
```

The parameter “meal” has no default value. Because of Python’s dynamic typing, when calling the function, I can pass any type of data for “meal.”

The Python style guide recommends function names begin with a lowercase letter. Class names should begin with an uppercase letter.

The Chapter 6 topic, “The Function Call Signature,” explains how to use the **signature()**function to see what parameters another function expects, what that function does, and the function’s return object. In Chapter 7, example 20 uses the **signature()** function to retrieve parameter information. In Chapter 6, the topic, “What are the Function Arguments,” explores function definitions.

Calling or Invoking a Function or Method

When calling or invoking a function, you pass arguments with values to the function inside the parenthesis. If there are no arguments, the parenthesis are empty but are still required to indicate the function call, as shown in Examples 7.30 and 7.47 in Chapter 7. In the example below, the last line calls the function “**menu**.”

```
def menu(meal, special=False):
    msg = “”
    if special is True:
```

```
        msg = 'The specials today are Mimosas. '
    if meal == 'breakfast':
        msg = 'Breakfast is eggs and toast. '
    else:
        msg = 'Sorry, we ran out of food. '
    return msg
print(menu('breakfast'))
```

The two statements below call the "menu" function and produce the same result. In the second example, I omit the optional keyword argument. When calling the function, the parameter "meal" is referred to as a positional argument that has a value of "**breakfast**."

```
menu('breakfast', special = False)
menu('breakfast')
```

Parameters

In the previous example, there are two parameters in the function definition, "meal" and "special."

	Parameter Name	Default Value	Required/Optional
Positional	meal		Required
Keyword	special	False	Optional

Table 3.27 Parameters

Arguments

Arguments are the values you pass to a function when calling the function. Not all functions have arguments. In this example, the function call has two arguments.

menu('breakfast', special=True)

Order	Parameter Name	Argument Value
1	meal	breakfast
2	special	True

Table 3.28 Arguments

When I call this function, the parameters are now referred to as "arguments" because I am calling the function. Example 7.21 in Chapter 7 demonstrates an argument that is the wrong type for a particular function.

Keyword (Optional) Arguments

PEP 3102 defines keyword arguments which are optional because there is a default value in the function definition. When calling a function, a name or "keyword" precedes the keyword argument. The second parameter in my earlier function definition includes the **keyword** "special" with a default value of "False."

In Chapter 7, Example 7.6 illustrates an **AttributeError** caused by missing keyword names when calling a method.

Positional Arguments

The "meal" argument is a positional argument because it does not have a keyword and default value. Positional arguments are mandatory or required since there is no default value. You must list **positional arguments** before any **keyword arguments**. The example below is **invalid** because a positional argument is after a keyword argument.

def **menu**(special=False, meal):

Example 7.36 in Chapter 7 raises an error because it is missing one positional argument.

In the previous example of the menu() function, the "special" argument has a default value. When calling the menu() function, "special" is an **optional** argument. If you don't provide the argument when calling this function, Python uses the default value "False" specified in this function's definition.

If a function has optional keyword arguments with default values, the values are assigned using the "scope" that exists at the time of the function definition. The global scope is used in the previous example where the menu() function definition is on line 1. In the case of nested functions, the function definition might be in the enclosing scope, as shown at the end of this Chapter in the namespace topic.

> An optional argument with a default value is another way to implement the concept of a "global variable." Let's say you want a running "total" value. The first time you call the function, you set the optional argument "total=0". Within the function, you update the total value. As you make recursive function calls, you pass the latest "total" value as an argument to the recursive function call statement.

Unpacking Operator Arguments

Occasionally, you may need to set an arbitrary number of arguments for a function. In the function definition, an asterisk * prefaces arguments to indicate the function can use an arbitrary number of objects. A variable number of positional arguments is often shown as myfunction(*args) and a variable number of keyword arguments is shown as myfunction(*kwargs).

Let's say you have a function that prints personalized movie tickets for each patron. The patron names vary from day-to-day. In the next code example, on line 1, there are two **parameters** enclosed in parenthesis:

```
1 def print_tickets(number_of_tickets, *name):
2       i = 0
3       while i < number_of_tickets:
4             print(name[i])
5             i += 1
6
7 print_tickets(2, ‘John’, ‘Alice’)
```

The function definition on line 1 includes an asterisk * or "unpacking operator" to indicate there is an arbitrary number of **name** arguments passed to the function. For more information on unpacking operators, see the next sections. There are two paramters in the function definition.

number_of_tickets

***name**

When I call the function on line 7, I pass it three arguments. Two of the arguments are names.

print_tickets(2, ‘John’, ‘Alice’)

Unpacking Operators

PEP 448 defines "Additional Unpacking Generalizations." You can define functions to take *x and **y arguments. Unpacking operators allow a function to accept any number of arguments that aren't specifically named in the declaration.

The asterisk * or ‘iterable unpacking operator’ unpacks the iterable into positional arguments.

The double asterisk ** or ‘dictionary unpacking operator’ provides the same behavior for dictionaries. You can pass arguments stored in a dictionary to a function using **, as shown below. This example is an arbitrary keyword argument dictionary.

```
In [1]: kwargs = {color: 'blue', height: 4}
In [2]: myfunction(**kwargs)
```

To pass arguments stored in an iterable to a function, use the * unpacking operator. An iterable might be a list or tuple. This example uses the "names" list to provide the arbitrary positional arguments.

```
In [1]: names = ['John', 'Alice']
In [2]: print_tickets(2, *names)
```

If you leave off the * unpacking operator in the function call on line 2, an error is raised, as shown in Example 7.52 in Chapter 7. Example 7.41 demonstrates an error when there are too many values to unpack.

The PEP 3132 "Extended Iterable Unpacking" specifies a "catch-all" name which is assigned to a list of all items not assigned to a "regular" name. In the next example, an asterisk * indicates "b" is assigned all remaining values.

```
a, *b = (1, 2, 3, 4)

a = 1
b = (2, 3, 4)
```

How to View the Function Argument Definition

To view arguments accepted by a function or method, you can use the help() function or inspect the function's **call signature**. For example, to see the arguments of the meal() function, run the program to create the function. In the **Console**, import the inspect library, and type the print statement shown below. The Python Interpreter returns the parameters for the menu function.

```
In [4]: from inspect import signature
In [5]: print(str(signature(menu)))
(meal, special=False)
```

In Chapter 6, the topic, "What are the Function Arguments," explores function definitions. In Chapter 7, Example 7.6 illustrates an **AttributeError** caused by missing keyword names when calling a method.

The devguide.python.org has details of the style guide for Python's documentation, and PEP 257 is specific to docstrings.

Function Return or Yield Objects

A function "returns" or "yields" one object; however, that object might be a container like a tuple with several items. When a function doesn't specify a return value, it returns the special value "NoneType" discussed earlier. As the Python Interpreter moves through the code in a function, when it encounters the keyword "return," it stops execution and returns the value in the return expression. Nothing after the return statement is executed.

> When a function uses the 'yield' statement instead of the 'return' statement, the function is a **generator**, as discussed previously.

In Chapter 6, the topic, "What Type of Object Does a Function Return?" has additional information on return objects. For debugging purposes, let's look at the function return object in terms of:

- What **type** of return object does the function return?
- Does the function return a value of "**None**?"
- Does the function return a tuple with several items?

This function returns a tuple with three strings and an int. When I call the function on line 6, I pass the return tuple elements to my variables "mystr1", "mystr2", "myint", and "mystr3".

```
1 def myfunction():
2       print('hi')
3       return 'str1', 'str2', 5, 'str3'
4
5
6 mystr1, mystr2, myint, mystr3 = myfunction()
```

Once I run the code, and the function definition is created, I can use the "type()" function in the Console to find what type of object the function returns.

In [3]: type(myfunction())

Out [3]: tuple

We looked at a return tuple object earlier in the topic, “Tuples and Function Return Objects.”

> The absence of a function return object may cause an error, if the original **function call** expects a function return object. When debugging you might comment all code in a function, and an error still occurs because of a discrepancy in the return object.

Boolean Return Object

The next two functions both return “True.” Because the second function, “**myfunction2**” is simpler, it is considered more “Pythonic.”

```
def myfunction():
    if 2 == 2:
        return True

def myfunction2():
    return 2 == 2
```

Return the Statement that is True

The next example of a return statement would return the value of “y” or ‘hello’ because Python returns the True statement. It is “True” that **y** is a string; and “False” that **x** is an integer. In this case, whichever expression is “True” would be returned.

```
x = ‘john’

y = ‘hello’

return isinstance(x, int) or isinstance (y, str)
```

All Paths Do Not Have a Return Value

Previously, the “menu” function returned a value on line 10. A return value **must exist for all paths** through the function. In the next example, I modified the program to have different return values for several paths. The “if” suites of code on lines 3-5 and 6-10 both have return values.

```
1  def menu(meal, special=False):
2      msg = “”
```

```
3        if special is True:
4              msg = 'The specials today are Mimosas. '
5              return msg
6        if meal == 'breakfast':
7              msg = 'Breakfast is eggs and toast. '
8              return msg
9        else:
10             msg = 'Sorry, we ran out of food. '
11 print(menu('lunch'))
```

Do you see the problem with this code? The "else" suite of code beginning on line 9 does not have a return value. When there is no return value, the Python Interpreter returns the value "**None**," which may not be what you wanted. The topic "Does the Object have a Value of None" in Chapter 6 explains the pitfalls of the value "**None**." Example 7.17 in Chapter 7 illustrates how to identify the value "None."

Index Example for a Tuple Return Object

In the next example, on line 14 I pass the function's return values to **mytxt**. Because the function returns two values on line 10, "**mytxt**" is now a tuple. When I try to print **mytxt** on line 17, the Console displays an error. Example 7.33 and 7.53 in Chapter 7 demonstrates this behavior.

```
1  def menu(meal, special=False):
2        msg, msg2 = "", "Thank you."
3        if special is True:
4              msg = 'The specials today are Mimosas. '
5        if meal == 'breakfast':
7              msg = 'Breakfast is eggs and toast. '
9        else:
10             msg = 'Sorry, we ran out of food.'
11             return msg, msg2
12
13
14 mytxt = menu('lunch')
15 if mytxt is None:
16       pass
17 else:
18       print(mytxt)
```

To fix my program, I need to change line 18 to print each element in the “**mytxt**” tuple, as shown below. The variable “mytxt” is now a tuple, so I may want to rename the variable.

```
print(mytxt[0], mytxt[1])
```

The Type of Return Value

The type of return value is important if you're using it as the argument for another function. In the earlier example, the “print” function expects a string, and my “**menu**” function returns a tuple. In this new example, the Python Interpreter raises an error. Using the previous function as an example, in the **Console**, I could use the function “type” to identify the type of object the “**menu**” function returns.

```
In [1]: myTuple = (msg, msg2)
In [2]: type(myTuple)
Out [2]: tuple
```

Recursive Functions

A recursive function calls itself until a statement, or base case, terminates the function. Typically a recursive call solves problems at a high level, reducing the problem's size at each recursive call, until finally, you reach your base case, which is the simplest form of the problem. The recursive call terminates at your base case. The solution to the “Towers of Hanoi” is a famous example of a recursive problem.

In the next example, the function calls itself recursively on line 5 until **bookcnt** is more than the length of “books” on line 2. If you omit the termination expression on line 2, the program runs continuously until a **RecursiveError** is eventually raised.

```
1  def printbooks(books, bookcnt=0):
2      while bookcnt < len(books):
3          print(books[bookcnt])
4          bookcnt += 1
5          bookcnt = printbooks(books, bookcnt)
6      return bookcnt
7
8
9  books = ['bk1', 'bk2', 'bk3']
10 cnt = int(printbooks(books))
```

```
print(‘There are %d books in %s’ % (cnt, books))
```

Recursive Memory Stacks

This topic looks at what happens with memory stacks as you make recursive calls. The code below includes a function “c” and a recursive call within the function on line 10.

```
1  def c(b, bc=0):
2      i = ‘\nStack’
3      j = ‘ - bc value is’
4      k = “‘bc’ identifier is ”
5      while bc < len(b):
6          bc += 1
7          i = i + str(bc + 1) + j + str(bc)
8          print(i)
9          print(k, id(bc))
10         bc = c(b, bc)
11     return bc
12
13
14 books = [‘bk1’, ‘bk2’, ‘bk3’]
15 print(‘\nStack 1 (global namespace)’)
16 cnt = c(books)
17 print(‘\nThere are %d books in %s’ % (cnt, books))
```

When I run the program, the **Console** outputs the following.

```
Stack 1 (global namespace)

Stack2 - bc value is 1
‘bc’ identifier is  4485190800

Stack3 - bc value is 2
‘bc’ identifier is  4485190832

Stack4 - bc value is 3
‘bc’ identifier is  4485190864

There are 3 books in [‘bk1’, ‘bk2’, ‘bk3’]
```

Let's look at a visual picture of how the Python Interpreter moves up and down the stacks.

When the program initially runs, it creates the global namespace or **Stack 1**. Line 16 calls the function **c()** and creates memory **Stack 2**. In memory **Stack 2**, after the program runs line 6, my counter "bc" has a value of 1, and the identifier for "bc" is 4485190800. On line 10, the program makes a recursive call to function **c()** and creates memory **Stack 3**.

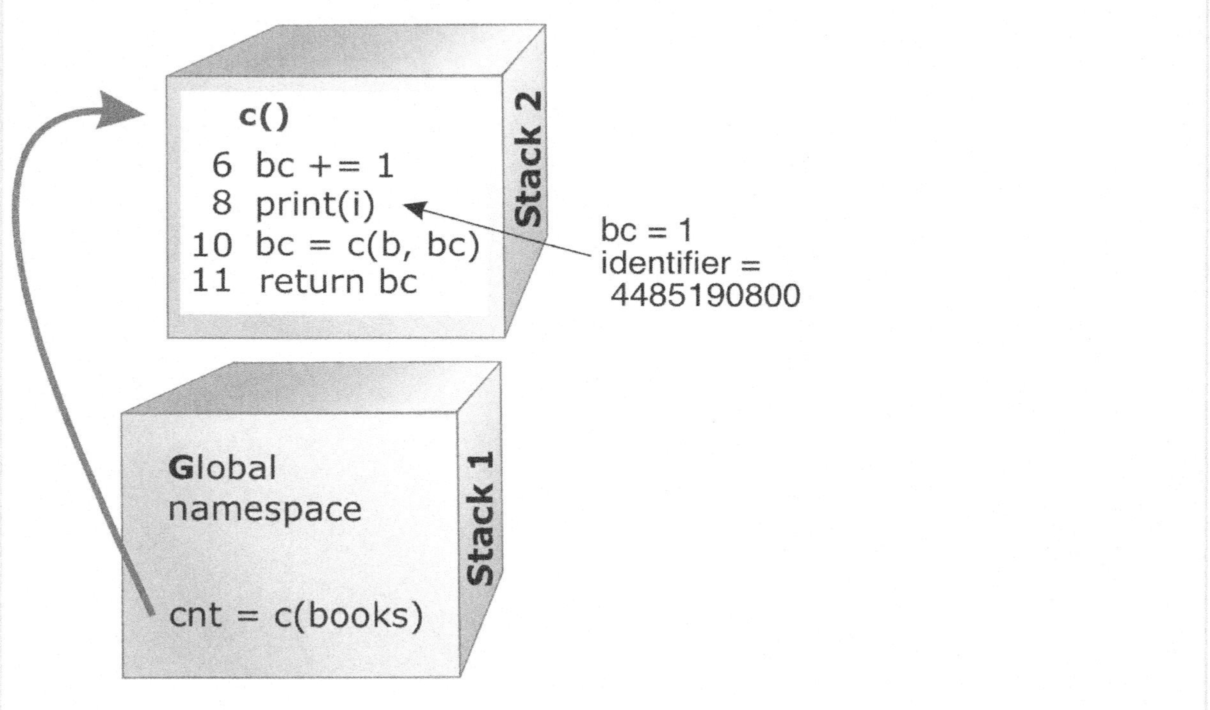

In memory **Stack 3**, after the program runs line 6 again, "bc" has a value of 2, and the identifier for "bc" is 4485190832. While "bc" has the same name, the identifiers are different, indicating these are two different variables. On line 10, the program makes a recursive call to function **c()** and creates memory **Stack 4**.

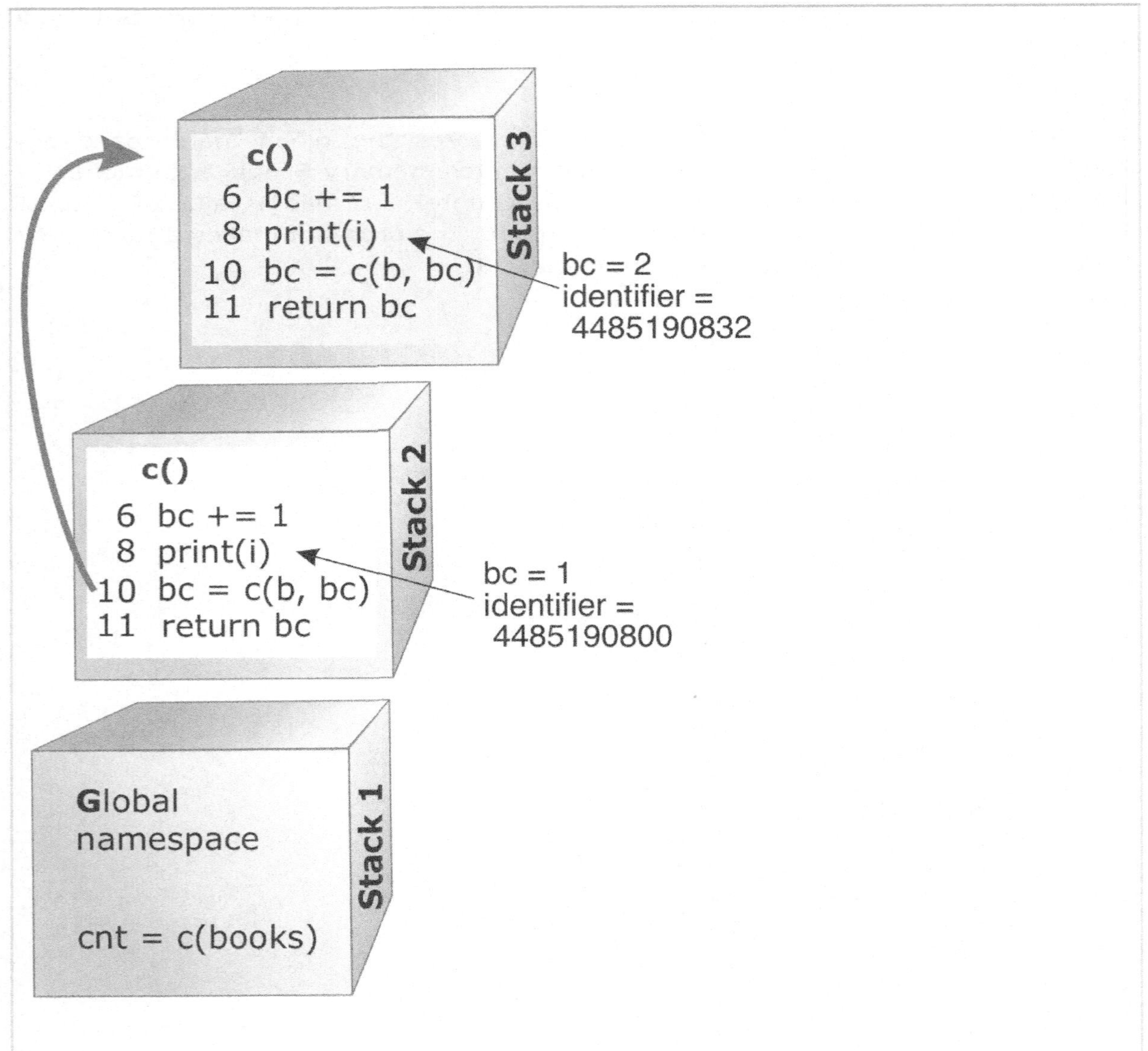

In memory **Stack 4**, the program again runs line 6. Now "bc" has a value of 3, and the identifier is 4485190864. On line 10, the program makes a recursive call to function **c()** and creates memory **Stack 5**.

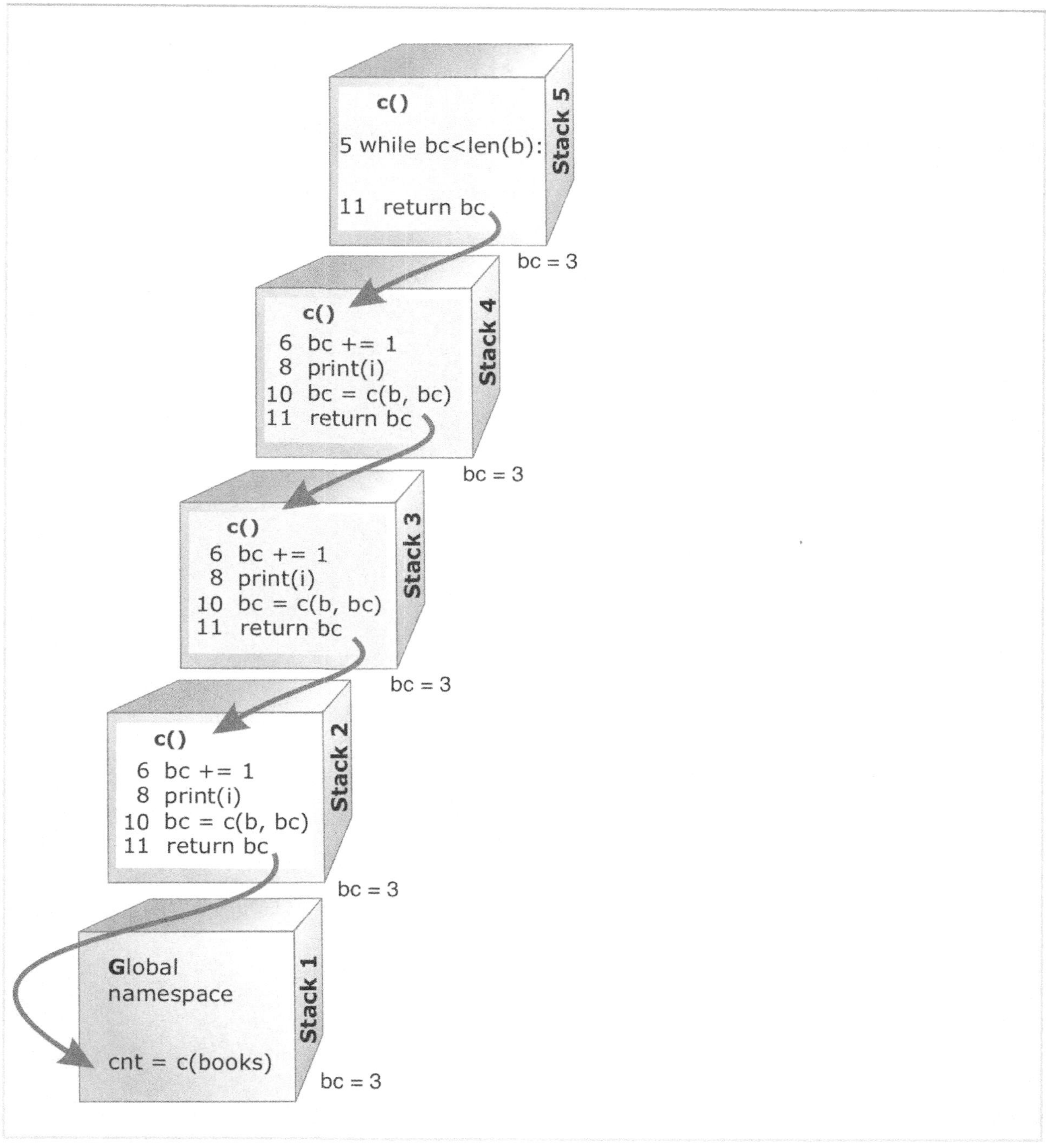
c()
5 while bc<len(b):
11 return bc
Stack 5
bc = 3
c()
6 bc += 1
8 print(i)
10 bc = c(b, bc)
11 return bc
Stack 4
bc = 3
c()
6 bc += 1
8 print(i)
10 bc = c(b, bc)
11 return bc
Stack 3
bc = 3
c()
6 bc += 1
8 print(i)
10 bc = c(b, bc)
11 return bc
Stack 2
bc = 3
Global
namespace
cnt = c(books)
Stack 1
bc = 3

In memory **Stack 5**, when line 5 compares the value of bc to the length of "b," the Python Interpreter returns False. At this point, "bc" has a value of 3, and the length of "b" is 3.

line 5: 3 < 3 is False

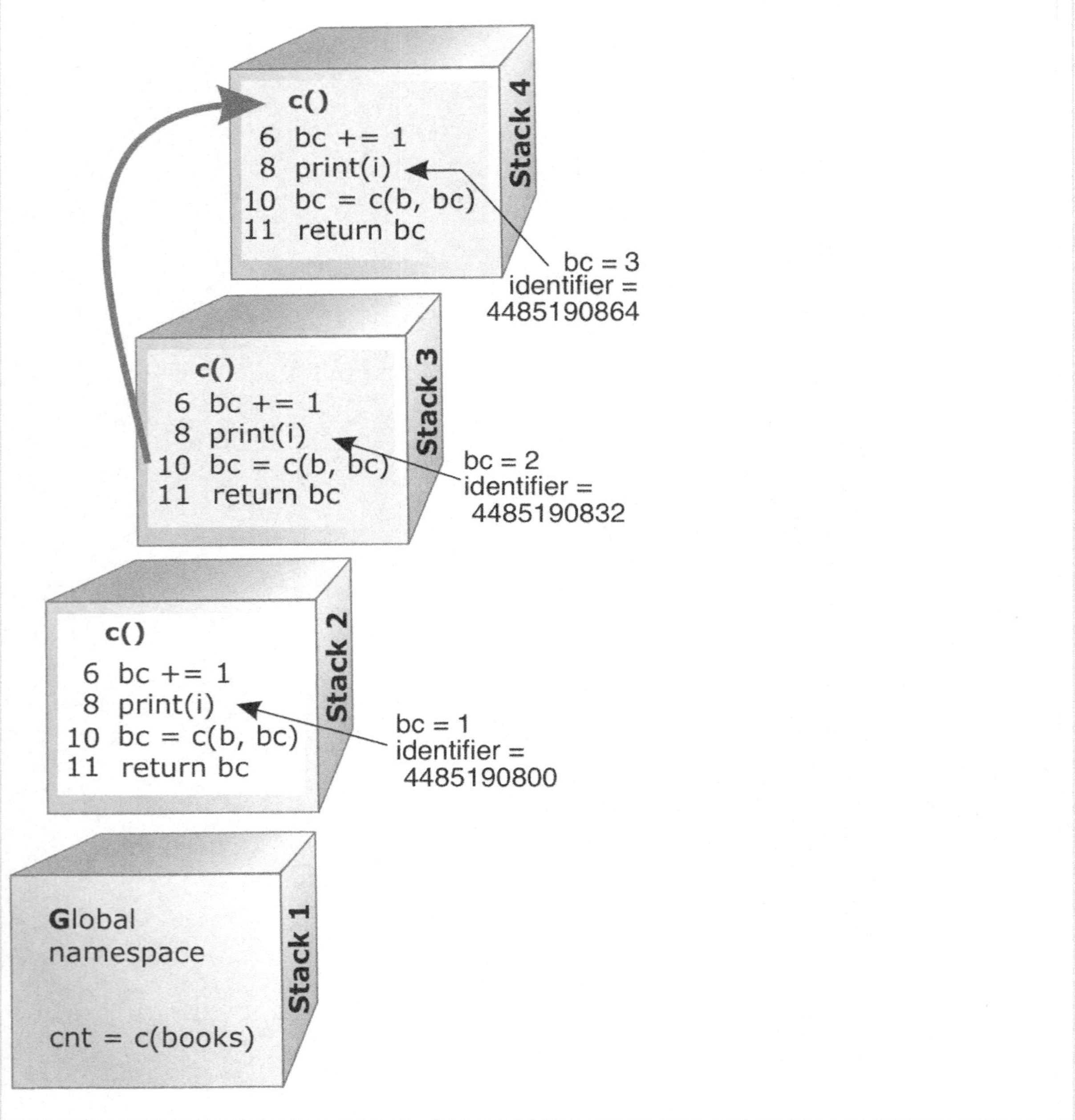

In **Stack 5**, the Python Interpreter runs line 11 and returns the value of "bc" to the calling function in **Stack 4**, as shown in the next diagram. In **Stack 4**, the Python Interpreter runs line 11 and returns the value of "bc" to the calling function in **Stack 3**. Next, the Python Interpreter returns "bc" to the calling function in **Stack 2**. Finally, "bc" is returned to **Stack 1** to line 16, the initial function call.

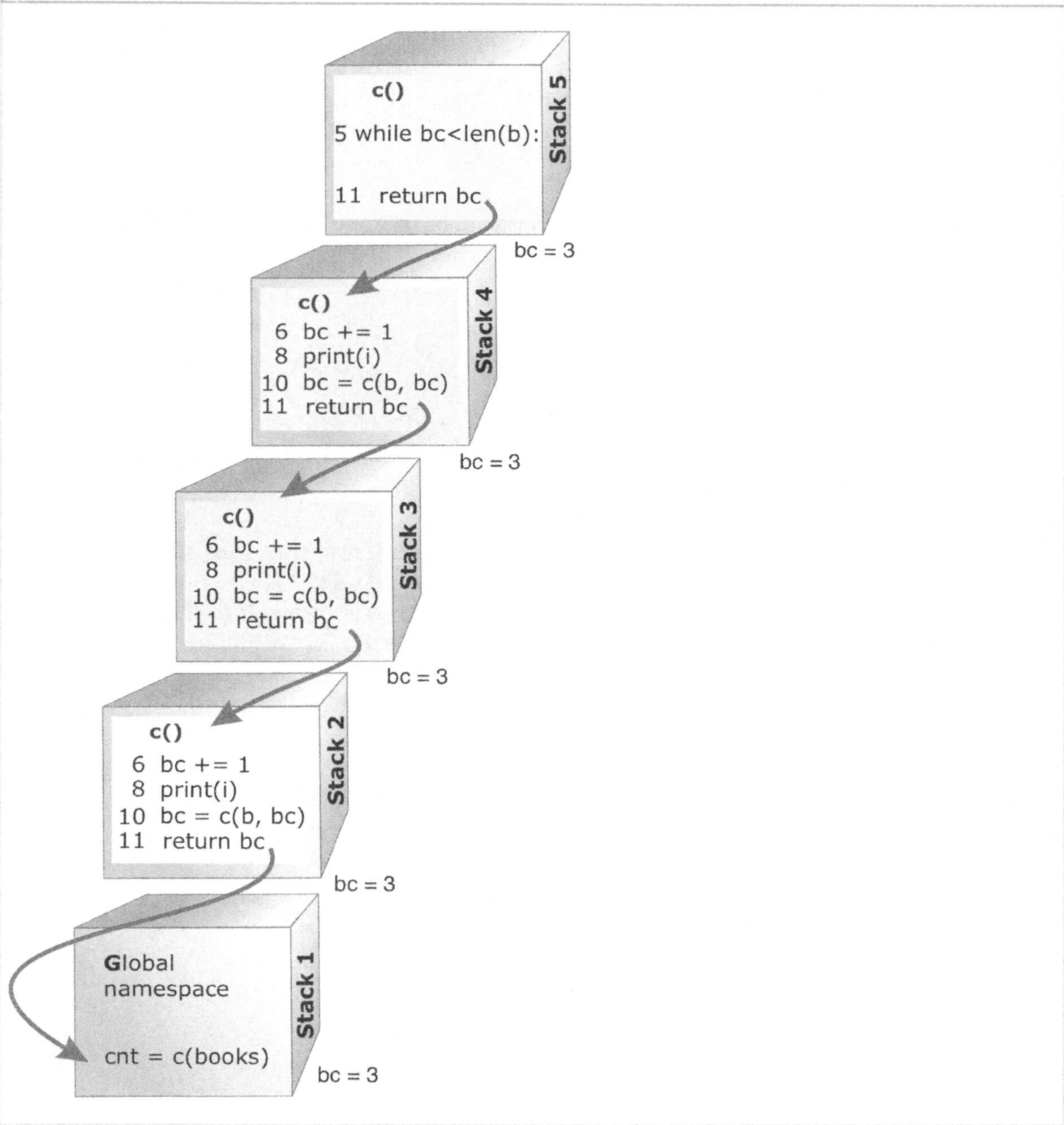

The Zip Function

Now let's look at several interesting functions. The **zip()** function takes two or more iterables as arguments and returns a "zip" object that behaves like tuples. For example, when you pass two lists with three elements each, zip() returns three pairs in a "zip" object.

The first example uses the **zip()** function with two lists, and returns a zip object that is unpacked to the "order" and "color" variables.

```
for order, color in zip([1, 2, 3], ['green', 'red', 'blue']):
    print(order, color, '\n')
```

When I run the code, the Console prints the following text.

```
In [1]:
1 green
2 red
3 blue
```

In the next example, I want to create a range of scores for a plot chart with the matplotlib library. To view more information on the matplotlib library, in Chapter 7 see examples 7.19 and 7.22.

I'm going to use 'school_Dict' as my iterable for the **zip()** function, and convert "zip" objects into a **tuple**, **dictionary**, and a **list**. The expression is a list comprehension that combines two zip objects to create 'newList.' The next figure shows the objects in "school_Dict." There are three keys with list values. The keys are:

Herman

John

Mary

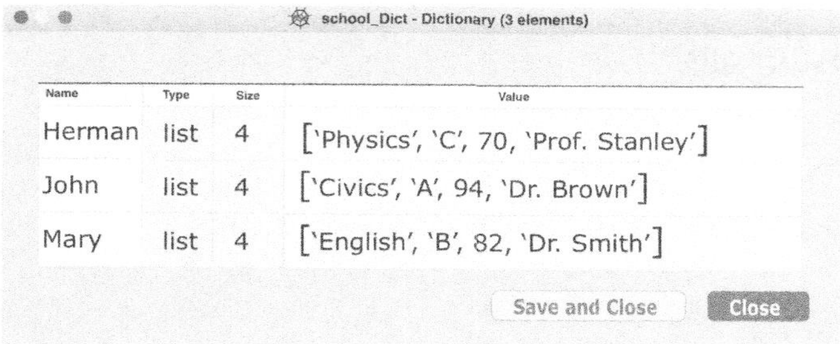

Name	Type	Size	Value
Herman	list	4	['Physics', 'C', 70, 'Prof. Stanley']
John	list	4	['Civics', 'A', 94, 'Dr. Brown']
Mary	list	4	['English', 'B', 82, 'Dr. Smith']

Figure 3.9 The school_Dict

In the first half of the expression I use the zip() function to combine objects together into a zip object. In the second half of the expression, I "unzip" the dictionary objects using an unpacking * operator. Now, we'll experiment in the Console and gradually work up to the final list comprehension.

```
newList = [dict(zip(school_Dict, x)) for x in zip(*school_Dict.values())]
```

1. The first half of the expression creates a zip object using "x" from the second half of the expression. As a demonstration, I'm going to temporarily provide "x" values in a tuple. In Step 4, we'll replace "x" when we use zip() to unpack the iterable from "school_Dict.values()."

```
x=(('Physics', 'Civics', 'English' ),
   ('C', 'A', 'B'),
   (70, 94, 82),
   ('Prof. Stanley', 'Dr. Brown', 'Dr. Smith'))
```

This "x" tuple contains the four tuples shown below. If you look back at the original **school_Dict** you can see that here I've grouped the three list items differently.

```
('Physics', 'Civics', 'English')
('C', 'A', 'B')
(70, 94, 82)
('Prof. Stanley', 'Dr. Brown', 'Dr. Smith')
```

2. Let's continue looking at the first half of the list comprehension, which returns a zip object. In the **Console**, I'm going to use the tuple() function to temporarily convert this zip object to a tuple.

```
In [1]:tuple(zip(school_Dict, x))
```

```
Out[1]:

(('Herman', ('Physics', 'Civics', 'English')),
 ('John', ('C', 'A', 'B')),
 ('Mary', (70, 94, 82)))
```

3. The "x" tuple in **Step 1** has the same values as the last half of the list comprehension statement.

```
tuple(zip(*school_Dict.values()))
```

When I remove the tuple() function, this is now the same expression as the second half of the list comprehension.

```
zip(*school_Dict.values())
```

4. Now that we've looked at different zip statements, I'm going to repeat Step 1. This time I am using the **dict()** function instead of the **tuple()** function.

```
dict(zip(school_Dict, x))
```

5. Earlier, when we looked at list comprehensions, I said a list comprehension follows this format:

newlist = **[expression(variable) - for item in iterable- if]**

In Step 4 we created the "expression." In Step 3 we created the **iterable** statement.

expression	dict(zip(school_Dict, x))
for item in	for x in
iterable	zip(*school_Dict.values())

The two zip statements are combined into the list comprehension that follows.

```
newList = [dict(zip(school_Dict, x)) for x in zip(*school_Dict.values())]
```

Finally, to create my graph, I create a "graphNums" object using the objects in newList[2].

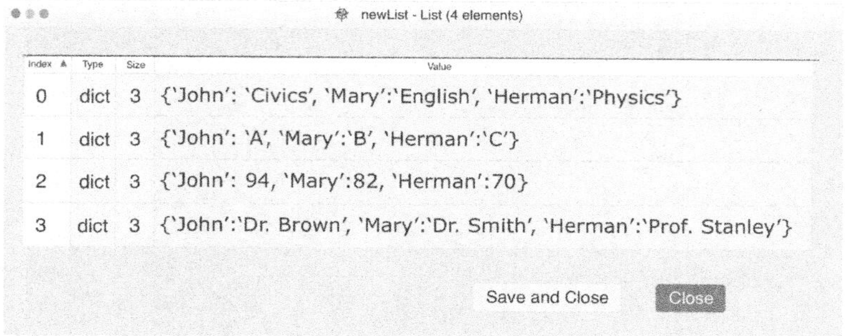

newList - List (4 elements)

Index	Type	Size	Value
0	dict	3	{'John': 'Civics', 'Mary':'English', 'Herman':'Physics'}
1	dict	3	{'John': 'A', 'Mary':'B', 'Herman':'C'}
2	dict	3	{'John': 94, 'Mary':82, 'Herman':70}
3	dict	3	{'John':'Dr. Brown', 'Mary':'Dr. Smith', 'Herman':'Prof. Stanley'}

Figure 3.10 newList

```
graphNums = list(newList[2].values())
```

Then, I assign "graphNums" to the third element in newList[2].

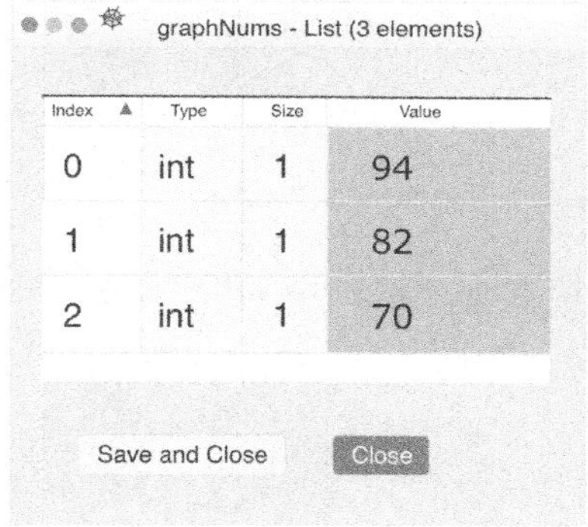

graphNums - List (3 elements)

Index	Type	Size	Value
0	int	1	94
1	int	1	82
2	int	1	70

Figure 3.11 graphNums

In the next example, I create a tuple for the grades using the unpacking asterisk symbol, as shown below. The asterisk * unpacks the sequence into positional arguments and behaves like an "unzip." The "grades" are the third element in the "s" tuple.

```
school_Dict = {'John': ['Civics', 'A', 94, 'Dr. Brown'],
               'Mary': ['English', 'B', 82, 'Dr. Smith'],
               'Herman': ['Physics', 'C', 70, 'Prof. Stanley']}

    c, g, s, t = list(zip(*myDict.values()))
```

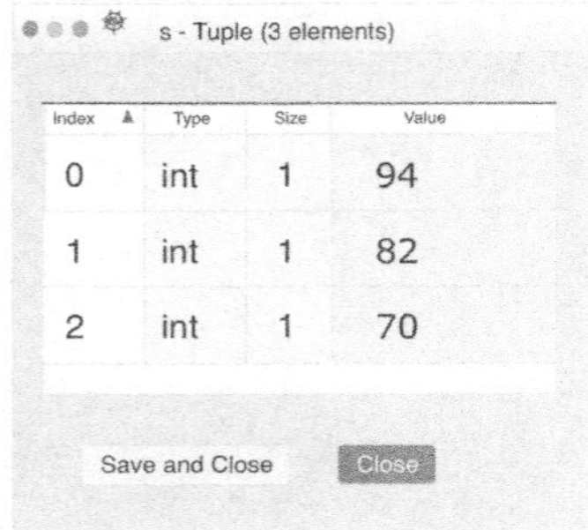

s - Tuple (3 elements)

Index	Type	Size	Value
0	int	1	94
1	int	1	82
2	int	1	70

Figure 3.12 The Tuple 's'

The Map() Function

The map() function takes a unary function and a **data structure** or "iterable" as arguments and returns an iterator of type "map" that applies the function to all items in the **data structure.**

map(*<function>*, *<iterator>*)

In this example, the map() function applies the function str() to all elements in "mylist."

map(str, mylist)

The map() function arguments can also be a function with several arguments. In the code below, the function "max" takes two list arguments and returns a "map" object.

```
list1, list2 = [2, 4, 6], [1, 3, 5]
map(max, list1, list2)
```

In the next example, I convert the "map" object type to a "list," so you can see the values returned. The max() function is applied to each list item, so the statements are 2 > 1, 4 > 3, and 6 >5.

```
In [1]: list1, list2 = [2, 4, 6], [1, 3, 5]
In [2]: list(map(max, list1, list2))
Out [2]: tuple [2, 4, 6]
```

This next example uses map to invoke the **gbp_to_usd** function for each element in the **gbp** list and return a new **usd** list.

```
1 def gbp_to_usd(temp)
2       return round(temp * .8, 2)
3
4
5 usd = []
6 gbp = [6.70, 32.51]
7 for m in map(gbp_to_usd, gbp):
8       usd.append(m)
9 print(usd)
```

The Console prints the following.

```
In [1]:
[5.36, 26.01]
```

Earlier, when we looked at list comprehensions, I compared them to the map() function. Lines 7 and 8 in the previous example could be rewritten as a list comprehension, as shown below on line 7.

```
1 def gbp_to_usd(temp)
2       return round(temp * .8, 2)
3
4
5 usd = []
6 gbp = [6.70, 32.51]
7 usd = [gbp_to_usd(temp) for temp in gbp]
8 print(usd)
```

Lambda Functions

Lambda expressions are used to create anonymous functions. These functions are not bound to a name and typically are simple expressions, often used with the map() or filter() functions. The format of a lambda expression is shown below. The <*parameters*> are variable names.

lambda *parameters*: *expression*

In the next lambda expression, on line 2 I am passing the sort() function the second element [1] in the list "pairs." The parameter is "m."

```
1    pairs = [(1, 'Jan'), (2, 'Feb'), (3, 'April')]
2    pairs.sort(key=lambda m: m[1])
```

Now the Console prints out "pairs" with the values sorted by the second element.

```
In [2]: pairs
Out[2]: [(3, 'April'), (2, 'Feb'), (1, 'Jan')]
```

In this next example, a lambda expression is combined with the map() function. The lambda parameter is "x" and the expression is **x * 4**.

```
for i in map(lambda x: x * 4, [1, 3, 6, 7]):
print(i)
```

The Console prints out the value shown below.

```
In [1]:
4
12
24
28
```

The Filter() Function

The filter() function takes a *function* and a **data structure** (*iterable*) as arguments. Filter() returns items in an iterable (of "filter" object type) for each <*iterator*> where the <*function*> returns **True** for that <*iterator*>.

filter(<*function*>, <*iterator*>)

In this example, filter() returns matched items from **myvar** as a "filter" object type, which I convert to a "list" on line 8.

```
1 def myfunc(mystr):
2       if mystr in 'Hello':
3             return True
4       else:
5             return False
6
7 myvar = ('H', 'i')
8 print(list(filter(myfunc, myvar)))
```

The Console prints out the value shown below, because "H" is in the string "Hello."

```
['H']
```

Lambda with Filter

You can also use a "lambda" expression as your function. Line 1 returns an object of type "filter" and assigns the values to "myvar." I convert the "filter" type to a "tuple" on line 2.

```
1  myvar = filter(lambda x: x > 4, [1, 3, 6, 7])
2  print(tuple(myvar))
```

The Console prints out the value shown below, because 6 and 7 are > 4.

```
(6, 7)
```

Let's look at this expression in detail. First, we'll look at the lambda function, keeping in mind the format of a lambda expression.

lambda *variable names*: *expression*

lambda expression: lambda x: x > 4	
parameter (variable names)	expression
x	x > 4

Now, let's focus on the filter part of the expression, given this format of a filter expression.

filter(<*function*>, <*iterator*>)

filter expression: filter(<*function*>, [1, 3, 6, 7]	
function	iterator
<*the lambda function*>	[1, 3, 6, 7]

Finally, let's put all the pieces back together.

expression: filter(lambda x: x > 4, [1, 3, 6, 7]	
function	iterator
lambda x: x > 4	[1, 3, 6, 7]

The iter() Function

The iter() function has two very different behaviors. If a second argument, *sentinel*, is given, the object must be a callable object, like a function. If the function call **iter(mylist)** includes one argument, like a list, the function iterates over the list.

iter(myfunction, *sentinel***)**

The Print() Function

Throughout this chapter, you've seen many examples of the print() function. The print() function prints out to the Console and is a handy debugging tool.

The default behavior is to print a line return, but if you provide the "**end**" keyword argument as shown below, there is no line return. In this example, the **\n** adds a line feed before 'Hello World.'

print('\nHello World', end='')

We've seen several examples already where I changed an integer to a string before using the print() function. You can also print integers or floats. This example demonstrates how to print the result of an arithmetic expression.

print(2*3)

The console output is "6."

When we looked at recursive functions, you may have noticed the last line printed an integer and strings.

```
print('There are %d books in %s' % (cnt, books))
```

3.25 Classes

This topic provides a brief overview of classes. The **docs.python.org** website has a tutorial on classes and explains the concept of "self" in great detail.

- Create a Class
- The DocString
- Variables - Attributes
- Create an Instance of the Class
- Methods
- Dotted Notation for Attributes
- Calling a Method

When working with classes, first you define or create a "class," then you create an "instance" of the class. In the examples that follow, my class name is "Car," and my instance of "Car" is "my_car." I can reuse the class "Car," creating many instances of "Car."

Classes implement data abstractions. To work with a class, you don't need to know the details inside the class or how it gets the job done. You only need to understand the data attributes and methods of the class.

You can define a class based on another class. So, for example, I could define a class Convertible(Car). When you create a class, the superclass is in parenthesis. The class Convertible(Car) is using "Car" as the superclass. "Convertible" is the subclass of "Car."

The variable "*self*" refers to any object you create of type "Car." Continuing the earlier example, "*self*" refers to the instance "my_car." The variable "*self*" is implicitly passed as the first parameter to class attributes and methods.

Special Methods and Override Behavior

Earlier, we looked at special method names that refer to system-defined or "dunder" names that begin with two underline characters. PEP 8 covers Module Level Dunder Names. Classes inherit these special methods from parent classes but can override that behavior.

For example, in Python, you see **<** in comparisons, but you could override the **__lt__ (less than)** behavior to do something entirely different. "Data attributes" associated with a class definition are called "class variables." When associated with an instance of a class, they are called instance variables. Sometimes you'll see a class variable used instead of a global variable, for example to increment a counter.

A class definition begins with **def __init__(self)**, as shown below on line 4.

```
1  class Car():
2      """This class represents a car."""
3      yr = 2020
4      def __init__(self, model, make, year):
5          """Initialize model, make, and year variables."""
6          self.model = model
7          self.make = make
8          self.year = year
9      def drive(self):
10         """Move the car."""
11         print(self.model.title() + " is now moving.")
12     def parallelpark(self):
13         """Parallel park the car."""
14         print(self.model.title() + " is now parking.")
15
16
17 my_car = Car('Subaru', 'Crosstrek', 2019)
18 print(my_car.model, my_car.make, my_car.year)
19 my_car.parallelpark()
```

Create a Class

In the previous class example, line 1 creates a class named "Car." Class names begin with a capital letter to differentiate them from function names, which should be lowercase.

The DocString

Lines 2, 5, 10, and 13 look like comments but are actually examples of a "DocString." The Chapter 6 topic, "The <u>Function Call Signature</u>," explains how to work with the "inspect" module and view a DocString signature.

The function help() reads the docstring when gathering information about an object.

Class Variables - Attributes

Continuing with the car class example, beginning with the function definition on line 4, you can see the four parameters in the class.

```
def __init__(self, model, make, year):
    self
    model
    make
    year
```

When working with the "my_car" instance of the Car class, I can use dotted notation to reference the variables.

```
my_car.model
my_car.make
my_car.year
```

When referring to the state of an object, you are referring to variables or **data attributes**. The variables **model**, **make**, and **year** on lines 6, 7, and 8, respectively, are accessible through instances.

```
self.model = model
self.make = make
self.year = year
```

The statement below is **invalid** because there is no attribute named "**color.**" When I run this program, the Python Interpreter raises an **AttributeError** in the **Console**.

```
my_car.color
```

In Chapter 7, Example 7.6 illustrates an error with an incorrect call for a class method, which causes an AttributeError.

Instance Variables and Class Variables

Instance variables are unique to each instance of the class. For example, **my_car.model** is different than **my_car2.model**. However, all instances of a class share class variables and methods. All instances of the **Car** class share the class variable "**yr**" I created on line 3.

Create an Instance of the Class

Instantiation is when you create an instance of an object from a class. On line 17, I create an instance of the Car class named "**my_car**."

```
my_car = Car('Subaru', 'Crosstrek', 2019)
```

Instance objects have attribute references. Valid attribute names include "**data attributes**" and "**methods**."

Methods

Functions that are part of a class are referred to as a "**methods**" or "**method attributes**." When referring to the behavior of an object, you are discussing the function or method. The "Car" class has two methods, defined in lines 9 and 12. The "drive" method is shown below.

```
def drive(self):
    """Move the car."""
    print(self.model.title() + " is now moving.")
```

Dotted Notation for Attributes

The normal dotted notation "**object.variable**" is used to access the instance of the class (the object) and the attribute. In this example, the syntax is "**my_car.model**." The primary object instance is "**my_car**," and the attribute identifier name is "**model**." To refer to the model, make, or year attributes, follow the syntax on line 18, as shown below.

```
print(my_car.model, my_car.make, my_car.year)
```

Calling a Method

To call a method in a class instance, use the syntax shown in line 19.

```
my_car.parallelpark()
```

These two statements call a method. The statement syntax varies, but the statements do the same thing.

```
Car.drive(my_car)
my_car.drive()
```

Superclass and Subclass

In this example the subclass "Family(Person)" is reusing the Person.__ init__(self, name). This makes the superclass attributes "name" and "alive" available to the class "Family."

```
class Person(object):
    def __init__(self, name):
        self.name = name
        self.alive = True

class Family(Person):
    def __init__(self, name, relationshiop):
        Person.__init__(self, name)
        self.relationship = relationship
```

At the end of this book, the **Appendix - Reference** has links for more information on Classes, Functions, Methods, Attributes, and Instances.

3.26 Modules and Libraries

Variables in Imported Modules

Often modules are broken into separate files or libraries, and you add these to your code with the **import** statement. This idea of breaking code into smaller chunks of code that are easy to debug and reuse independently is known as **modularity**. Typically you don't need to know anything about the internal code in a function or module. All you really care about is the function inputs (arguments), what the function does, and what the function outputs (the return object.) This concept is known as **abstraction**.

To reference a variable inside another module, use dotted notation. In this example, I import a module "mymodule2" that has the variable "mystr2." The expression **mymodule2.mystr2** returns the value of **mystr2**.

```
import mymodule2

print(mymodule2.mystr2)
```

To avoid name conflicts, you can also provide a function "alias" with your import statement. In Chapter 7, Example 7.19 demonstrates a ModuleNotFound error caused by an incorrect alias. The syntax to assign an alias "plot" is shown below.

import matplotlib pyplot as plot

3.27 Attributes

The Chapter 4 topic, "Variables and Objects in Memory," discusses the current namespace and the concept of attributes. The Python glossary entry for "attributes" is "a value associated with an object which is referenced by name using dotted expressions."

In the Chapter 2 example, we looked at a line of code with a number variable.

```
myint = 57
print(myint.upper)
```

When this program runs, it causes an unhandled exception, and the **Console** Traceback message is "**AttributeError**," because there is no attribute "upper" for a variable of type "int."

When looking at Classes in this chapter, we saw that attributes could be variables or methods within a class instance. In our earlier Class example, we saw that instance objects have attribute references. Valid attribute names include "**data attributes**" and "**methods**." In the example below of attributes, "**yr**" is a class variable, and "**drive**" is a method in the **my_car** instance of the "**Car"** Class.

```
my_car.yr
my_car.drive()
```

3.28 Scope, Namespace & Memory

Each time a program runs and creates variables, the Python Interpreter adds the variables to the "global namespace" or "**Stack 1**." This top-level code executes at the '**__main__**' scope, as outlined at docs.python.org. The *global namespace* is the first memory "stack."

Variable Explorer displays objects in the current "scope." Variable Explorer is empty until you run the program to create the program's memory "namespace."

The variable "name" combined with the memory "space" (or namespace) uniquely identifies a variable. When you step through your code, the "local scope" or local namespace reflects the objects in memory at that point in time. Scope changes when your code moves into a method or function, and a new "local scope" is created while you're inside that function. Lexical scoping or "static scoping" refers to the line of code that created a variable and limits the variable to that local scope or namespace.

In Chapter 7, Example 7.10 demonstrates how to reset namespace to insure your variables are current.

The LEGB rule refers to the **L**ocal -> **E**nclosing -> **G**lobal -> **B**uilt-in namespaces. Nested functions consist of a "local" namespace located within the "enclosing" function. All functions are stacked onto the "global" namespace, which in turn is stacked on top of Python's built-in namespace. We'll look at several examples of local and global scope at the end of this chapter.

In Python, you can read, but not change, the value of a global variable at any point in your program and from within functions, as long as everything is within the **same *.py file**. It is possible to have two variables with the same name and different values because they are in two different "scopes." You'll notice this behavior as you step through the code and watch the list of variables in Variable Explorer. When you step into a function, the variable names reflect the "local scope."

If you want to change a variable in different "scopes," you can use the "**global**" keyword to change the variable into a "global variable" so that you can change the variable within that paritcular local scope. We looked at global variables earlier with an example of how object values change as "scope" changes. In Chapter 7, Example 7.50 demonstrates a scope issue.

There are several functions to view scope, and we'll look at a few in the following pages. For example, the keyword "**nonlocal**" refers to a variable in the "enclosing" namespace. As you work with these functions, you'll see that namespaces in Python are stored in the form of a dictionary.

dir(__builtins__)

locals()

globals()

id()

> We looked at memory stacks for recursive functions earlier.

A Function that Accesses a Global Variable

We'll begin looking at namespaces and scope in the example below. The function definition for **blockParty()** begins on line 1, and the function has no arguments. The indented lines that follow through line 3 make up the body of the **blockParty()** function. Lines 1 to 3 are a "suite of code." The main body of the program begins on line 6.

- The "food" variable is defined on line 6 in the main body of the program, which means "food" is in the *global namespace*. Any function in this *.py file can access the global "food." In this example, within the **blockParty()** function, the global variable "food" is accessed on line 3.
- The **blockParty()** function is **not allowed to change** the value in the global "food" variable.

```
1  def blockParty()
2      name = 'John'
3      print(name, 'has', food)
4
5
6  food = 'chips'
7  blockParty()
```

Variables in the main program are in the *Global Namespace* of the program. The main program begins on line 6. In the diagram that follows this is memory "Stack 1." In order to see the scope changing "live" in Variable Explorer, we're going to debug the file.

1. Type the sample code into the **Editor**. If it's not already open, open Variable Explorer from the **View** menu by clicking on **Panes**. At this point,

there are no variables displayed because we haven't run the program to initialize the variables and assign values. That's about to change!

On the Spyder toolbar, click on **Debug file** (Ctrl+F5).

2. In the **Editor** pane, line 1 is highlighted. Because line 1 is a function definition, when I click **Run current line** (Ctrl+F10), the Python Interpreter analyzes the function definition and then moves to line 6.

In the **iPython Console**, to the left of line 6 is an arrow ----> indicating the Python Interpreter is about to run line 6.

In the Spyder toolbar, click **Run current line**. Line 6 runs. Now, in the **Editor** pane, the cursor moves down and highlights line 7. In the iPython Console, the arrow ----> now points to line 7.

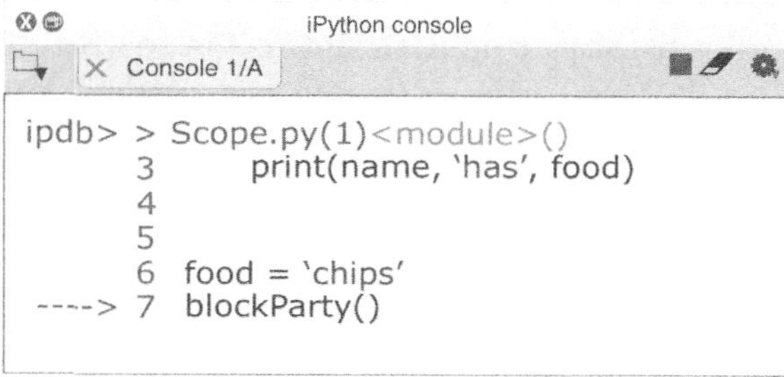

Variable Explorer displays the variable "food" with a value of "chips." Notice the variable is a "str" type.

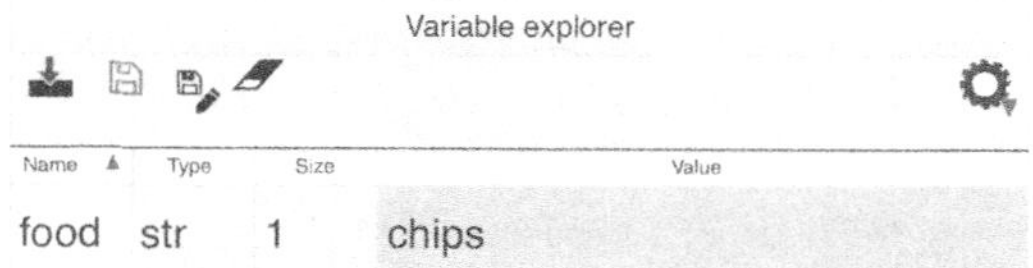

3. Line 7 invokes the function **blockParty()**. We want to step through the code inside the function. In the Spyder toolbar, click on Step into function or method of current line (Ctrl+F11). Line 7 runs invoking the **blockParty()** function.

If you click **Run current line** instead of "Step into function or method of current line," *the program runs all lines in the* **blockParty()** *function and exits debug mode.*

In the iPython Console, debug moves the cursor to the function **blockParty()** on line 1. An arrow ----> points to line 1.

The Editor highlights line 1.

```
1 def blockParty()
2       name = 'John'
3       print(name, 'has', food)
4
5
6 food = 'chips'
7 blockParty()
```

In the Spyder toolbar, click **Run current line** to run line 1. The local scope changes to the **blockParty()** function and a new "stack" of memory is created. In the next diagram, this is "**Stack 2**." Variable Explorer still shows the "food" variable because "food" is in the *global namespace*. The global scope variables can be accessed or "read," **but not changed**, within the **blockParty()** function.

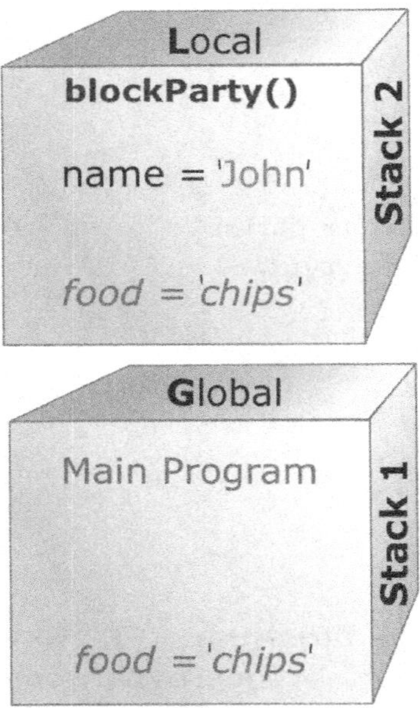

4. The previous diagram outlines the *global namespace* in **Stack 1**, and the *local namespace* of the function **blockParty()** in **Stack 2**.

   In the **iPython Console**, let's look at the *global namespace* with the built-in function **globals()**. Below, I've abbreviated the output text to show the last line, which is my global variable "food." The interpreter actually prints out a large dictionary for the namespace, as indicated by the curly braces **{}**.

ipdb> globals()

{ .... 'food': 'chips'}

5. Continue stepping through the code. In the function **blockParty()** after line 2 runs, Variable Explorer also shows the "name" variable. This variable is in **Stack 2** or the *local namespace*.

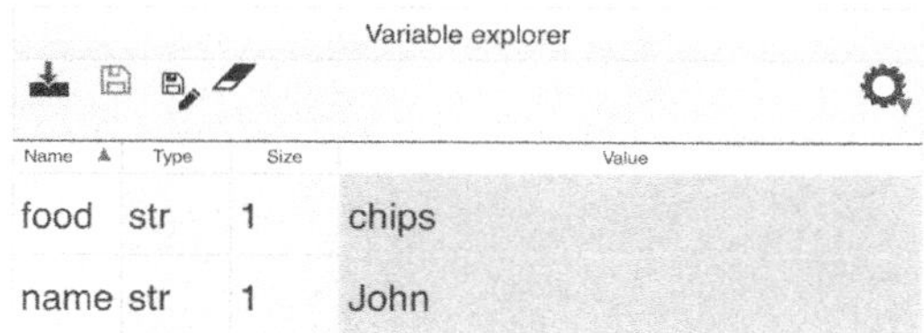

When you run line 3, the iPython Console output is "John has chips."

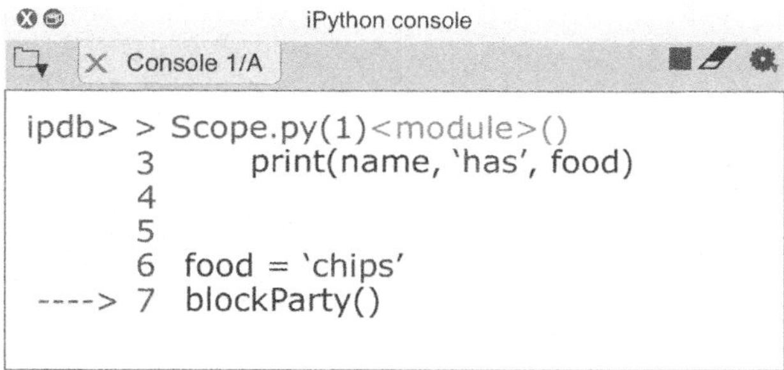

6. The locals() function shows all variables in the current or *local namespace* **Stack 2**. In the iPython Console, type "locals()." Because "food" is in the global namespace, it is not shown.

ipdb> locals()

{'name': 'John'}

7. Continue stepping through the code. In the function **blockParty()**, after line 3 runs, the Python Interpreter moves down to line 7. When line 7 is highlighted, you are back in the main program or *global namespace*. The *global namespace*, or **Stack 1**, has the "food" variable with a value of 'chips.'

Variable Explorer no longer shows the "name" variable because **Stack 2** is discarded when you exit the **blockParty()** function.

A Function Variable with the Same Name as a Global Variable

The previous example is pretty straightforward. Now we are going to repeat the same steps with a small variation. This time we add a "food" variable assignment on line 3 within the function "**blockParty()**."

As we step through the code, you'll see two variables named "food," but with different values and identifiers.

```
1 def blockParty()
2       name = 'John'
3       food = 'salsa'
4       print(name, 'has', food)
5
6
7 food = 'chips'
8 blockParty()
```

The main program begins on line 7. The "food" variable from line 7 is in the *Global Namespace* or main scope of the program. The diagram in Step 4 that follows shows this as memory "**Stack 1**."

Now we'll debug the file.

1. Type the sample code into the **Editor**. On the Spyder toolbar, click on **Debug file** (Ctrl+F5).

   If it's not already open, open Variable Explorer from the **View** menu by clicking on **Panes**.

2. In the **Editor** pane, line 1 is highlighted. Because line 1 is a function definition, when you click **Run current line** (Ctrl+F10) the Python Interpreter evaluates the function definition and moves on to line 7.

   In the **iPython Console**, to the left of line 7 is an arrow ----> indicating the Python Interpreter is about to run line 7.

   In the Spyder toolbar, click **Run current line**. Line 7 runs. The program is still in the "*global namespace*" or "**Stack 1**."

   In the Editor pane, debug moves down and highlights line 8. The iPython Console displays an arrow next to line 8, as shown in the next diagram.

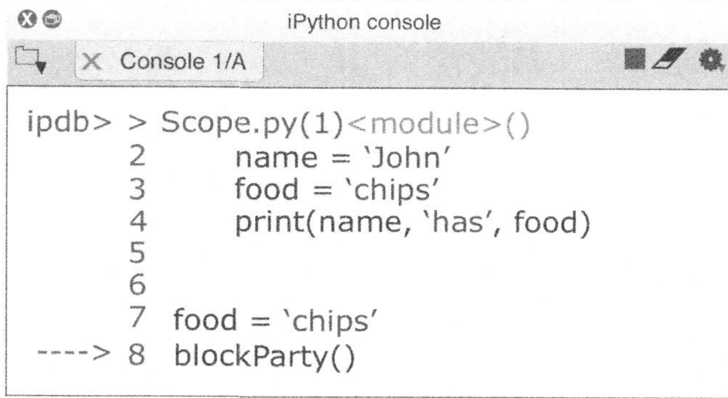

3. Line 8 invokes the function **blockParty()**. We want to step through the code inside the function. In the Spyder toolbar, click on Step into function or method of current line (Ctrl+F11). Line 8 runs invoking the **blockParty()** function.

In the **iPython Console**, debug moves the cursor to the function **blockParty()** on line 1. In the Console, an arrow ----> points to line 1. In the Editor, line 1 is also highlighted. In the Spyder toolbar, click **Run current line** to run line 1.

The local scope changes to the **blockParty()** function, and a new "stack" of memory is created. This is "**Stack 2**" and is now the "local scope." Variable Explorer still shows the "food" variable with a value of "chips" from the *global namespace*.

4. Continue stepping through the code. In the function **blockParty()**, after line 2 runs, Variable Explorer shows the "name" and "food" variables. The "food" variable is from the *global namespace*.

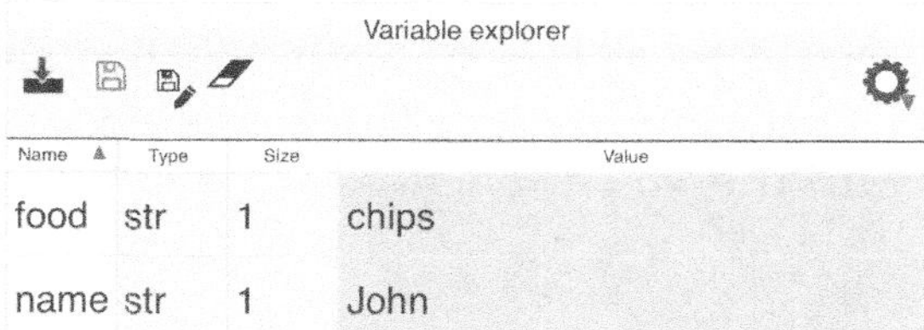
Variable explorer

Name	Type	Size	Value
food	str	1	chips
name	str	1	John

Stack 2 now has two variables: the local variable "name" and the global variable "food."

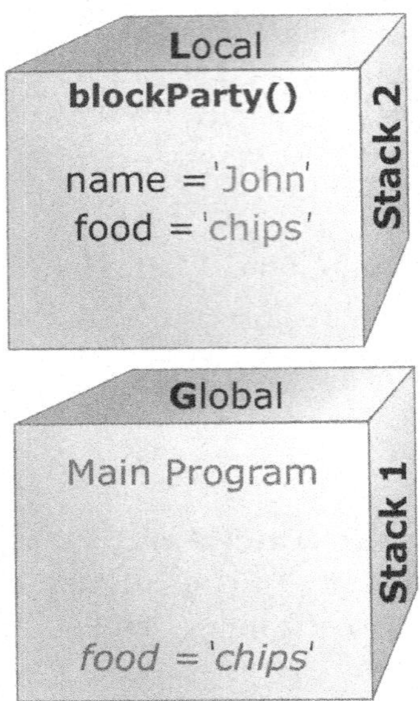

5. When you run line 3, a new variable called "food" is created in "**Stack 2**" with a different value of "salsa," as shown below in Variable Explorer.

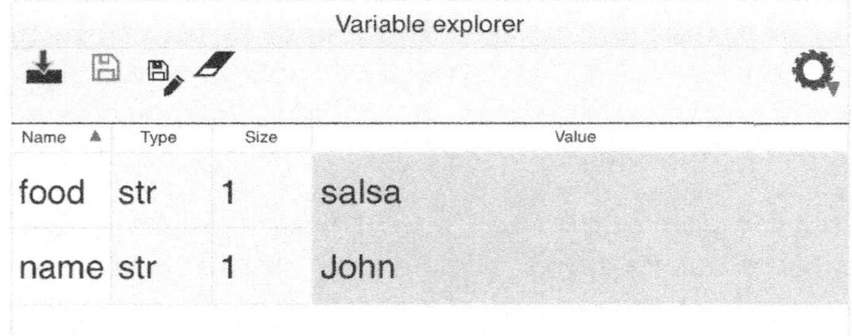

This local variable "food" in **Stack 2** has the same name as the global variable but points to a different location in memory - in this case, **Stack 2**'s "food" with the value "salsa."

6. This time, the locals() function shows two variables in the current or *local namespace*, which is **Stack 2**. In the iPython Console, type "locals()."

ipdb> locals()

{'name': 'John', 'food': 'salsa'}

Looking at the printout in the **iPython Console**, you can tell the namespace variables are stored in a dictionary because of the **curly**

braces {}. The program is within the **Stack 2** *local namespace* of **blockParty()**. If I were to update the local variable "food," the other "food" variable in the outer scope or *global namespace* would not change.

To see the identifier of the objects, let's use the **id()** function to get the ID for the **Stack 2** "food" variable. Because line 4 is highlighted in the Editor, I know I am still in the *local namespace* of the blockParty() function. Your computer output for ID will be different than what is shown below.

ipdb> id(food)

140309822725104

7. Continue stepping through the code. After line 4 runs, the code moves down to line 7. When line 7 is highlighted, you are back in the *global namespace* or **Stack 1**.

Variable Explorer no longer shows the "name" variable because *Stack 2 is discarded* when you exit the "blockParty()" function. Also, you'll notice the value of the "food" variable changed back to "chips." The program is back in the *global namespace* or "Stack 1.

8. In the iPython Console, use the id() function to view the identifier for this "food" variable in the *global namespace*. This output will show a different ID number.

ipdb> id(food)

140309822723824

Scope in Nested Functions

Earlier we looked at the LEGB rule for **L**ocal -> **E**nclosing -> **G**lobal -> **B**uilt-in namespaces. Nested functions consist of a function's "local" namespace located within the "enclosing" function. To illustrate the "enclosing namespace," the next example has a nested function, "**games()**."

```
def blockParty()
    def games()
        game = 'darts'
        print(game, 'starts at noon')
    name = 'John'
    food = 'salsa'
    print(name, 'has', food)

```

```
9
10 food = 'chips'
11 blockParty()
```

The scope of the function **blockParty()** is the "enclosing namespace" of the **games()** function, and is **Stack 2**. The function **games()** is nested inside **blockParty()** and will be **Stack 3**.

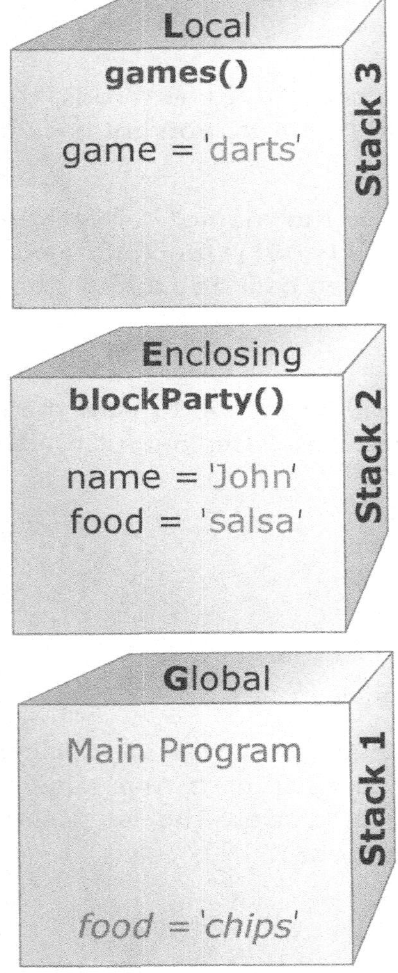

Earlier I said the "global" keyword is used when you want to update a global variable from within a function. Similarly, the nested function **games()** can update "name" in **blockparty()'s** "enclosing" namespace if you add a statement on line 3 with the keyword "nonlocal."

```
def blockParty()
      def games()
            nonlocal name
            game = ‘darts’
            print(game, ‘starts at noon’)
      name = ‘John’
      food = ‘salsa’
      print(name, ‘has’, food)
      games()


food = ‘chips’
blockParty()
```

Let’s add another function to the code and review scope. In this example, the **events()** function definition is on line 11 in the main body of the program.

```
1  def blockParty()
2        def games()
3              game = ‘darts’
4              print(game, ‘starts at noon’)
5        name = ‘John’
6        food = ‘salsa’
7        print(name, ‘has’, food)
8        games()
9
10
11 def events()
12       type = ‘party’
13       print(type)
14
15 food = ‘chips’
16 blockParty()
18 events()
```

In this case, the main program has two paths. The functions blockParty() and games() have no access to the variables in the events() function, and vice versa.

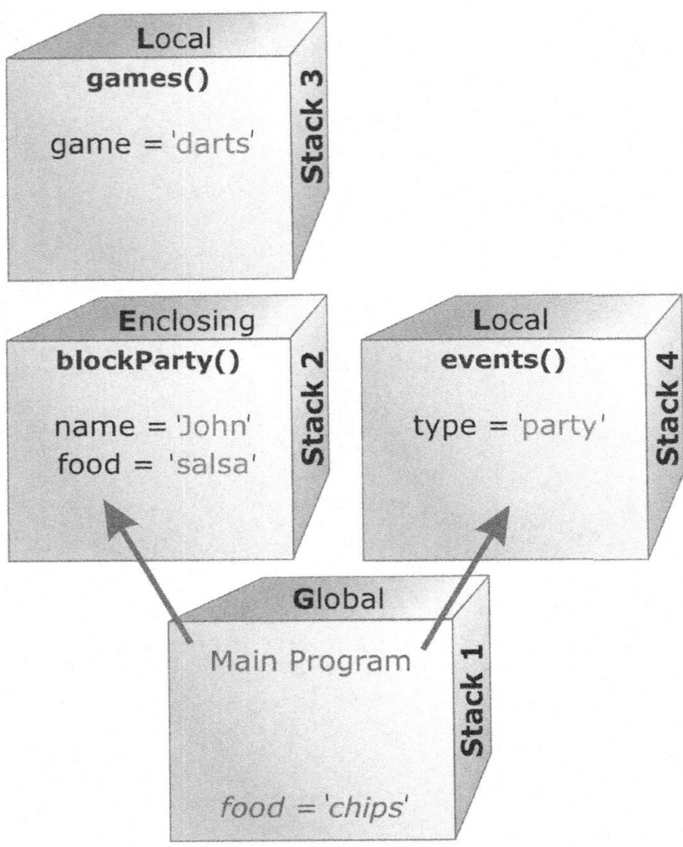

When you're analyzing scopes, *diagram the path* through the program to determine namespaces.

4. Debugging Tools

In this Chapterwe discuss

This Chapter outlines a few ways to use the Spyder IDE to debug your program. With a few simple commands, there is a wealth of information available about your variables, functions, data structures, and more. We'll look at:

- Adding Print Statements to code in the Editor, and viewing the results in the Console (the Python Shell.)
- Using Debug Mode in Spyder.
- Using Interactive Mode in the **Console**.

4.1 Debugging Overview

When debugging code, I inspect values, types, function arguments, and function return objects. "Introspection" functions like help() and dir() also provide information on methods, functions, and objects. In the topic "Introspection" that follows, we'll touch on the Inspect library. There are also libraries for "logging" and functions to identify bottlenecks and timing issues. Finally, I'll demonstrate how to focus on a specific area of code for testing and how to create test data.

1. Inspect Objects and Variables
2. Add Print Statements to a Script
3. Debug Mode
4. Variable Explorer
5. Interactive Mode

1. When you're working in the **Editor,** if you place your cursor over an object name and pause a few seconds, the Editor **highlights** all instances of that variable or object name. This is a quick way to spot inconsistencies with variable names, and to locate where a variable is used or changed.

2. In the **Editor**, add **print statements** to your script, and run the program. The **Console**, also known as the Python Shell, displays the results of print statements.

> In the Run menu select "Run selection or current line" to run only the selected lines of code.

3. Run your program in Debug mode, stepping through the lines of code. The **Console** prompt changes to **ipdb** in Debug mode. In Debug Mode, you step through the lines of code, pausing to look at the **Variable Explorer** pane or type commands at the **Console** prompt. You can also set a "breakpoint" to move to a particular location in your program when using Debug mode. The Outline pane is a great way to see nested control statements. In Spyder, select "Outline" from the View, Panes menu.

4. The **Editor** pane highlights the next line to execute when you click "run current line" on the debug toolbar. Variable Explorer displays the values of each variable in the local scope.

5. Interactive Mode in the **Console** allows you to type commands that display object values. In the Console type the name, or identifier, of the object. The Python Interpreter returns the value of the identifier. The object can be an integer variable, a list item, tuple, or another type of object.

In the **Console**, you can also type individual lines of code while developing or testing your code. Interactive Mode is a great way to test code before adding it to your script.

> The topic "Variables and Objects in Memory" later in this chapter outlines how Python creates variables and objects when you run a program or script. If you type your object name in the **Console** and the Traceback says "NameError," insure that you already ran the line of code that **creates the object** in the local scope.

Backup Files

Keeping frequent backups and backing up before you start debugging can save a lot of frustration and time. On my Mac, I run a Python script to backup my files every five minutes. The script runs every five minutes until I break out of the program, usually when I'm done for the day. This particular script backs up my Indesign files for this book, and is an example of how Python can help with every day tasks.

When I double click this b.command file in Finder, it opens a **Terminal** window on my Mac and runs my Python script, "backup_files.py."

b.command
cd /Users/rlz/Python_Coding/Bkups
python backup_files.py

This Python script imports three libraries. Every five minutes, the script gets the current date and time for the name of a new directory. After copying files to the new directory, the script "sleeps" for five minutes.

```
import os
import shutil
import time
def savework():
      while True:
            t = time.strftime('%m-%d-%Y %H_%M', time.localtime())
            p2 = os.path.join(os.path.join(p1, "Bkups"), t)
            if not os.path.exists(p2):
                os.makedirs(p2)
            for f in os.listdir(p1):
                if f[-5:] == '.indd' and f[0] != '~':
                   shutil.copyfile(p1 + '/' + f, p2 + '/' + f)
time.sleep(300)  # sleep 300 seconds
p1 = os.path.join(os.environ['HOME'], 'Python_Coding')
savework()
```

4.2 Print Statements

A popular debugging choice is to add print statements to your code. A print statement is a quick and easy way to inspect an object's type, value, or length, while your code is running. Add a print statement to your script in the **Editor** window, and on the **Run** menu execute your program.

While it's not exactly elegant, I frequently add a print statement to my code that simply says something like, "about to have a problem." Then I add a debug "**breakpoint**" at that location. The **Console** displays output from the print statement. The Console is the Python Shell.

In the next example, I added two print statements to help me follow my running code.

```
meals = ['breakfast', 'lunch', 'snack', 'dinner']
fruits = ['apple', 'orange', 'grape']
i = 0
while i < 4:
      j = 0
      print("my meal is: ",  meals[i])
      while j < 4:
            print("My choice of fruit is: ", fruits[j])
            print ("j is: ", j)
            j = j + 1
      i = i + 1
```

```
In [1]: my meal is: breakfast
my meal is: breakfast
my meal is: breakfast
my meal is: breakfast
my meal is: breakfast
my meal is: breakfast
my meal is: breakfast
```

Try This 4.1   Print Statements

While helpful, in this example the print statements in the Console window quickly scroll by, because this program is in an infinite loop. Scrolling output is where Debug mode, text output to file, or logging comes into play. We'll look at all three options in the next sections. In the next example, I create a file, write some data, and close the file.

```
fh = open('myfile.txt', 'w')
notes = 'Sample text'
fh.write(notes)
fh.close()
```

Chapter 6 has several examples of print statements. In Chapter 7, Example 7.15 uses print statements with exception handling logic. Example 7.35 uses print statements to debug a generator script. Chapter 6 explores the syntax to view an object's type, length, and value.

Indenting Loop Print Statements

Another print option is "indenting" the print statements each time the program loops through a Suite of code. In Python, a "Suite" of code is a block of indented code, as discussed in Chapter 3. These print statements provide a visual representation of how many times the loop has run.

```
meals = ['breakfast', 'lunch', 'snack', 'dinner']
fruits = ['apple', 'orange', 'grape']
i = 0
level = ""
while i < 4:
      level = level + ".... "
      print("my meal is: ", fmeals[i])
      i = i + 1
```

In this example, the **Console** shows the print output with a series of dots representing the depth of the loops. I use the "level" string variable to create the effect.

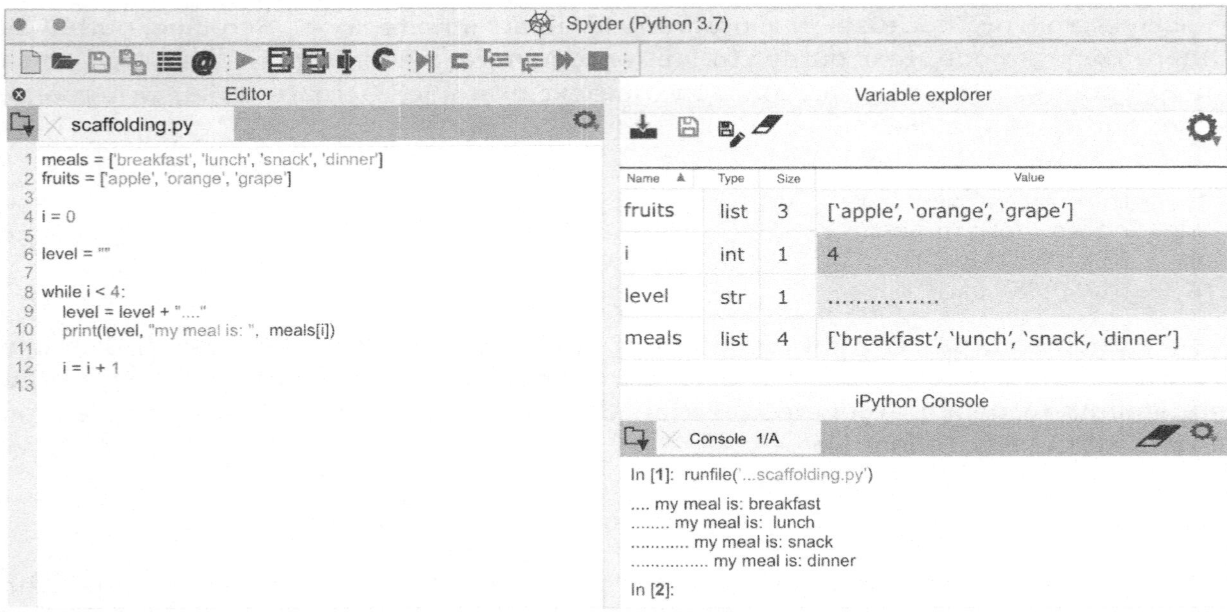

Figure 4.1 Indenting Loop Print Statements

4.3 Overview of the Editor

The **Editor** automatically suggests relevant code completion, based on the particular object you are working with. For example, if you create and assign a date to the variable "thedate," the Editor will display a pop-up window after you type "thedate" followed by a dot. In the next figure, I am scrolling through the pop-up items to select "year." You can turn off code-completion in Preferences, Editor, Code Introspection/Analysis.

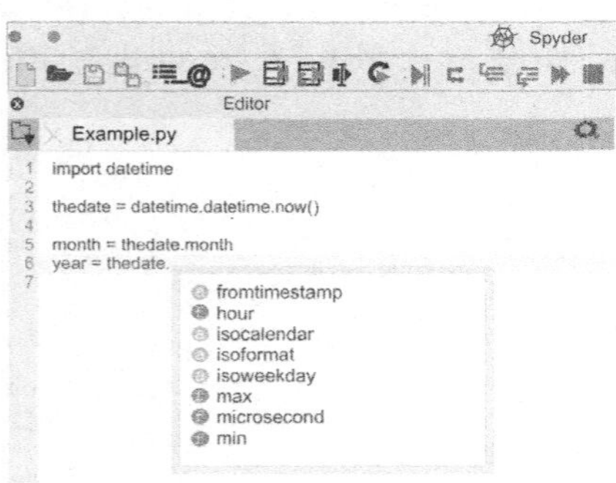

Figure 4.2 Code Completion

In the previous example, when I scroll down an orange icon indicates "year" is an attribute of the datetime.datetime object "thedate", and is referenced using dotted notation, as shown below.

print(thedate.year)

If you want more information on "year" you can use introspection functions, which we'll look at in the topic "Introspection" that follows. In the **Console** pane, type **dir(thedate)** to see attributes and methods for "thedate" object.

dir(thedate)

In the Console pane, when you type **help(thedate)** the object attributes are displayed, as shown below. The syntax for help with objects is **help(*object*)**.

help(thedate)

```
| ----------------------------------------------------------------------
| Static methods defined here:
| __new__(*args, **kwargs) from builtins.type
|     Create and return a new object. See help(type) for accurate signature.
|
| ----------------------------------------------------------------------
| Data descriptors defined here:
|
| fold
|
| hour
|
| microsecond
|
| minute
|
| second
|
| tzinfo
|
| ----------------------------------------------------------------------
| Data and other attributes defined here:
|
| max = datetime.datetime(9999, 12, 31, 23, 59, 59, 999999)
|
| min = datetime.datetime(1, 1, 1, 0, 0)
|
| resolution = datetime.timedelta(microseconds=1)
```

Figure 4.3 Console Display of Object Attributes

To open Python's interactive help system type **help()** with no argument. The prompt changes to **help>**. Type "**q**" to exit the help system.

In [**1**]: help()

help> False

To see a list of Python's reserved keywords, you can also type **help("keywords")**.

- In the **Editor**, position your cursor over "thedate" variable and wait a few seconds. All instances of "thedate" variable are highlighted in yellow. This is a great way to find when a variable is used.
- The **Editor** has a **red** circle with an "x" to indicate an error, and a **yellow triangle** to the left of a line number to indicate a warning. When I hover over the yellow triangle, a pop-up message is displayed, "unexpected indentation."
- When you hover your mouse over a parenthesis, the paired parenthesis is highlighted in green. If a parentheses is missing, the starting parenthesis is highlighted in orange.
- On my computer, the **Editor** highlights functions and methods in purple, and variables are black. Numbers are a brownish-red color, and strings are green. Keywords like "def," "import," "for," and "while" are blue. Your settings may vary, but I wanted to point out that color coding is another indicator that syntax is correct. In Chapter 7, Example 7.12 illustrates how to "debug" using color coding.

Code Completion Pop-up

The purple icon in the pop-up window indicates methods or functions. The **max(**thedates**)** class atrribute in the example below displays the oldest date in the list "thedates."

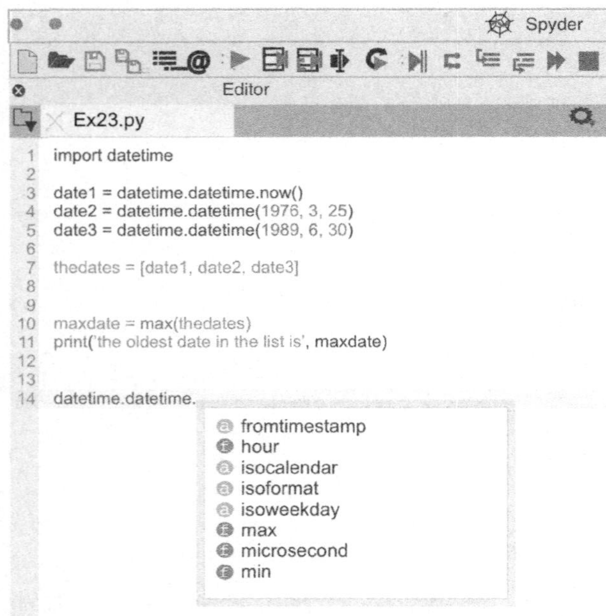

Figure 4.4 The max() Function

In the Editor, if you type your object name "datetime." with a period at the end, the code completion pop-up includes the "date" method.

dob = datetime.date(1972, 12, 3)

> A function created in a class is called a method.

4.4 The Help Pane

The Help pane can display details about functions and methods. In the next example, information for the object "datetime.date" is displayed in the Help pane. This datetime.date() method takes 3 arguments: year, month, day.

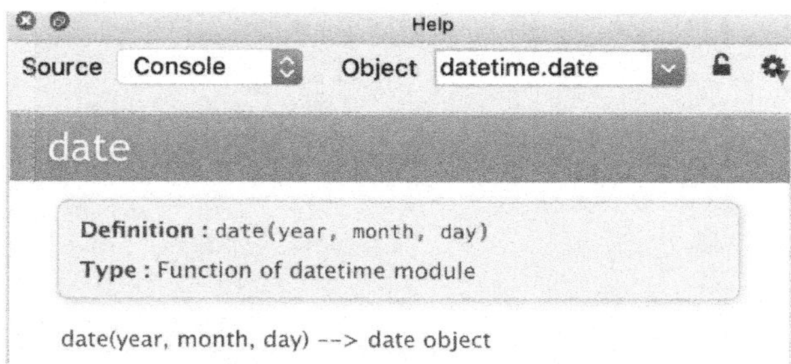

Figure 4.5 Help for datetime.date Function

4.5 Debug Mode

Use the **Debug** menu commands to step through the lines of code, or press Cntrl + F12 on a Windows computer to move to the next breakpoint. The Variable Explorer displays object values, changing over time as you step through the program code and the local scope changes.

In the **Editor**, double click on a line of code to set a **breakpoint** or press F12 on a Windows computer. When running a program in Debug Mode, a breakpoint pauses the program at that point, so that you can inspect the variable and object values in Variable Explorer or the Console. In the Editor, a red dot appears to the left of the line number with the breakpoint.

On the **Debug** menu, select 'debug' to launch the iPython debugger, or press Cntrl + F5 on a Windows computer. The prompt in the **Console** changes to **ipdb>**, indicating the iPython debugger is active.

> If a program halts and displays a Traceback error, you can type **%debug** to start "Debug Mode," as demonstrated in Examples 7.2, 7.20 and 7.52. Later in this chapter, we'll look at "magic functions" that begin with a percent symbol.

In the next example, there is a breakpoint • on line 3. The figure shows the **Editor** pane, as well as the **Console** pane, after I pressed Cntrl + F5 on a Windows computer to start debugging. Notice the **Console** prompt changed to **ipdb>**.

```
1 mystring = 'purple peanuts'
2
●3 print(mystring)
```

```
In [1]: debugfile('C:/SampleScript.py', wdir='C:')
>C:\SampleScript.py(1)<module>()
---->1 mystring = "purple peanuts"
      2 print (mystring)

ipdb>
```

Table 4.1 Setting a Breakpoint

In the **Console** pane, an arrow indicates the current line number, in this case, line 1. If Variable Explorer is not already open, on the **View** menu select "Panes," and then click on Variable Explorer. As I "**step-through**" the code, I want to watch the "mystring" object in Variable Explorer. At this point, Variable Explorer is empty because we have yet to run the first line of code to create the program's "namespace" in memory.

As you step through the code, the Editor highlights the current line.

Click the icon to **Run the current line of code** or press **Cntrl + F10** on a Windows computer. The Python interpreter creates the object "mystring" and assigns the value "purple peanuts." This example of dynamic typing is one of the reasons I love Python. With one line of code, Python figures out the type of object to create and assigns a value.

In Chapter 7, Example 7.2 illustrates Debug Mode. Chapter 6 has several examples that use Debug mode.

End Debug Mode

To exit the debugger, type **q** or **quit** at the **Console** prompt and press enter, as shown below. If you are in an iPython Session in the **Console**, you may have to press **Esc + Enter**. You can also restart the kernel when you select "Restart Kernel" from the **Consoles** menu.

```
ipdb>C:\SampleScript.py(1)<module>()
    1 mystring = "purple peanuts"
    2
---->3 print (mystring)

ipdb>
ipdb>quit

In [2]:
```

Table 4.2 Quit Debug Mode

4.6 Variable Explorer

As variables are created in your main program they are added to the "global scope" or namespace, as discussed in Chapter 3, "Scope, Namespace & Memory." The global scope is the first memory "stack." Variable Explorer displays objects in the current "scope" and is empty until you run the code to create the program's memory "namespace." In Chapter 7, Example 7.50 explores scope.

At this point in our example, **Variable Explorer** displays a row with the type of the "mystring" object, and the value I assigned in line 1.

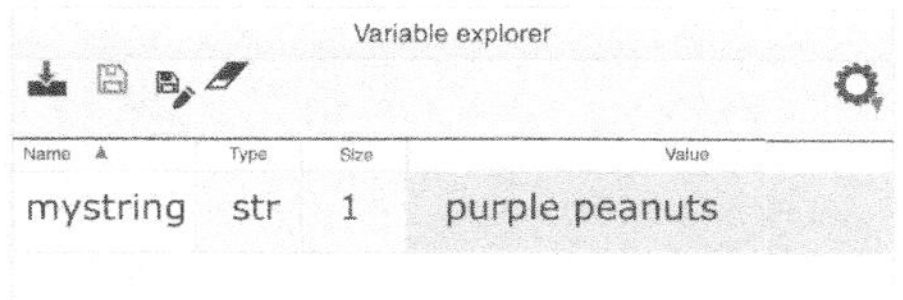

Figure 4.6 The Variable Explorer Pane

Variable Explorer shows variables and objects in memory. If you don't see your object displayed in Variable Explorer, you need to execute that part of the program. If you're unsure if the variables are in scope, you could use the **locals()** function in the Console to see local variables.

To start fresh and clear program memory, in the Console use the magic function **%Reset**. See the topic "Variables and Objects in Memory" later in this Chapter for information on namespaces. In Chapter 7, examples 7.1-7.3 demonstrate using Variable Explorer.

4.7 Example: My Program Loops & Never Ends

Let's briefly look at an example of **Debug Mode** in action. When I run this test program, it never ends. In other words, it loops continuously. My hypothesis is the while loop that begins on **line 8** needs adjusted. First, I'll stop the running program. Next, I'll use Debug Mode to step through the code and identify what is happening.

1. On the **Consoles** menu, select "Restart Kernel" to interrupt the running program.
2. Double click to the left of line 9 to add a breakpoint. A **red** dot appears to the left of the line number.
3. On the **Debug** menu, select "Debug" or click on the Debug control.

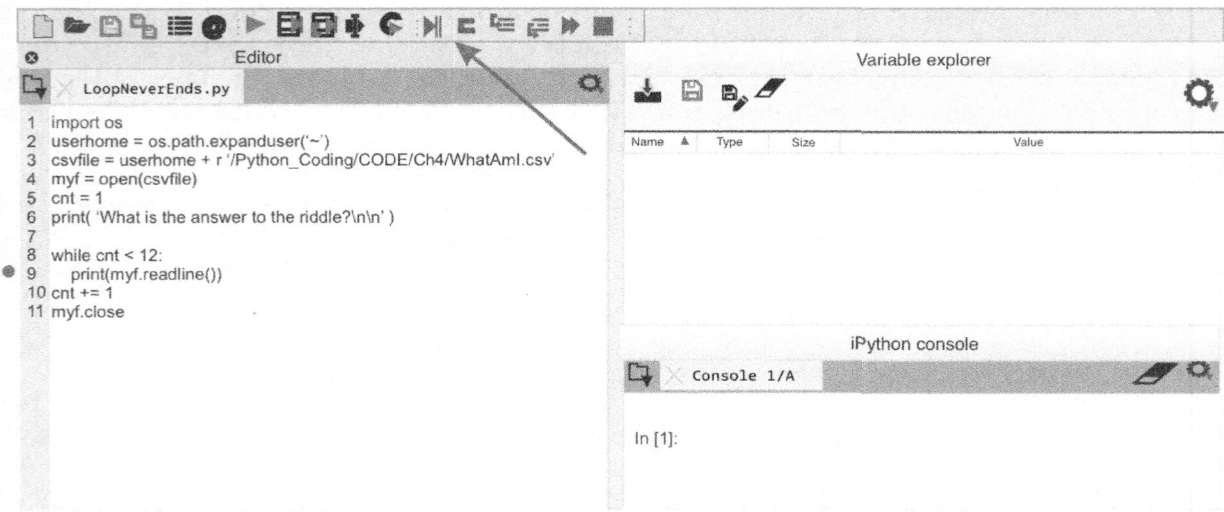

Figure 4.7 Add a Breakpoint

4. The **Console** prompt changes to **ipdb>** to indicate the iPython Debugger is active, and **Variable explorer** displays values for variables in the current active local scope. At this point in the code, the variable **cnt** has a value of **1**.

   The **Console** displays a few lines of the code, with an arrow indicating the current line 9. Line 9 runs when I click on "Continue Execution."

> The Debug Mode commands "u" or "up" move backward in your program. These commands are useful to find where the value was assigned to a variable. The Console prompt changes to ipdb> when in Debug Mode.

5. When I click on "Continue Execution" again, line 9 runs and moves back to line 8. The variable **cnt** still has a value of **1**. At this point in the program, I expected the value of **cnt** to be 2.

   If I use the command "Run Current Line," in the **Console** pane, I can see the program moving continuously from line 8 to line 9 and then moving back to line 8. This program is in an infinite loop.

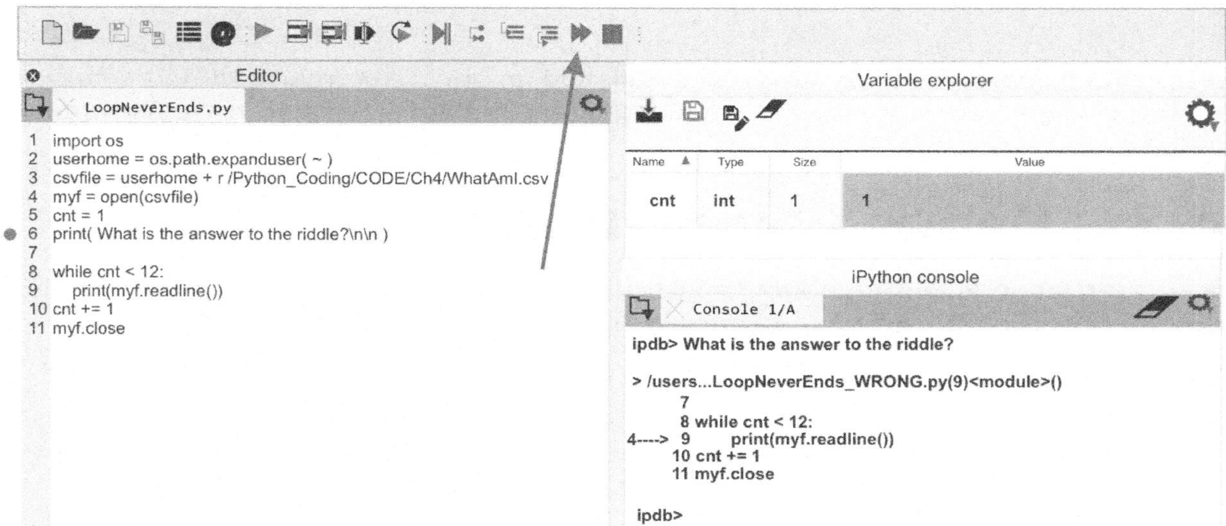

Figure 4.8 Continue Execution

6. To resolve the issue, I need to indent line 10, so this statement that increments the **cnt** variable is part of the while loop. The concept of a "Suite" of Indented Code was discussed in Chapter 3.

In the next figure, the output is correct in the **Console**. In the Editor pane, you can see line 10 is now indented.

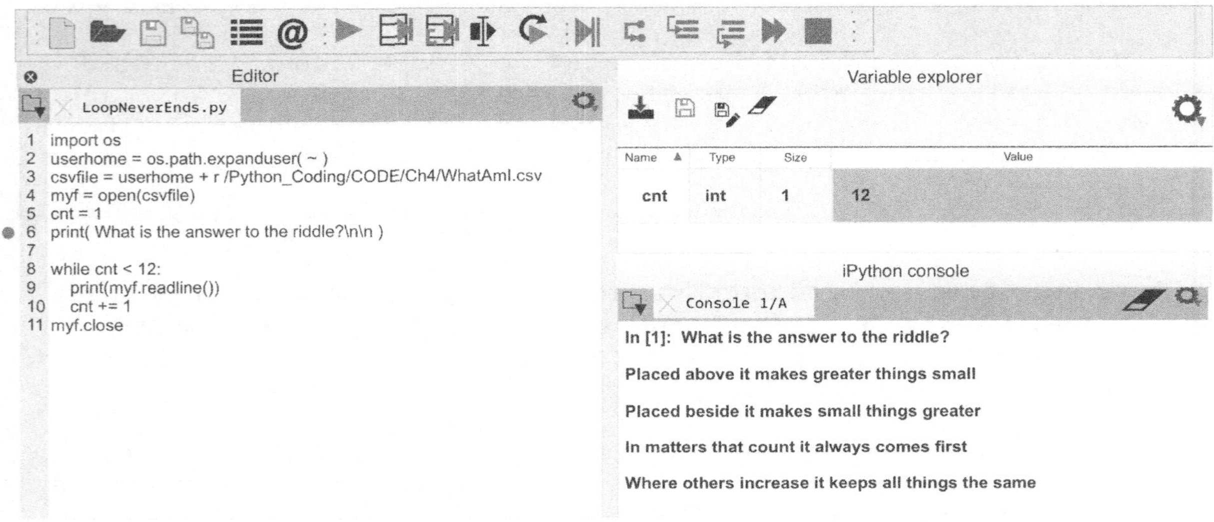

Figure 4.9 The Finished Program

To complete the program, I could add a print statement with the answer to the riddle - the number one. In Chapter 7, Example 7.1 also demonstrates an infinite loop.

4.8 Debug Commands

In Debug Mode, type **?** in the **Console** and press enter to see a list of Debug Commands. A brief list of popular commands is shown below.

ipdb> ?

For specific details on a particular command, type help, and the command name. For example, type "**help next**."

?	Help with Debug commands
b or **break**	Add a break

c	Continue
cl or **clear**	Clear breaks
d or **down**	Move down in the stack trace
exit	Exit Debug Mode
h or **help**	Help on Debug Mode
j or **jump**	Jumps to line number with a block of code
n or **next**	Move to next line
u or **up**	Move up in the stack trace
q or **quit**	Exit Debug Mode

4.9 Console Interactive Mode

Another option to view object values involves typing in the **Console** in **Interactive Mode**, which is similar to typing in the **Console** while in Debug Mode. In the **Console**, type the identifier (the name) of the object. The Python interactive interpreter displays the value in the **Console**, as shown below.

```
In [1]: mystring
Out[1]: 'purple peanuts'
```

> You must run the program statement that creates or sets the object value in the current <u>namespace</u> or local <u>scope</u> before the Python Interpreter, or Variable Explorer, can display a value.

At any time, you can type the name of an object in the **Console**, and the Python Interpreter displays the value. This "Interactive Mode" also allows you to perform calculations or use functions and methods, as shown in the next example.

```
ipdb> mystring
'purple peanuts'

ipdb> 2+3
5

ipdb> import math

ipdb> math.sqrt(16)
4.0

ipdb>
```

Table 4.3 Type in Console

The special identifier _ underscore is used in the interactive interpreter (or Console) to store the result of the last evaluation.

Chapter 6 has several examples that use Interactive Mode.

The iPython kernel also has several "magic commands" that begin with the percent % character.

%debug

%reset

Click in the Console window and press **Ctrl C** to cancel program execution. **Ctrl L** clears the namespace memory.

In Chapter 7, examples 7.1, 7.2, and 7.6 demonstrate Interactive Mode.

Increment Counters

One of my **favorite debugging shortcuts** is to change a counter so that I can move forward when I'm looping through the code. For example, I can change a "while loop" to move from the 2nd iteration to the 1200th iteration. Let's say I'm debugging, and my program normally starts with a "bfr" counter = 2. In the Editor, I increment the "bfr" counter to **bfr = 1200**.

Watch Out for Changing Values

While most functions or methods provide useful results when typed in the Console, you can get unexpected results. In Chapter 7, Example 7.14 reads a TXT file with the OS library. The function **readline()** moves to the next line of the TXT file every time you type it in the Console, which may not be what you were expecting.

iPython Session

The **Console** prompt changes to three dots and a colon **...:** to indicate you are in an **iPython Session**. Press enter twice, or press **Esc + Enter**, to exit the iPython session.

In [**1**]: def myfunction(str)

```
...: print(str)
```

> When the newline prompt ...: is displayed, press Shift Enter to execute the commands.

4.10 Variables and Objects in Memory

The Python Interpreter creates variables and objects when you run a program or script. The collection of these objects is the "**Namespace**." If you're debugging a line of code and a function uses an object, you want to ensure the object exists in memory before trying to view the object in **Variable Explorer**. The Variable Explorer shows active variables in memory for the current scope. Take, for example, this line of code that uses a variable "**myint**" of type "int."

```
myint = 57
print(myint.upper)
```

If the program ran and created "myint" already, the **Console** Traceback message is "**AttributeError**," because there is no attribute "upper" for a variable of type "int." **If the program hasn't run and created the variable "myint,"** the **Console** Traceback message is "**NameError.**" In this example, a misleading Traceback message "NameError" is hiding the Traceback message you want to see, "AttributeError."

In Chapter 3, we looked at an example of a "global variable," and how object values change as scope changes. For more information on scope, refer to the topic, "Scope, Namespace & Memory." In Chapter 7, Example 7.50 also demonstrates scope.

When you change a function definition and want to use the new version of the function, you can run just that part of your code. In the **Run** menu select "Run selection or current line" to run only the selected lines of code.

> Use the %reset magic command in the **Console** to reset the namespace.

4.11 Introspection

Introspection is the ability to determine information about live objects such as modules, classes, methods, and functions. You can easily tell the type of the object at runtime. Several functions help with introspection, as well as the "**inspect**" library.

*objectname***?**

dir()

help()

id()

repr()

type()

locals()

globals()

To inspect objects, we'll execute statements in the **Editor** and **Console**, including statements with "Instrospection" functions that provide details about objects. The syntax varies depending on whether you are typing in the **Editor** or **Console** pane. The syntax is also specific to the type of object. We'll look at those differences in depth in Chapter 6. In the case of data structures like lists, tuples, or dictionaries, you may want to see values for the entire list or the value of only a particular list item.

Editor

Console (Python Shell)

Using ? in the Console

For details on any object, in the **Console** type the object name followed by a question mark. There is no space between the object name and the question mark. For details on the object "**myfunction**," in the **Console** type the function name followed by a question mark, as shown below. The output includes the Signature, DocString, and the type of object.

```
In [2]: myfunction?

Signature: myfunction(str)
Docstring: <no docstring>
File:      ~//Ch 3 code/Functions/<ipython-input-8-df3069fd62ae>
Type:      function
```

This next example returns help for the max() function. You may want to compare this output to the __doc__ attribute in the "docstring" topic that follows.

```
In [5]: max?

Docstring:
max(iterable, *[, default=obj, key=func]) -> value
max(arg1, arg2, *args, *[, key=func]) -> value

With a single iterable argument, returns its biggest item. The default keyword-
only argument specifies an object to return if the provided iterable is empty. With
two or more arguments, return the largest argument.

Type:      builtin_function_or_method
```

dir()

The function **dir()** displays all objects in the current local namespace, as shown in the next figure. After running the sample "*Project1.1.py*" script, the local scope changes. This script uses the "openpyxl" library to create the **ws4** object. For example, after running the "*Project1.1.py* script, the dir() function displays relevant information about the program objects in the **Console**. Type the dir() command in the **Console** window.

```
In [2]: dir()
```

In Chapter 7, Example 7.38 uses "dir()" to debug an AttributeError.

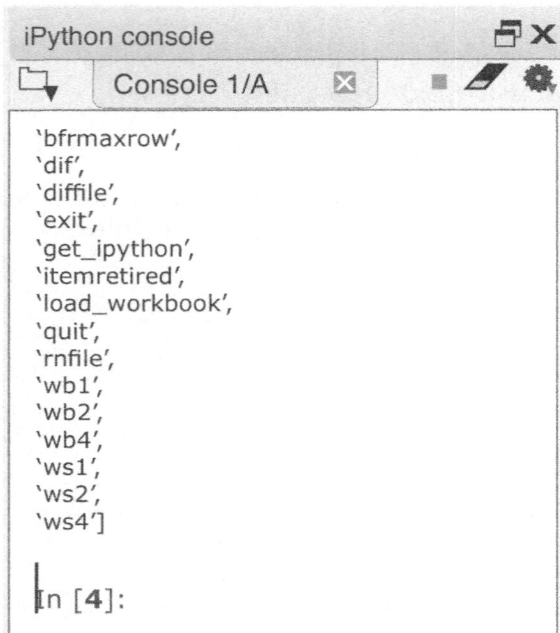

Figure 4.10 Objects in Current Local Scope

> In Chapter 7, Example 7.38 uses "dir()" to debug an AttributeError.

dir(object)

While the **dir()** function looks at all objects, the statement **dir(ws4)** takes the argument "ws4" and retrieves information on that particular object. In the **Console** window attributes specific to the **ws4** object are displayed, as shown below. The dir(*<object>*) function displays different attributes depending on the type of object you use for the argument.

There is quite a long list of valid attributes for the **ws4** object, and the next example only shows a few of the attributes. In particular, I'm interested in what functions I can use with the **ws4** object, and I've highlighted the "**delete_cols**" method.

Note, if you're using an older version of **openpyxl**, "**delete_rows**" might not be available. The **dir()** function is an easy way to check if a particular function or method should work with your code.

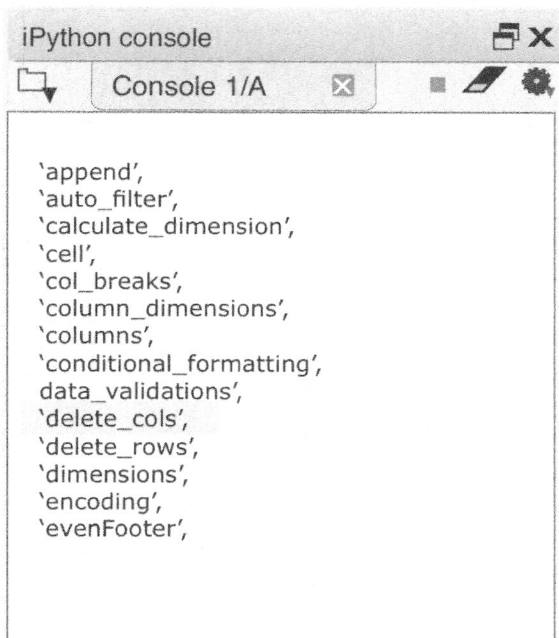
iPython console
Console 1/A
'append',
'auto_filter',
'calculate_dimension',
'cell',
'col_breaks',
'column_dimensions',
'columns',
'conditional_formatting',
data_validations',
'delete_cols',
'delete_rows',
'dimensions',
'encoding',
'evenFooter',

Figure 4.11 Valid Attributes for the ws4 Object

help()

The **help()** function invokes the help system for help with a module, function, class, method, or keyword; for objects in the current namespace. For example, when I type **help(load_workbook)** in the **Console** window, Python displays information specific to the method "load_workbook" from the "openpyxl" library.

In [**2**]: help(load_workbook)

We looked at help() earlier in the topic, "Overview of the Editor." We also looked at a datetime.date method in the "Help" pane.

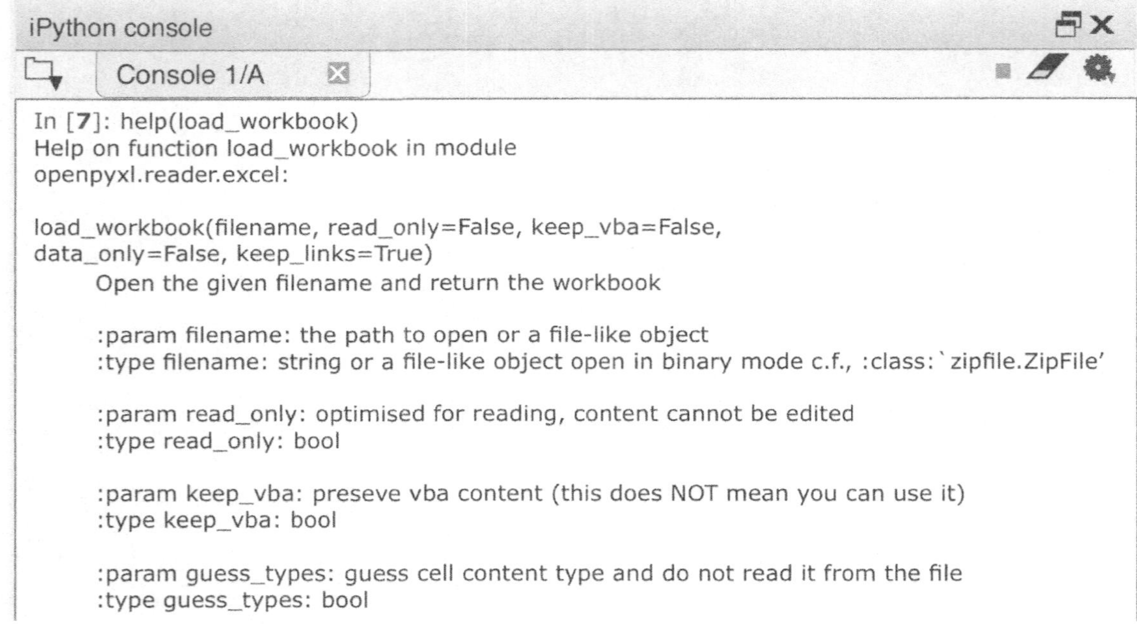

Figure 4.12 Help for load_workbook Method

The help() function reads the **docstring** if available and inspects objects to gather the output. Example 7.19 in Chapter 7 uses the help() function. Example 7.23 invokes help with the shortcut **Cntrl + I**.

The Inspect Library

Use the "inspect" library for additional information on an object, including the Docstring or call signature of a function or method. There are many functions available in the inspect library. Details are available on the docs.python.org website. The next example uses the **signature()** function in the **Console**.

```
In [2]: from inspect import signature
In [3]: from openpyxl import load_workbook
In [4]: str(signature(load_workbook))

(filename, read_only=False, keep_vba=False, data_only=False, keep_links=True)
```

What Version of Python?

The **version_info** attribute displays the current version of Python, as shown below.

```
In [5]: import sys
In [6]: sys.version_info

Out[7]: sys.version_info(major=3, minor=7, micro=4, releaselevel='final',
serial=0)
```

The type() Function

In the Chapter 3 topic, "What is the Data Type?," we used the **type()** function to examine the type of an object. Chapter 6 also includes numerous examples using the type() function.

```
print(type(my_var))
```

The id() Function

When dealing with immutable objects or scope issues, the **id()** function is useful in isolating which object you are referencing. The id() function displays the identity of the object. Scope has to do with global vs. local variables.

```
print(id(bfr))
bfr = bfr + 1
print(id(bfr))
```

The repr() Function

The **repr()** function returns a string representation of an object, and is useful in finding "whitespace," special characters like new line **\n**, or float rounding errors. Example 7.45 in Chapter 7 demonstrates a float comparison error.

The len() Function

The len() function shows the length of the string or the number of items in a data structure. For example, len(mydictionary) would return the number of dictionary key:pairs. You can find the number of items in a list with **len(mylist)**.

The locals() Function

You may recall from Chapter 3, the locals() function shows all objects in the current or local namespace. In the iPython Console, type "locals()."

```
In [5]: locals()
```

The globals() Function

The globals() function shows all objects in the current or global namespace. In the iPython Console, type "globals()."

```
In [5]:  globals()
```

The docstring

The **__doc__** attribute prints a function's docstring if it exists. A *docstring* might cover these topics.

- What the function does.
- What type of arguments the function takes.
- What the function returns, if anything.

This next example is the docstring for the max() function. Earlier we used **?** to see information on the max() function.

```
In [5]: max.__doc__

Out[5]: 'max(iterable, *[, default=obj, key=func]) -> value\nmax(arg1, arg2,
*args, *[, key=func]) -> value\n\nWith a single iterable argument, return its
biggest item. The\ndefault keyword-only argument specifies an object to return if\
nthe provided iterable is empty.\nWith two or more arguments, return the largest
argument.'
```

4.12 Logging

Logging is a simple way to capture debugging data. Use logging when the output in the **Console** pane scrolls and is lost because there is too much data. Logging is also useful when you're working out code logic, or have a live program with user reports of erratic behavior.

The python.org website has a "Logging HOWTO" and a "Logging Cookbook" topic in the documentation section.

This script has a logging level set to ERROR, which means it logs errors and critical events. For a thorough look at logging, please refer to the docs.python.org.

```
logging.basicConfig(format='%(asctime)s - %(message)s',
        datefmt='%d-%b-%y %H:%M:%S',
        filename='test.log',
        level=logging.ERROR)
```

When there is an exception on line 9 in the statement **10/my_int**, the Python Interpreter logs a critical error to the **test.log** file.

```
1  import logging
2  logging.basicConfig(format = '%(asctime)s - %(message)s',
3          datefmt = '%d-%b-%y %H:%M:%S',
4          filename = 'test.log',
5          level = logging.ERROR)
6  logging.error('The logging level is ERROR and above.')
7  my_int = 0
8  try:
9      10/my_int
10 except Exception:
11     logging.critical("my_int is %s", my_int, exc_info = True)
```

The first time you run the program the logfile **test.log** is created. The default mode is "append." If the log file is not created, try restarting Spyder. This is the output in the log file:

```
29-Jan-19 10:29:33 - Logging level is ERROR and above.
29-Jan-19 10:29:33 - my_int value is 0
Traceback (most recent call last):
    File "/Ch 4 code/Logging/logging.py", line 13, in <module>
    10/my_int
ZeroDivisionError: division by zero
```

To disable logging, use the "disable" method with the appropriate argument, as shown below.

```
logging.disable(logging.CRITICAL)
```

4.13 The timeit() Function

The timeit() function can identify bottlenecks in your code. Let's say we want to time this block of code.

```
colors = ('blue', 'red', 'green')
for color in colors:
    print(color)
```

Import the **timeit** module. Create a string "**mycode**" that encloses the code statements in triple quotes. In the example below, the last line invokes the

timeit method to run the code 100 times.

```
from timeit import timeit
mycode = '''
colors = ('blue', 'red', 'green')
for color in colors:
      print(color)
'''
print(timeit(stmt=mycode, number=100))
```

4.14 Logging Time and Loop Counters

When writing new code, sometimes I add print statements to display the time, as well as loop counters. This is similar to the topic "Indenting Loop Print Statements" we looked at earlier. I have to admit, watching a Python program take 30 seconds to complete 75 million comparisons makes me very happy I use Python!

This is an example showing process time, the current local time, and a counter.

```
import time
i = 1
j = 50
start = time.process_time()
start1 = time.localtime()
thestarttime = time.asctime(start1)
print('Start time is: ', thestarttime,
                'and start process time is', start, '\n')
while i < 10000:
      if i == j:
            end = time.process_time()
            print('Time so far is:', start - end)
            print("i is", i)
            j += 1000
      i += 1
end = time.process_time()
print('Time to complete is: ', start - end)
start2 = time.localtime()
theendtime = time.asctime(start2)
print("\nStarted at:", thestarttime)
print("Ended at:", theendtime
```

The Console output is shown below:

```
Start time is:  Sun Jun 14 19:25:05 2025 and start process time is 11.184358

Time so far is:  -0.0003019999999995804
i is 50
Time so far is:  -0.0014359999999999928
i is 2050
Time so far is:  -0.0018299999999999983
```

```
i is 3050
Time so far is:  -0.0022180000000009414
i is 4050
Time so far is:  -0.002792000000001238
i is 5050
Time so far is:  -0.0032180000000003872
i is 6050
Time so far is:  -0.0036020000000007713
i is 7050
Time so far is:  -0.003984000000000876
i is 8050
Time so far is:  -0.00436800000000126
i is 9050
Time to complete is:  -0.005131999999999692

Started at: Sun Jun 14 19:25:05 2020
Ended at: Sun Jun 14 19:25:06 2020
```

4.15 Focused Testing

Sometimes I need to focus on one part of my code, or cell, to the exclusion of other areas. In the Editor, use a hashtag and two percent signs to indicate the start of a cell. I also might make a very simple "function" that I can test and debug, and later merge it into a library. By providing test data for the steps I'm excluding, I can focus on the defect. Let's look at my program that has five tasks.

1. Get KDP royalites.
2. Get the GBP exchange rate.
3. Calculate total sales for the month.
4. Calculate the average daily sales for the month.
5. Calculate the expected monthly sales.

Actual Result

When I run the code, the program halts. The Traceback shows a ZeroDivisionError on line 65. I haven't changed anything in the program in several weeks. Until today the program ran successfully. This is the code on line 65.

dailysales = (total/myday)

Incorrect Code

The value of "**myday**" is set on line 64, as shown below. As it happens, on the first day of the month, the statement on line 64 evaluates to zero.

myday = (datetime.datetime.today().day-1)

dailysales = (total/myday)

While this particular example is easy to troubleshoot, when you have a program with external connections, it can be a challenge to isolate the defect. With a slight modification, I can use a variable "**testmode**" as a switch to use test values. When I want to test 'datecalculations,' I set all the other conditional statements to use test data. In effect, I remove all the other code from the equation and only run lines 62-68.

For example, the "else" statement on line 55 sets **gbp** to a value of 999.99 when **testmode** is "**tst_datecalculations**."

test_mode.py

```
44
45 # Get exchange rate
46 if testmode == '' or testmode == 'tst_exchangerate':
47     url2 = 'https://usd.fxexchangerate.com'
48     html2 = urlopen(url2)
49     soup2 = BeautifulSoup(html2, 'lxml')
50     tables2 = soup2.findChildren('td')
51     gbpex = float(tables2[3].string[:6])
52     gbp = gbp/gbpex
53     print("gbp converted to USD is:", gbp)
54 else:
55     gbp = 999.99
56
57 # Calculate total sales for the month
58 total = usd + gbp
59 print("total sales this month  ", round(total, 2))
60
61
62 if testmode == '' or testmode == 'tst_datecalculations':
63     # Calculate average daily sales
64     myday = (datetime.datetime.today().day-1)
65     dailysales = (total/myday)
66     print("average daily sales ", dailysales)
67 else:
68     dailysales = 2.22
```

Figure 4.13 test_mode.py

4.16 Create Test Data

Use the smallest subset of data possible for testing. After removing a chunk of data, ensure you still have enough data for your program to function. If you're debugging an error, be careful to keep the data that recreates the error.

In this example, I changed the code on line 13 and created an HTML data file. Rather than connecting to a live website, I copied the "HTML" data to a file. I also removed unnecessary headings and tables from the HTML file.

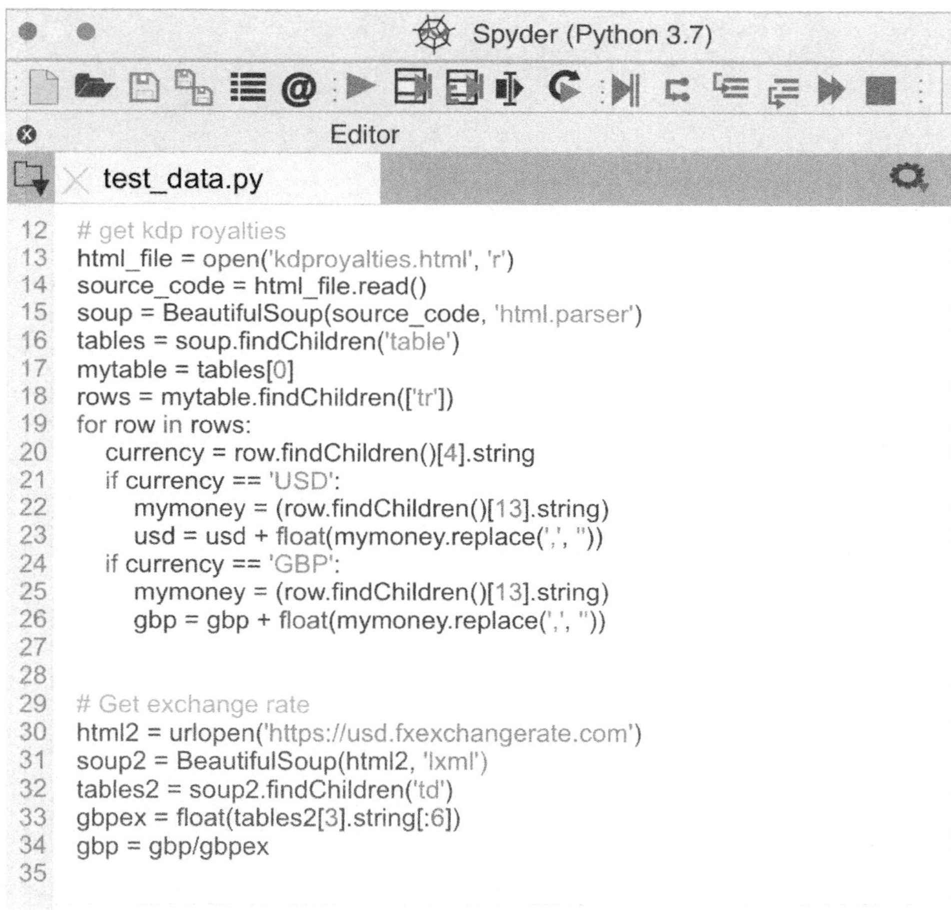

Spyder (Python 3.7)
Editor
test_data.py
12 # get kdp royalties
13 html_file = open('kdproyalties.html', 'r')
14 source_code = html_file.read()
15 soup = BeautifulSoup(source_code, 'html.parser')
16 tables = soup.findChildren('table')
17 mytable = tables[0]
18 rows = mytable.findChildren(['tr'])
19 for row in rows:
20   currency = row.findChildren()[4].string
21   if currency == 'USD':
22   mymoney = (row.findChildren()[13].string)
23   usd = usd + float(mymoney.replace(',', ''))
24   if currency == 'GBP':
25   mymoney = (row.findChildren()[13].string)
26   gbp = gbp + float(mymoney.replace(',', ''))
27
28
29 # Get exchange rate
30 html2 = urlopen('https://usd.fxexchangerate.com')
31 soup2 = BeautifulSoup(html2, 'lxml')
32 tables2 = soup2.findChildren('td')
33 gbpex = float(tables2[3].string[:6])
34 gbp = gbp/gbpex
35

Figure 4.14 Test Data.py File

Below is a small excerpt of the html data, with the data I need for my program.

try and except.py | royalties_divide_and_conquer.py | kdproyalties.html*

```
    </tr>
    <tr>
      <td valign="middle" class="td1">
        <p class="p2"><span class="s1">Amazon.co.uk</span></p>
      </td>
      <td valign="middle" class="td2">
        <p class="p2"><span class="s1">GBP</span></p>
      </td>
      <td valign="middle" class="td3">
        <p class="p2"><span class="s1">0.00</span></p>
      </td>
      <td valign="middle" class="td4">
        <p class="p2"><span class="s1">0.00</span></p>
      </td>
      <td valign="middle" class="td5">
        <p class="p2"><span class="s1">2.43</span></p>
      </td>
    </tr>
    <tr>
      <td valign="middle" class="td1">
        <p class="p2"><span class="s1">Amazon.de</span></p>
      </td>
      <td valign="middle" class="td2">
        <p class="p2"><span class="s1">EUR</span></p>
      </td>
      <td valign="middle" class="td3">
        <p class="p2"><span class="s1">0.00</span></p>
      </td>
      <td valign="middle" class="td4">
        <p class="p2"><span class="s1">0.00</span></p>
      </td>
      <td valign="middle" class="td5">
        <p class="p2"><span class="s1">0.00</span></p>
      </td>
    </tr>
    <tr>
      <td valign="middle" class="td1">
```

Figure 4.15 Test HTML Data File

Test Objects

In Chapter 2 we talked about focused testing, and a simple way to create test objects. I wanted to recap that information again because it's such a time saver.

For testing purposes, I only need **mydictionary** with a few elements. To create a dictionary for testing purposes let's look at two ways to create a test dictionary. The first example is best suited to dictionaries with only a few elements.

1. Run the main program to create **mydictionary**.
2. In the Console, type **mydictionary**.

3. The Console prints out all the values. Copy the data to create a test version of **mydictionary**.

4. In the main program or test script, I use the data in an assignment statement for a new "test" dictionary.

To simply output an object's value to a file, you could create a file and write the object values. In this example I output "myList" values to "myfile.txt."

```
fh = open('myfile.txt', 'w')
fh.write(myList)
fh.close()
```

Create a Test Dictionary

When my dictionary has a lot of data, I prefer to output the data to a file instead of the Console. The process is the same, but I use a helper program "**createTestDataFromDict()**" to create the output file. The output file is a complete assignment statement to create a new dictionary.

The main body of the original program "**ePub_index.py**" is shown on lines 15-20. I want to make a copy of the "index" dictionary.

1. On line 21, I invoke the "createTestDataFromDict()" function to make the output file "**testDictionary.txt**."

2. In case the dictionary has data I can't convert to a string, I use "try and except" syntax on lines 4-7.

3. On line 5, I add each key:value pair to "myStr." The key is **str(k)** and the value is **str(d[k])**. I also add a line return "**\n**" character at the end of each key:value pair.

4. On line 9, I remove whitespace from the end of "myStr." The last line of data in "mystr" has an extra "**\n**" that I don't need.

5. On line 10, I use slicing to remove the comma from the end of "myStr." The statement below is similar but uses the **rstrip()** method to remove the comma.

   ```
   myStr = myStr.rstrip(',')
   ```

6. On line 8, I create a new file "**testDictionary.txt**" using the **open()** function.
7. On line 11, I write "myStr" data to the file.
8. Finally, on line 12, I save the file with the **close()** function.

```
1   def createTestDataFromDict(d):
2       myStr = “testDict = {”
3       for k in d:
4           try:
5               myStr += “‘” + str(k) + “’: “ + str(d[k]) + “,\n”
6           except Exception:
7               print(‘exception converting key:’, k)
8       myFile = open(‘testDictionary.txt’, ‘w’)
9       myStr = myStr.rstrip()          # remove whitespace on right
10      myStr = myStr[:-1] + ‘}’        # remove last comma from string
11      myFile.write(myStr)
12      myFile.close()
13
14
15  index = {‘1’: 1.0,
16          ‘49’: [‘3.9’, ‘Strings’],
17          ‘59’: [‘3.10’, ‘Lists’],
18          ‘60’: [‘3.11’, ‘Methods for Lists’],
19          '73': ['3.12', 'Tuple'],
20          ‘74’: [‘3.13’, ‘Dictionary’]}
21  createTestDataFromDict(index)
```

The new "testDictionary.txt" file is shown below.

```
testDict = {‘1’: 1.0,
‘49’: [‘3.9’, ‘Strings’],
‘59’: [‘3.10’, ‘Lists’],
‘60’: [‘3.11’, ‘Methods for Lists’],
‘73’: [‘3.12’, ‘Tuple’],
‘74’: [‘3.13’, ‘Dictionary’]}
```

5. Exceptions

In this Chapter we discuss

Kinds of Errors

The Stack Trace or Traceback Message

Try and Except

Raise

Assert

Built-in Error Types

To begin our discussion of exceptions, we'll look at the basic kinds of programming errors. When I say "kind" of error, this is just a general classification to characterize programming errors. When an event happens that the Python Interpreter can't process successfully, it stops the program with an exception.

After an unhandled exception occurs, the Python Interpreter displays the stack trace in a "**Traceback**" message in the **Console** pane with details about the exception. In the topic, "Traceback Message," you'll see there is a wealth of information in a Traceback message. Often the Traceback message immediately points to the cause of the error.

To handle exceptions, you can add "**try and except**" statements to deal with exceptions gracefully. For critical events, we'll look at the "**raise**" command where you raise your own exception. When an object must be a certain value, adding an "**assert**" statement to trigger an exception when a value is outside your parameters alerts you to the problem.

Finally, we'll briefly look at the Python built-in exceptions you're likely to encounter when programming in Python.

5.1 Kinds of Errors

Generally, when things go wrong in a program, they fall into one of three categories.

- Syntax Errors
- Logic or Semantic Errors
- Runtime Errors

Syntax Errors are usually obvious, and the Spyder Editor points out Syntax errors with a yellow triangle. Runtime errors occur when the Python Interpreter halts and displays an exception. I find my "Logic" errors the most difficult to identify, because the program does what I told it to do, but my initial design or logic is flawed.

Syntax Errors

A syntax error is raised by the parser when the parser encounters a syntax error. The Spyder Editor makes it virtually impossible to have Syntax errors. A yellow triangle appears to the left of the line number if there is a Syntax error in the code.

Chapter 7 demonstrates syntax errors in Examples 7.8, 7.9, 7.11 and 7.12.

Logic or Semantic Errors

With a logic error, the flaw is in the design on my script. In Chapter 7, Example 7.25 demonstrates a logic error where I told the program to do something, but the outcome isn't what I wanted. To identify logic errors, I find it helpful to go back to the drawing board and look at my initial "Intended Outcome" or pseudocode. Pseudocode is an outline of your program design in simple terms, often written in plain English.

Runtime Errors

The challenge with debugging runtime errors is a line (or suite) of code runs as expected several times, and then suddenly halts with an error. As a program runs, variable values change. Another example of a RunTime error is when a program takes too long to run.

While general RunTime errors are flagged as a "RunTimeError" by the Python Interpreter, what I am referring to as "Runtime" is the overall kind of error. The actual Traceback message displayed in the Console may vary, as shown in Chapter 7 in Examples 7.5 and 7.12.

To research a runtime error, we need to look at the values at the moment the error occurred. When looking at values, you may have a critical variable that must be a certain value for your code to function. Assert statements halt the program and warn you when values are outside the parameters you require.

Another example of a Runtime error is a block of code that takes too long to run. In this case, the function "timeit" calculates program execution and can identify timing issues. Chapter 7 looks at these kinds of errors in Examples 7.1, 7.4, 7.6, 7.14, 7.15, and 7.17.

5.2 The Stack Trace or Traceback

The Traceback includes this basic information.

- File
- Line Number
- Module
- Exception
- Exception Description

The next example demonstrates a sample **Console** Traceback message. I abbreviated the file path for readability.

In [**1**]: File "workbook.py", line 289, in __getitem__
raise KeyError("Worksheet {0} does not exist.".format(key))
KeyError: 'Worksheet Sheet1 does not exist.'

The Traceback details are as follows:

File: "workbook.py"
Line Number: 289
Module: __getitem__
Exception: **KeyError**
Exception Description: Worksheet Sheet1 does not exist.

Traceback information provides the clues needed to research many issues. In Chapters 6 and 7, I'll often refer back to the "Exception" in the Traceback. In Chapter 7, Examples 7.1, 7.2, 7.3, and 7.6 demonstrate traceback screens.

Don't Be Fooled

A misleading Traceback message "**NameError**" could be hiding the Traceback message you want to see. In the Chapter 4 topic, "Variables and Objects in Memory," we looked at how the Python Interpreter creates variables and objects when you run a program or script. In this example, there is a variable "myint" of type "int."

```
myint = 57
print(myint.upper)
```

If the program ran and created "myint" already, the **Console** Traceback message is "AttributeError" because there is no attribute "upper" for a variable "myint." If the program hasn't run and created the variable "myint," the **Console** Traceback message is "NameError."

When the program encounters an **Out of Memory** error, the Traceback exception is rarely the actual cause of the defect.

5.3 Try and Except

Unhandled exceptions halt the program and display a Traceback message with an exception error. When you add "try" and "except" statements to your code, you add handlers to control how exceptions are handled, and prevent your program from unexpectedly halting. There are four blocks to a try:except statement. The "else" block of code runs only if there isn't an exception. The "finally" block always runs, and is often used to close files and cleanup memory.

```
try:

except Exception:

else:

finally:
```

In this next example with "except," you can see where I added custom messages.

```
1   try:
2       gbpex = float(tables2[3].string[:6])
3       gbp = gbp/gbpex
4       print("gbp converted to USD is:", gbp)
5   except TypeError:
6       print("Type error when converting exchange rate")
7   except ZeroDivisionError:
8       print('ZeroDivisionError where gbpex is:', gbpex)
9   except Exception as exceptdetails:
10      print(exceptdetails, 'gbpex is:', gbpex)
11  finally:
12      print("Done calculating the gbp exchange rate.")
```

The **finally** block of code on line 11 runs whether the **try** clause has an exception or not. You can also raise your own type of error, as shown on line 6.

```
try:
    <some code>
except Exception:
    raise ValueError(mymsg)
```

Examples 7.15, 7.21, and 7.24 in Chapter 7 demonstrate the try and except syntax.

5.4 Raise

At any point in your program, you can add your own "raise" statements to raise an exception, as shown below.

```
raise Exception("I broke my program.")
```

5.5 Assert

With an "**assert**" statement, program execution stops or halts when an expected condition is not met. When your program depends on a statement to be true, consider adding an "assert" statement to alert you if the statement does not evaluate to "True." Some interesting assertions are:

- A number is > 0
- A variable is a particular type (datetime)

- There are no duplicates
- A string or value is not None

> In debugging when your program stops at an assert statement, you know the "bug" must be somewhere before the assertion. There are several ways to disable all assertions at runtime, so use care with asserting confidential values.

When I was calculating KDP royalties earlier, I found the GBP exchange rate on a web site. In order for my program to calculate GBP royalties in USD currency, "**gbpex**" must be greater than zero.

```
assert gbpex > 0, 'gbpex must be > ' + str(gbpex)
```

Now when my program runs and "**gbpex**" is not greater than zero, an exception is raised. The **Console** displays a Traceback message, as shown below.

```
AssertionError: gbpex must be > 0
```

In the example below, I check that the variable "thedate" is a *datetime* type. This time "thedate" is valid and no exception is raised.

```
1  import datetime
2  thedate = datetime.datetime.now()
3  assert type(thedate) == datetime.datetime, "this isn't a date"
4  if thedate is not None and type(thedate) == datetime.datetime
5        print('everything is ok')
```

With a small modification on line 2 "thedate" becomes an "int." Now "thedate" is not a datetime type, and the assertion fails.

```
1  import datetime
2  thedate = datetime.datetime.today().day - 1
3  assert type(thedate) == datetime.datetime, "this isn't a date"
4  if thedate is not None and type(thedate) == datetime.datetime
5        print('everything is ok')
```

5.6 Built-in Error Types

The following list of built-in exceptions is a reference for the examples that follow. For a complete list of exceptions, visit https://docs.python.org/3/library/exceptions.html.

ArithmeticError

ArithmeticError is the base class for built-in exceptions for various arithmetic errors.

AssertionError

An **AssertionError** is raised when the assert statement fails.

AttributeError

An **AttributeError** is raised on attribute assignment or when the reference fails. When an object does not support attribute references or attribute assignments at all, a **TypeError** is raised. For example, an "int" object has no attribute "upper." The code below would cause an **AttributeError**:

```
myint = 57
print(myint.upper)
```

Because a "string" object does have an attribute "upper," this code for a string is valid.

```
mystr = 'age'
print(mystr.upper())
```

To view attributes of an object named **"mystr,"** first run the program, then type **"dir(mystr)"** in the Python **Console**. You must run the program for the Python Interpreter to create the variable "mystr." **If you haven't run the program**, the Python Interpreter displays a **NameError** exception. See Chapter 7, Example 7.6, for a description of debugging an **AttributeError**.

Earlier in Chapter 3 we looked at strings in dictionaries. Examples 7.6, 7.38 and 7.39 demonstrate an AttributeError. The "AttributeError 'list' object 'extend' is read only" means you forgot the parentheses at the end of a function call.

```
mylist.extend()
```

In Python, objects have attributes. So, for example, the object "**ws1**" has an attribute named "**.cell**." In this example, the dotted notation would be **ws1.cell()**.

EOFError

An EOFError is raised when the input() function hits the end-of-file condition without reading any data. This is common if you forget the closing quote or apostrophe in a string assignment.

FloatingPointError

The FloatingPointError is raised when a floating-point operation fails.

ImportError

When the Python Interpreter has trouble loading a module, the Interpreter raises an ImportError.

Indentation Error

An IndentationError is raised when there is incorrect indentation in the code. In Chapter 7, Examples 7.5 and 7.7 demonstrate an IndentationError. For more information, see the topic "Indented Code" in Chapter 3.

IndexError

An IndexError is raised when the index of a sequence is out of range as discussed in Chapter 3. If the index is not an integer, a **TypeError** is raised. The base class of an IndexError is a LookupError. See Examples 7.1-7.2 in Chapter 7.

As an example, if the code moves beyond the limits of the list an **IndexError** is raised. If I have four objects in the list and use index "5" or mylist[4], and IndexError occurs. Python starts counting at 0, so this example is beyond the bounds of the list.

If you try to assign a value to an index that doesn't exist, it causes an error.

IndexError list assignment index out of range.

Instead, to add add items to a list, use .insert(), .extend(), or .append().

IOError

Starting from Python 3.3, an IOError is an OSError.

KeyError

A KeyError is raised when a key is not found in a dictionary, and is a subclass of LookupError. In Chapter 7, see Examples 7.20 and 7.31 that demonstrate this type of error.

KeyboardInterrupt

A KeyboardInterrupt is raised when the user hits the interrupt key (Ctrl + C or delete).

LookupError

A LookupError is the base class for KeyError and IndexError.

MemoryError

A MemoryError is raised when an operation runs out of memory.

ModuleNotFoundError

The ModuleNotFound error indicates a module could not be located and is a subclass of ImportError. In Chapter 7, Example 7.19 demonstrates a ModuleNotFoundError.

NameError

You've probably noticed I often say, "run the program to create variables, then..." If an object doesn't exist in the namespace it means the variable hasn't been created in memory. The **NameError** is raised when a variable is not found in the local or global scope. This exception occurs when an identifier is invalid or is an unknown name.

For example, a misspelled identifier can cause a NameError. The

Spyder IDE highlights a NameError. In Chapter 7, Examples 7.3, 7.10, 7.13, and 7.22 demonstrate NameErrors. We also looked at the related **UnboundLocalError** exception in the Chapter 3 topic, "Global Variables."

> The Chapter 4 topic, "Variables and Objects in Memory," outlined how the Python Interpreter creates variables and objects when you run a program or script. If you type your object name in the Console and the Traceback says "NameError," ensure that you ran the line of code that creates the object in the local scope.

OSError

An OSError is raised when a system operation causes a system-related error, such as failing to find a local file on disk.

OverflowError

The OverflowError is raised when the result of an arithmetic operation is too large to be represented. The OverflowError is a subclass of an ArithmeticError.

RecursionError

A RecursionError is derived from the base class RuntimeError. A RecursionError is similar to an IndexError where the index is out of bounds. A recursive loop counts down to the end of the loop as shown in the Chapter 3 topic, "Recursive Functions." A RecursionError is raised when the maximum recursion depth is exceeded.

RuntimeError

A "RuntimeError" is raised when an error is detected that does not fall under any other category.

StopIteration

A StopIteration exception is raised by the **next()** function to indicate that there is no further item to be returned by the iterator. In Chapter 7, Example 7.35 raises a StopIteration error.

SyntaxError

A SyntaxError is raised by the parser when it can't parse the program. The Spyder Editor makes it virtually impossible to have Syntax errors. A yellow triangle appears to the left of the line number if there is a Syntax error in the code.

SystemError

A SystemError occurs when the interpreter detects an internal error.

SystemExit

The sys.exit() function raises a SystemExit exception.

TabError

A TabError occurs when code inconsistently uses tabs and spaces. The TabError is a subclass of IndentationError.

TypeError

A TypeError is raised when a function or operation is applied to an object of an incorrect type. A TypeError occurs when you are attempting to perform an operation on an incorrect object type. Examples of TypeErrors you might see are:

- tuple object does not support item assignment
- string indices must be integers
- divide int by a string (3/'a')
- mixing types
- missing a function argument

Tuple Object does not Support Item Assignment

As an example, if you try to assign a new value to an item in a **tuple**, a TypeError is raised.

```
In [3]: mytuple[1] = 'three'

Traceback (most recent call last):
      File "<ipython-input-3-db66c3391d15>", line 1, in <module>
       mytuple[1] = 'three'

TypeError: 'tuple' object does not support item assignment
```

String Indices Must be Integers

In Chapter 3, we saw a TypeError when iterating over a string. The "print" statement shown below would cause an error because the values 'abc' are not integers.

```
mystr = 'abc'
for i in mystr:
      print('mystr char is:', mystr[i])
```

The **Console** would display a traceback message with a "**TypeError.**" I've abbreviated the Traceback message below for readability.

```
In [2]:

Traceback (most recent call last):
TypeError: string indices must be integers
```

A slight modification in the code would prevent the error. In the example below, I am using the "**range()**" function combined with the length function "**len()**" to find the length of the list. We looked at the "range" function in Chapter 3.

```
mystr = 'abc'
for i in range(len(mystr)):
      print('mystr char is:', mystr[i])
```

UnboundLocalError

An UnboundLocalError is raised when you assign a value to a variable that doesn't exist in the program scope. In Chapter 3, in the topic "global variables" we looked at an example of this type of error. In Chapter 7, Example 7.50 demonstrates an UnboundLocalError.

ValueError

A ValueError is raised when a function gets an argument of correct type but improper value. For example, a datetime object considers a time value for seconds < 60 or a month between 1 and 12 to be valid. A datetime month value of 13 creates an exception, and the Python Interpreter displays a ValueError. The syntax below is invalid for a datetime object:

d1 = datetime(**1999**, 13, 31)

ZeroDivisionError

A ZeroDivisionError is raised when the second argument of a division or modulo operation is zero. The ZeroDivisionError is a subclass of ArithmeticError. Example 7.24 in Chapter 7 shows a divide by zero error.

6. Try This

In this Chapter, we discuss

What is the Object Value?
String and Number Variable Values
True & False Vlues
Tuple Objects and Values
List Objects and Values
Dictionary Objects and Values
Does the Object Have a Value of None?
What is the Object Type?
What is the Length of the Object?
What are the Function/Method Arguments?
What Type of Object Does a Function Return?

While the examples in Chapter 7 do have several suggestions on how to identify a particular bug, they are only helpful if you're experiencing the same problem; in the real world, that's not likely to happen. My concern with only using "Examples," is you'll rarely encounter the same issue when working with your code. Your situation is unique, and probably won't match one of the examples.

To provide the missing piece of the debugging puzzle, I'm going to take some time in this chapter to break down the debugging process into a reusable format. I'll cover some common issues. Unfortunately, my issue list isn't going to be all-inclusive, but I hope it kickstarts your debugging experience.

While an odd chapter title, "Try This" is a fitting name. When I was learning to program, I would share my dilemmas with a good friend. He would say, "Try this..." and offer a few suggestions. That little nudge in the right direction was a godsend that helped me find my way. I'm not sure if I can create that experience for you, but I'm going to try.

As we work through the next sections, you'll notice a common theme, where we look at these topics in different contexts.

- Object Values
- Types of Objects
- Length of Objects
- Passing Arguments to Functions or Methods
- The Return Object of a Function

We'll look at the common objects outlined below. This list of objects isn't every possible Python object, but I think these are enough to get you started.

- Strings and Numbers
- Tuples
- Lists
- Dictionaries

It can be exasperating when you have a runtime or logic error and have no idea where to start debugging. The suggestions in this chapter may help you get started debugging your program.

6.1 What is the Object Value?

When I am debugging, often, the first thing I check is the object value. If you decide to take the hands-on approach and add print statements to your code or use Interactive Mode in the Console, the next few topics show you examples for strings, tuples, lists, and dictionaries. In the case of data structures like lists, tuples, and dictionaries, I'll also include the syntax to inspect all items or a single item. This content may be a bit repetitive, but on the plus side, this is a handy reference.

6.2 String and Number Variable Values

In this topic, I'll look at several ways to find the value of string and number variables.

Print the Value of a String Variable

Add a print statement to your script in the **Editor** window, and run your program.

mystring = "Purple Peanuts"

In the example the follows, I add a print statement in the **Editor** window to see the value of a string. When I run the program, the output of the print statement is shown in the **Console** pane. The Console is the Python Shell.

A String Identifier: mystring
Value: purple peanuts
Reference: Chapter 4 - Add Print Statements

```
mystring = "purple peanuts"
print(mystring)
```

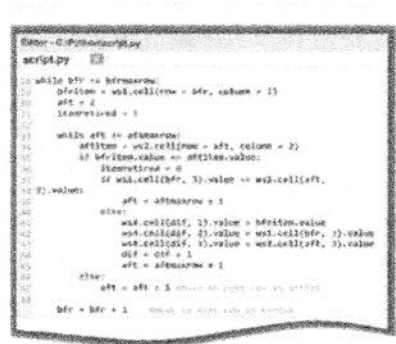

```
In [1]: runfile('C:/SampleScript.py', wdir='C:')
purple peanuts
```

Variables in Imported Modules

To reference a variable inside another library, module or class, use dotted notation. In this example, I import a module "mymodule2" that has the variable "mystr2." The expression **module2.mystr2** returns the value of **mystr2**.

```
import mymodule2
print(mymodule2.mystr2)
```

Inspect a Number Variable in Debug Mode

Debug Mode with Variable Explorer is a simple way to see object values as you step through your code. In this example, in one line the **Editor** creates a string variable named "mynumber" and assigns a value.

mynumber = 57

1. Run the program in Debug Mode to create the variable in memory.
2. Next, I type "**mynumber**" in the **Console**. Because I am in Debug Mode, the Console prompt is **ipdb>**.

   Variable Explorer also shows the value of the "**mynumber**" variable.

Inspect a String Value with Interactive Mode

To see the value of the string in Interactive Mode, type the string name "mystring" in the **Console**. The assignment statement that creates the variable is shown below.

mystring = "purple peanuts"

A String Identifier: mystring
Value: purple peanuts
Reference: Chapter 4 - Interactive Mode

1. Run the program to create the string variable in memory.
2. Type "mystring" in the Console.
3. The Python Interpreter displays the value of "mystring" on the next line in the **Console**.
   Because you are using the Console, quotes around the value indicate this is a string.

```
In [2]: mystring
Out[2]: 'purple peanuts'
```

6.3 True & False Values

Rather than just looking at a boolean variable in this topic, I also wanted to recap some of the boolean objects we looked at in Chapter 3.

- Logic tests
- Compound boolean statements ("is" and "is not")

- Function return values
- Conditional statements

Recall from Chapter 3, a boolean value is either "True" or "False" and behaves like the integers 0 and 1 respectively. Let's experiment with some statements in the **Console** that return True or False.

```
In [1]: not 0
Out[1]: True

In [2]: 3 is 0
Out[2]: False
```

The next example uses the "**modulo**" operator "**%**" that returns the remainder when dividing two numbers. This expression returns "0" indicating there is no remainder. The statement is "False." In simple terms I am asking, "does x % 7 have a remainder?" and the answer is "no" or "0."

```
In [1]: x = 21
In [2]: x % 7
Out[2]: 0
```

When combined with the boolean "not" operator the same expression is "True." In this example I am asking, "is it true that x % 7 does not have a remainder?" and the answer is "yes, that is true."

```
In [3]: x = 21
In [4]: not x % 7
Out[4]: True
```

While True

The "while" statement that follows is always **True**, so the program runs until you break out of the loop.

```
while True:
```

Boolean Return Object

The next two functions both return "True." Because the second function, "**myfunction2**" is simpler, it is considered more "Pythonic."

```
def myfunction():
    if 2 == 2:
        return True

def myfunction2():
    return 2 == 2
```

Conditional Statements

In Chapter 3 we looked at Conditional Statements. The Python Interpreter evaluates the statement and continues executing that block of code if the statement is True. If the statement is False, the loop ends.

```
for i in range(0, 20):
if i % 2 != 0:
    print("i is an odd number", i)
```

Return the Statement that is True

The next example of a return statement would return the value of "y" or 'hello' because Python returns the True statement. It is "True" that **y** is a string; and False that **x** is an integer. In this case, whichever expression is True would be returned.

```
x = 'john'

y = 'hello'

return isinstance(x, int) or isinstance (y, str)
```

Print the Value of a Boolean Variable

Add a print statement to your script in the **Editor** window, and ▶ run your program.

```
myBool = False
```

In the example that follows, I add a print statement in the **Editor** window to see the value of a bool. When I run the program, the output of the print statement is shown in the **Console** pane.

A Boolean Identifier: myBool
Value: False
Reference: Chapter 4 - Add Print Statements

```
myBool = False
print(myBool)
```

```
In [1]: runfile('C:/SampleScript.py', wdir='C:')
False
```

Inspect a Boolean Variable in Debug Mode

Debug Mode with Variable Explorer is a simple way to see object values as you step through your code. In this example, in one line the **Editor** creates a boolean variable named "myBool" and assigns a value.

myBool = True

1. Run ⏯ the program in Debug Mode to create the variable in memory.
2. Next, I type "myBool" in the **Console**. Because I am in Debug Mode, the Console prompt is **ipdb>**.

```
ipdb> myBool
False
```

Variable Explorer also shows the value of the "**myBool**" variable.

Inspect a Boolean Value with Interactive Mode

To see the value of the boolean variable in **Interactive Mode**, type the variable name "myBool" in the **Console**. The assignment statement that creates the variable is shown below.

myBool = True

A Boolea Identifier: myBool
Value: True
Reference: Chapter 4 - Interactive Mode

1. In the **Editor**, type the assignment statement to create the variable in memory and run your program.

```
myBool = True
```

2. Type "myBool" in the **Console**.

```
In [2]: myBool
Out[2]: True
```

3. The Python Interpreter displays the value of "myBool" in the **Console**.

Boolean Operations

In Chapter 3 we looked at the boolean operators "and," "or," and "not." These operators are sometimes referred to as short-circuit operators. The evaluation of a compound boolean expression stops when an outcome is reached. In this example, the Python Interpreter stops evaluating the expression after "5 == 4" because the statement evaluates to "False."

```
if 5 == 4 and 2 != 6:
```

6.4 Tuple Objects and Values

In this topic, I'll look at several ways to inspect tuple objects and tuple element values. To create a tuple, use this syntax in the **Editor**:

mytuple = ('Apple', 'Orange', 'Watermelon')

Print All Tuple Item Values

Add a print statement to your script in the **Editor** window and run your program. The output of the print statement is shown in the **Console** pane.

All Items in the Tuple
Identifier: mytuple
Values: Apple, Orange, Watermelon
Reference: Chapter 4 - Add Print Statements

```
print(mytuple)
```

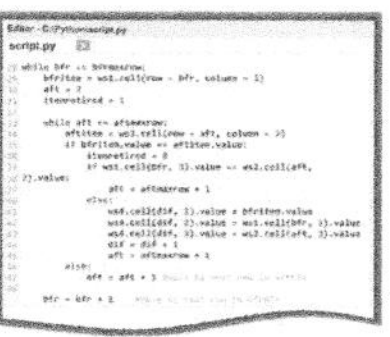

```
In [1]: runfile('C:/SampleScript.py', wdir='C:')
('Apple', 'Orange', 'Watermelon')
```

The parentheses around the value indicate this is a tuple.

Print a Tuple Item Value

To see the value of a tuple item, type **mytuple[0]**. The first item in the tuple has an index value of **0**.

A Tuple Item
Identifier: mytuple[**0**]
Value: Apple
Reference: Chapter 4 - Add Print Statements

1. Add a print statement to your script in the **Editor** window.
2. Run your program. The output of the print statement is shown in the **Console** pane.

```
print(mytuple[0])
```

```
In [1]: runfile('C:/SampleScript.py', wdir='C:')
Apple
```

Inspect All Tuple Items in Interactive Mode

Continuing on using the previous example, to see all the values of a tuple named "mytuple," type the tuple name "mytuple" in the **Console**.

All Items of the Tuple
Identifier: mytuple
Value: Apple, Orange, Watermelon
Reference: Chapter 4 - Interactive Mode

1. Run the program to create the tuple variable in memory.
2. Type "mytuple" in the Console in **Interactive Mode**. The Python Interpreter displays the value of "mytuple" on the next line in the **Console**. *The parentheses around the value indicate this is a tuple.*

Object Type	Identifier	Value
A Tuple	mytuple	purple peanuts

```
In [2]: mytuple
Out[2]: ('Apple', 'Orange', 'Watermelon')
```

Inspect A Tuple Item in Interactive Mode

To see the value of a tuple object "mytuple," type "mytuple" in the **Console**. The first element in the tuple has an index value of **0**.

A Tuple Item
Identifier: mytuple[**0**]
Value: Apple
Reference: Chapter 4 - Interactive Mode

1. Run the program to create the tuple variable in memory.
2. Type "mytuple[0]" in the Console in **Interactive Mode**. The Python Interpreter displays the value of the "mytuple[**0**]" object on the next line in the **Console**. *The parentheses around the value indicate this is a tuple.*

In [**2**]: mytuple[0]
Out[2]:('Apple')

6.5 List Objects and Values

In this topic, I'll look at several ways to inspect list objects and list item values. To create a list, use this syntax:

mylist = ['soda', 'water', 'coffee']

Print All List Item Values

In this example, I print out the three strings in "mylist" to the **Console** pane.

All Items of the List
Identifier: mylist
Value: soda, water, coffee
Reference: Chapter 4 - Add Print Statements

1. Add a print statement to your script in the **Editor** window.

2. Run your program. The output of the print statement is shown in the **Console** pane. *The brackets around the value indicate this is a list.*

```
mylist = ['soda', 'water', 'coffee']
print(mylist)
```

```
In [1]: runfile('C:/SampleScript.py', dir='C:')
['soda', 'water', 'coffee']
```

Print the Value of a List Item

To print the value of a list item, add a print statement to your script in the **Editor** window, and run your program. The second item in the list has an index value of **1**.

A List Item
Identifier: mylist[**1**]
Value: soda, water, coffee
Reference: Chapter 4 - Add Print Statements

1. Add a print statement to your script in the **Editor** window.

2. Run your program. The output of the print statement is shown in the Console pane. In the example below, the output is "water."

   The quotes or apostrophes around the value idicate the list item is a string.

```
mylist = ['soda', 'water', 'coffee']
print(mylist[1])
```

In [**1**]: runfile('C:/SampleScript.py', wdir='C:')
'water'

Inspect a List Item in Debug Mode

Debug Mode with Variable Explorer is a simple way to see object values as you step through your code. In this example, I run the program in **Debug Mode**. Because I am in Debug Mode, the prompt is **ipdb>**.

Notice **Variable Explorer** shows the values in the "**drinks"** list. The third item is "coffee" and has an index value of **2**.

A List Item
Identifier: drinks[**2**]
Value: coffee
Reference: Chapter 4 - Debug Mode

1. Run the program in Debug Mode to create the variable in memory.
2. Type **drinks[2]** in the **Console**, as shown below.

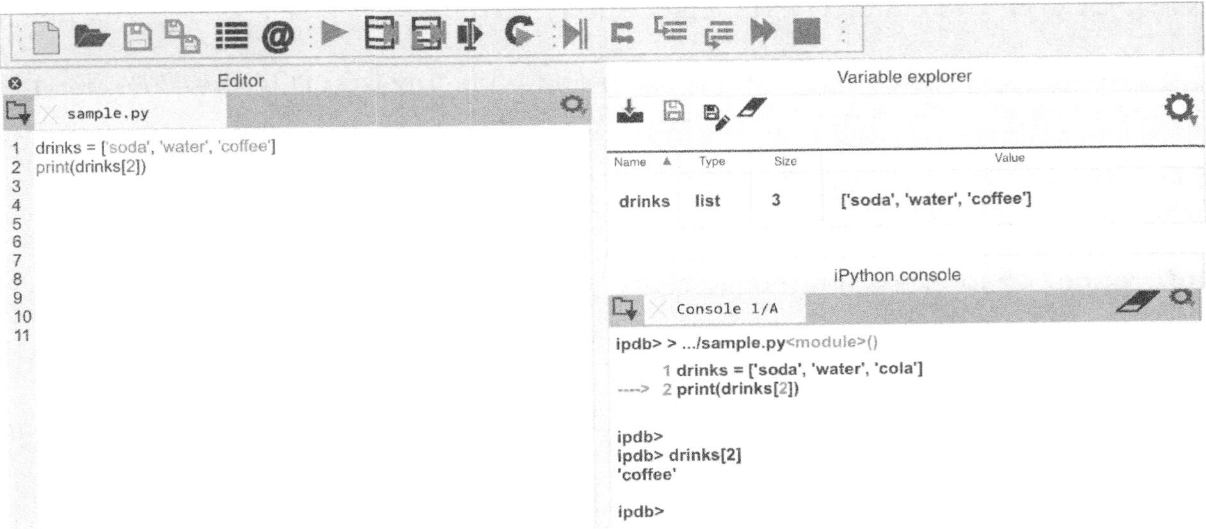

Figure 6.1

Inspect All Items of a List in the Console

To see all values of a list, type the list name in the **Console**.

All Items in the List
Identifier: mylist
Value: soda, water, coffee
Reference: Chapter 4 - Interactive Mode

1. Run the program.

2. Type "mylist" in the Console. The Python Interpreter displays the value of "mylist" on the next line in the **Console**.
   Because this is a list, the value is enclosed in brackets.

   The list elements are strings as idicated by the apostrophes.

```
In [2]: mylist
Out[2]: ['soda', 'water', 'coffee']
```

Inspect a List Item in the Console

In this example, I run the program and type "mylist[1]" in the Console. The second element in the list has an index value of **1**.

A List Item
Identifier: mylist[**1**]
Value: water
Reference: Chapter 4 - Interactive Mode

1. Run the program.

2. Type "mylist[**1**]" in the **Console**. The Python Interpreter displays the value of mylist[**1**] in the **Console**.

   Because this list element is a string, the value is inside quotes.

In [**2**]: mylist[1]
Out[2]: 'water'

6.6 Dictionary Objects and Values

In this topic, I'll look at several ways to inspect Dictionary objects and dictionary key:value pairs. To create a dictionary, use this syntax:

```
mydictionary = {'Name': 'Zimmerman',
                'Grade': 'A',
                'Course': 'Python Programming'}
```

Print the Value of a Dictionary Key:Value Pair

To print the value of a dictionary key, add a print statement to your script in the **Editor** window, and run your program.

A Dictionary Key:Value
Identifier: mydictionary[**'Name'**]
Value: Zimmerman
Reference: Chapter 4 - Add Print Statements

1. Add a print statement to your script in the **Editor** window.
2. Run your program. The output of the print statement is shown in the Console pane. In the example below, the output is "Zimmerman."

```
mydictionary = {'Name': 'Zimmerman',
                'Grade': 'A',
                'Course': 'Python Programming'}
print(mydictionary['Name'])
```

In [**1**]: runfile('C:/SampleScript.py', wdir='C:')
Zimmerman

Inspect All Dictionary Items in the Console

To see all the key-pairs of a dictionary named "mydictionary," type "mydictionary" in the **Console**. In this example, I run the program, and the Python Interpreter displays the key:value pairs of "mydictionary" on the next line in the **Console**.

All Dictionary Items
Identifier: mydictionary
Key-Pair Values: Name: Zimmerman, Grade: 'A', 'Course': 'Python Programming'
Reference: Chapter 4 - Interactive Mode

1. Run the program.

2. Type "mydictionary" in the Console. The Python Interpreter displays the value of "mydictionary on the next line in the **Console**.

   Because this value is a dictionary curly braces surround the elements.

In [**2**]: mydictionary
Out[2]: {'Name': 'Zimmerman', 'Grade': 'A'. 'Course': 'Python Programming'}

Inspect a Dictionary Item Value in the Console

Once you know a key name in a dictionary, you can find the value of the dictionary key:value pair. In this example, I run the program and type mydictionary['Grade'] in the Console. The key name is "Grade."

A Dictionary Item
Identifier: mydictionary['Grade']
Value: A
Reference: Chapter 4 - Interactive Mode , Chapter 3 - Find the Value of a Dictionary Item.

1. Run the program.

2. Type "mydictionary['grade']" in the **Console**. The Python Interpreter displays the value of "mydictionary['Grade']" on the next line in the **Console**.

If you don't know the key name, the next example shows how to iterate through key names.

```
In [2]: mydictionary['Grade']
Out[2]: 'A'
```

Inspect a Dictionary Item in Variable Explorer

Debug Mode with Variable Explorer is a simple way to see object values as you step through your code. In this example, I create a variable "schoolinfo" in a "for statement" on line 5. This variable "schoolinfo" is used to access the keys in **mydictionary**. When I step through the "for loop" twice in Debug Mode, the "schoolinfo" variable has the value of the second key in "mydictionary." Keys are in no particular order, which is why you have to iterate through the keys, or know the key name. After running the code, the Console shows the keys: "Name, Grade, Course."

A Dictionary Item
Identifier: mydictionary['Grade']
Variable: schoolinfo
Values: Name, Grade, Course
Reference: Chapter 4 - Debug Mode Variable Explorer

```
mydictionary = {'Name': 'Zimmerman', 'Grade': 'A',
                'Course': 'Python Programming'}
for schoolinfo in mydictionary:
      print(schoolinfo)
```

When you double click on the name of a dictionary in Variable Explorer, a pop-up window opens .

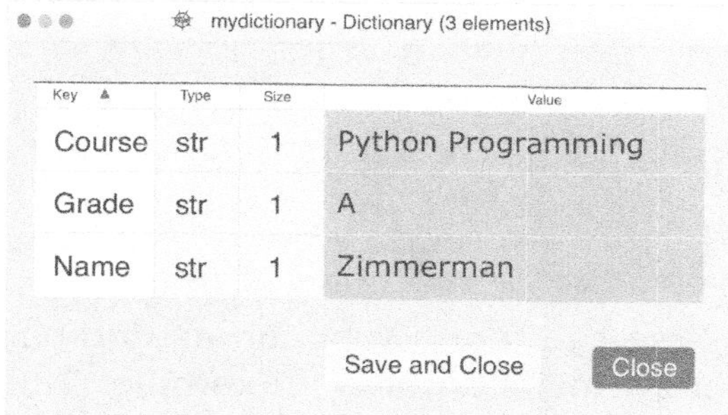

mydictionary - Dictionary (3 elements)

Key	Type	Size	Value
Course	str	1	Python Programming
Grade	str	1	A
Name	str	1	Zimmerman

Save and Close   Close

Figure 6.2 Pop-up in Variable Explorer

6.7 Does the Object have a Value of None or Whitespace?

When importing external data into Python data structures, it's not uncommon to have items with a value of "None" or unexpected whitespace. For example, if you import an Excel worksheet with empty cells, those items have a value of "None." Also, sometimes strings are equal to "".

Functions with no specified return value also return "None." The value "None" is returned when you don't have a return value for all paths in the function, as explained in the Chapter 3 topic, "Function Return Values." Example 7.17 in Chapter 7 also illustrates a function that returns "None."

The "None" value causes problems when passing arguments to functions that expect a particular type or value for an object. For example, the DateTime library function "**.strftime()**" expects an argument of type "datetime", "time", or "date." If you pass an object that has a value of "None" to the "**.strftime()**" function, the Python interpreter displays an error, as shown in Chapter 7, **Example 7.20**.

Sadly, this is also one way Divide by Zero errors happen in a program. When you convert an item in a data structure from a string to an "int," an item with a value of "None" becomes a zero. The Divide by Zero error is shown in the Chapter 7 **Examples 7.24 and 7.17**, and includes a sample "if statement" to test for a "None" value or "NoneType."

Whitepsace Characters

Another cause of unexpected consequences is whitespace. There may be a tab, line return, or some other character in your data that impacts a search or comparison. These string functions are useful for removing those unseen characters.

lstrip() Remove left whitepspace characters.
rstrip() Remove right whitespace characters.
strip() Remove whitespace characters from both sides.

To identify whitespace characters you can use the repr() function as outlined in the Chapter 3 topic, "Whitespace Characters." In Chapter 7, Example 7.29 demonstrates whitespace errors.

6.8 What is the Object Type?

In Debug Mode, Variable Explorer shows the type of the object. Another option to view whitespace is to add a print statement, or type commands in the Console, as outlined earlier. The second example below prints the type of the function's return object.

```
print(type(mystring))
print(type(myfunction())
```

Object	Syntax
number, string or data structure	type(mystring) type(mytuple) type(mylist) type(mydictionary)
a tuple item	type(mytuple[0])
a list item	type(mylist[0])
a dictionary item	type(mydictionary('Name'])

6.9 What is the Length of the Object?

The **len()** function shows the length of a string or the number of items in a data structure. For example, **len(mydictionary)** would return the number of dictionary key:value pairs, and **len(mylist)** would return the number of items in the list.:

Object	Syntax
number, string or data structure	len(mystring) len(mytuple) len(mylist) len(mydictionary)
a tuple item	len(mytuple[0])
a list item	len(mylist[0])
a dictionary item	len(mydictionary('Name']

6.10 What are the Function Arguments?

Before using a function, identify what type of arguments the Function expects. Then, check your arguments to be sure they are the correct type and value, as outlined previously. The **Help** pane and searching the Internet are a great way to review the definition of the function to ensure both the arguments and return objects are what you expect. In the Console, you can also use these introspection functions for more information about your object, as outlined in Chapter 4 in the topic "Interactive Mode."

```
In [1]: myfunction?
In [2]: dir(myfunction)
In [3]: help(myfunction)
```

The reference for built-in functions can be found on **docs.python.org**. Example 26 in Chapter 7 also looks at these options.

The Function Call Signature

Ideally every function has a "function call signature." The "inspect" module includes **signature(myfunction)** that returns a function's docstring. The **getfullargspec()** function displays the names and default values of a function. Chapter 7, Example 20 uses the **signature()** function to retrieve parameter information.

For additional information on the "**openpyxl**" method "**load_workbook**," I can look at the "call signature" for that callable object. In Python v3.x, PEP 362 specifies the function signature object and lists each parameter accepted by a function. In the **Console**, import the module and print the signature for the object, as shown below. In Chapter 7, Example 7.20 also illustrates this syntax from PEP 362. The inspect library displays the DocString, and is mentioned in the topic "Classes" in **Chapter 3**.

```
from inspect import signature
print(str(signature(load_workbook)))
```

Inspect the Docstring

Hopefully, functions include a "docstring" explaining the purpose of the function and what the function returns, if anything. In this next example, I'm inspecting the arguments, signature, and docstring of "myfunction." The last line retrieves the "docstring" using the dotted notation "**myfunction.__doc__**."

```
from inspect import *
#
#
def myfunction(a = myint, b = myfloat):
            '''
            this function takes an int and a float
            and doesn't do anything
            '''
            pass
#
#
from inspect import *
print(getfullargspec(myfunction))
print(signature(myfunction))
print(myfunction.__doc__)
```

6.11 What Type of Object Does a Function Return?

In Chapter 3, we looked at "functions that return a tuple" and "function return or yield objects." The "Interactive Mode" of the **Console** is a great way to check what a function returns. You may want to check the value, type, or length of the object.

```
print(myfunction())

type(myfunction())

len(myfunction())
```

The **Help** pane is another way to review the definition of the function and docstring, to ensure both the arguments and return object are what you expect. A function returns one object, but that object might be a tuple with several items as outlined in Chapter 3. Example 26 in Chapter 7 looks at these options.

7. Examples

In this Chapter, we take "debugging" for a spin. These examples build on everything we've looked at so far. It doesn't matter if you landed here first, or read everything to this point. Either way, I provide references to those previous topics, in case you want to take a brief sojourn to review them.

Ex	Description	Built-in Error Type
1	List index out of range	IndexError
2	List index out of range (Example 1 continued)	IndexError
3	Wrong Variable Name	NameError
4	Invalid assignment	Runtime
5	While statement not indented	IndentationError
6	Method arguments incorrect	AttributeError
7	Empty block is illegal	IndentationError
8	Parentheses not matched	SyntaxError
9	Colon misssing	SyntaxError
10	Case sensitive	NameError
11	Keyword missing	SyntaxError
12	Illegal characters or keyword	SyntaxError
13	Misspelled identifier	NameError
14	File doesn't exist	FileNotFoundError
15	Adding incorrect types	TypeError
16	Misspelled keyword	SyntaxError
17	Value is none	TypeError
18	Method attribute not found	AttributeError
19	Module not found	NameError
20	Key not in dictionary	KeyError
21	Arugment is incorrect type	ValueError
22	Object not found - NameError	NameError
23	Invalid data passed to method	ValueError
24	Calculation causes a ZeroDivisionError	ZeroDivision Error
25	There is a mistake in a math calculation	
26	Assigning datetime value causes ValueError	ValueError
27	Matching strings NoneType error	NoneTypeError
28	Matching strings fails	TypeError
29	Whitespace or special characters	
30	Debug: Step through your function	
31	Key not in dictionary	KeyError
32	'2' + 2 Concatenate fails	TypeError
33	Function returns 2 values	TypeError
34	Unsupported operand	
35	Generator object not subsciptable	StopIteration
36	Missing 1 required positional argument	TypeError
37	Reserved keyword	TypeError
38	Invoking a class method raises an error	AttributeError

Ex	Description	Built-in Error Type
39	Key error creating a dictionary key:pair.	AttributeError
40	Illegal target for annotation	
41	Too many values to unpack	ValueError
42	Tuple object does not support item assignment	TypeError
43	An object is not callable	TypeError
44	Can only concatenate tuple not 'str'	TypeError
45	Float comparison fails	
46	Unhashable type: 'dict'	TypeError
47	'builtin_function_or_method' object is not subscriptable	TypeError
48	String comparison error	TypeError
49	Invalid literal for int() with base 10	ValueError
50	A variable is referenced before assignment	UnboundLocalError
51	Plot - shape mismatch	ValueError
52	Unpacking operator	IndexError
53	Unpack non-iterable bool	TypeError

For each example that follows, I use a systematic approach to examine the program.

Intended Outcome: What I want the program to do is the Intended Outcome.

Actual Result: What the program did is the Actual Result.

Incorrect Code: The Incorrect Code is the actual code that is not working properly.

Debugging Experiment: The steps I use to "debug" what the program is actually doing comprise the Debugging Experiment.

How to Resolve the Issue: This section is a brief description of the change to the code to resolve the issue.

Correct Code: The Correct Code that works as I intended.

References: The References list previous topics related to this example.

7.1 List Index Out of Range

Description: The list index is out of range.

Intended Outcome

There are two lists in this program, "meals" and "fruits." I want the program to loop through each list and print the items in order.

Actual Result

The **Console** output shows the print statement on line 6 repeats with the first item in the List.

Incorrect Code

This is the Example 7.1 code before any changes. Can you spot the areas we need to fix? We'll look at each error in Examples 7.1 and 7.2.

```
1   meals = ['breakfast', 'lunch', 'snack', 'dinner']
2   fruits = ['apple', 'orange', 'grape']
3   i = 0
4   while i < 4:
5       j = 0
6       print("my meal is: ",  meals[i])
7       while j < 4:
8           print("My choice of fruit is: ", fruits[i])
9           j = j + 1
10  i = i + 1
```

Debugging Experiment

In this example, when I run the program, it loops continuously. First, I use **Debug Mode** to research what is happening. This is a good time to backup your files before making any changes.

1. Run the program. The program runs endlessly. The program is in an infinite loop. In the **Console**, the Python Interpreter repeatedly outputs the print statement from line 6.

2. To stop the program, in the **Consoles** menu, I select "Restart kernel."

   Double click twice on line 6 to add a breakpoint. Select "Debug File" on the menu, as shown below.

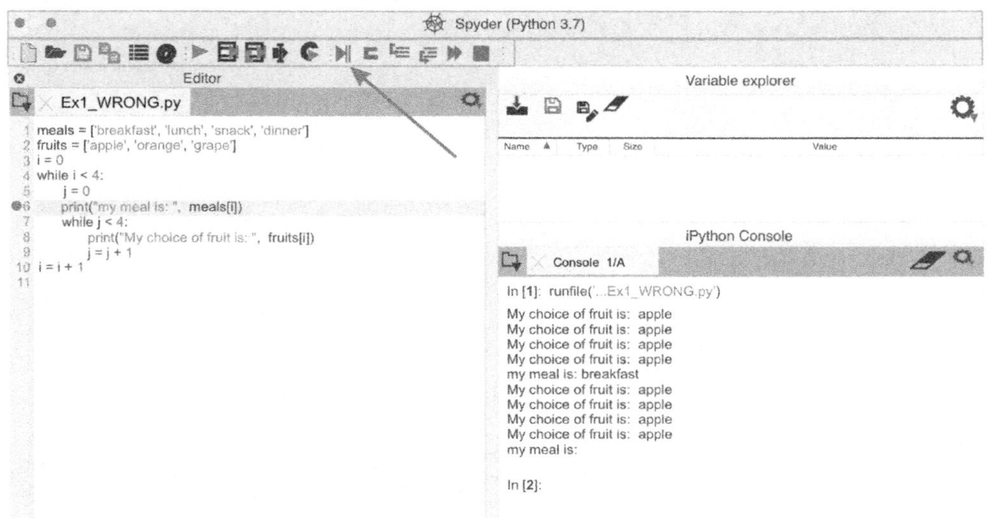

3. The **Console** prompt changes to **ipdb>** to indicate you are in **Debug Mode.** In the **Console**, type "**s**" to step through the program. The Python Interpreter moves to the next line.

   Type "**s**" a few times, and you'll notice the program loops back to line 4. Variable Explorer shows the value of "**i**" is 0 and is not changing as the program runs.

4. In the earlier figure, the print statement on line 6 was repeatedly output to the **Console**, indicating that the "while loop" on line 4 is looping continuously. I suspect that my counter "i" is not incremented properly on line 10.

   In the **Console** pane, type "**q**" to quit **Debug Mode**. The next topic outlines the change to resolve this issue.

> Press **Control** + **C** to stop a program, or choose "Restart kernel" from the **Consoles** menu.

5. On the **View**, Panes menu, select "Outline" to see your code grouped in "suites." Line 10 is not part of the suite of code that begins on line 4.

How to Resolve the Issue

In the **Editor** I indent line 10. Now line 10 is part of the suite of code that begins on line 4, with the "while" control statement. One error is fixed, but there is another error we'll look at in Example 7.2.

Good Code

```
1   meals = ['breakfast', 'lunch', 'snack', 'dinner']
2   fruits = ['apple', 'orange', 'grape']
3   i = 0
4   while i < 4:
5       j = 0
6       print("my meal is: ",  meals[i])
7       while j < 4:
8           print("My choice of fruit is: ", fruits[i])
9           j = j + 1
10      i = i + 1
```

Reference

These topics from previous chapters are a good reference for this example.

Chapter 2 - Debugging Steps
Chapter 3 - Control Statements
Chapter 3 - Iterate through Items in a List
Chapter 3 - Indexing
Chapter 3 - Suite of Code
Chapter 4 - Add Print Statements
Chapter 4 - Backups
Chapter 4 - Interactive Mode
Chapter 4 - Debug Mode Variable Explorer
Chapter 4 - Infinite Loop
Chapter 5 - Traceback
Chapter 5 - IndentationError
Chapter 5 - IndexError
Chapter 6 - Check Object Type

7.2 Index Error

Description: The list index is out of range. This kind of runtime error appears when you run the program.

Intended Outcome

There are two lists in this program, "meals" and "fruits." I want the program to loop through each list and print the items.

Actual Result

The print statement on line 8 “**fruits[i]**” causes an IndexError because the index is out of range.

Incorrect Code

Example 7.2 code before any changes follows.

```
1    meals = [‘breakfast’, ‘lunch’, ‘snack’, ‘dinner’]
2    fruits = [‘apple’, ‘orange’, ‘grape’]
3    i = 0
4    while i < 4:
5        j = 0
6        print(“my meal is: “,  meals[i])
7        while j < 4:
8            print(“My choice of fruit is: ”, fruits[i])
9            j = j + 1
10       i = i + 1
```

Debugging Steps

In this example the program halts. I use Debug Mode to research what is happening.

1. Run the program. The Python Interpreter halts because of an exception and displays an **IndexError** in the **Console**.

In the **Console**, the Python Interpreter displays a Traceback message “list index out of range.” The error is in Line 8. If I click on “line 8” in the **Console**, it is a hyperlink to that location in my code in the **Editor** pane.

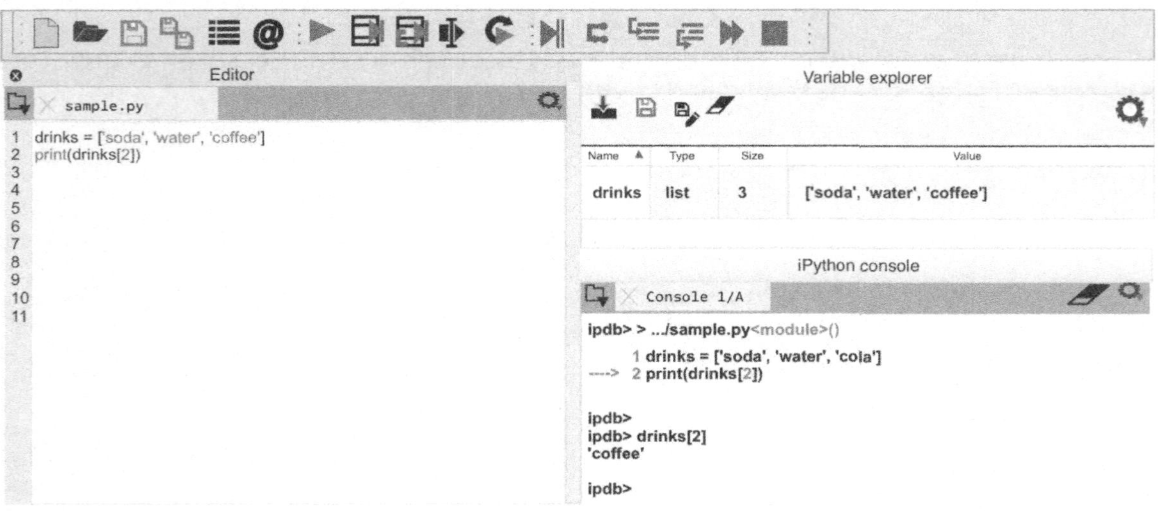

2. Type **%debug** in the **Console** pane to start Debug Mode. The **Console** prompt changes to **ipdb>**.

3. Type **fruits[3]** in the **Console** pane. **Variable Explorer** shows "**i**" has a value of 3, so fruits[i] evaluates to fruits[3]. The message "IndexError: list index out of range" is displayed.

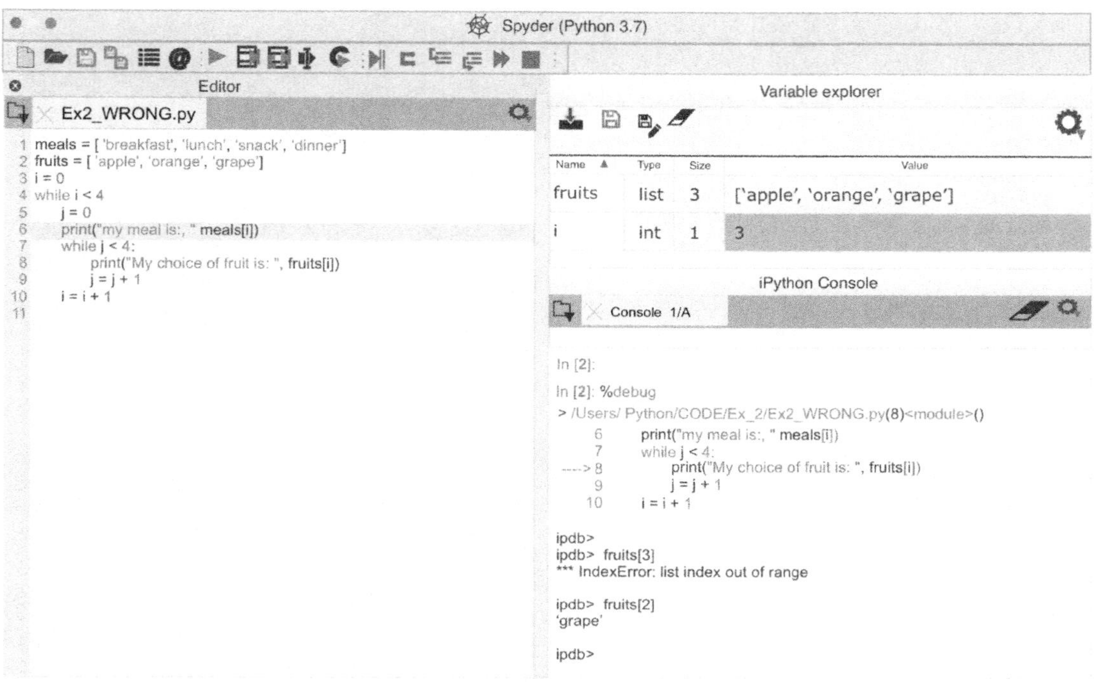

4. Now type **fruits[2]** In the **Console,** pane. The value 'grape' is displayed. Grape is the last item in the "fruits" list. The range of the fruits list is 0 to 2.

   If this had been a long list, I could have typed **len(fruits)** in the **Console**, to see how many items were in the list.

   In the **Console** pane type "**q**" to quit Debug Mode. The next topic outlines the change to resolve this issue.

How to Resolve the Issue

While the error occurred on line 8, the problem is actually on line 7. In the **Editor**, I update line 7 to use the variable "**j.**"

```
while j < 3:
```

Good Code

```
meals = ['breakfast', 'lunch', 'snack', 'dinner']
fruits = ['apple', 'orange', 'grape']
i = 0
while i < 4:
    j = 0
    print("my meal is: ",  meals[i])
    while j < 3:
        print("My choice of fruit is: ", fruits[j])
        j = j + 1
    i = i + 1
```

Reference

These topics from previous chapters are a good reference for this example.

Chapter 3 - Indexing
Chapter 3 - Iterate through Items in a List
Chapter 4 - Debug Mode
Chapter 4 - Interactive Mode
Chapter 4 - Debug Mode Variable Explorer
Chapter 5 - Traceback
Chapter 5 - IndexError
Chapter 6 - Check Object Type
Chapter 6 - Check Length of Object

7.3 Wrong Variable

Description: The code references the wrong variable name.

In this example, there is a flaw in the overall design or logic of my program. The program does what I coded, but the outcome is not what I intended. In the **Console**, my print statement does not iterate through my list of fruits. *This program is slightly different from the previous examples.*

Intended Outcome

The program should print a list of fruits for each meal.

Actual Result

The program halts with an IndexError: list index out of range.

Incorrect Code

Example 7.3 code before any changes follows.

```
1  meals = ['breakfast', 'lunch', 'snack', 'dinner']
2  fruits = ['apple', 'orange', 'grape']
3  i = 0
4  while i < 4:
5        j = 0
6        print("my meal is: ",  meals[i])
7        while j < 3:
8              print("My choice of fruit is: " fruits[i])
9              print("j is: ", j)
10             j = j + 1
11       i = i + 1
```

Debugging Steps

1. When I run the program, the Python Interpreter halts with an error. The Traceback shows the IndexError was caused by line 8.

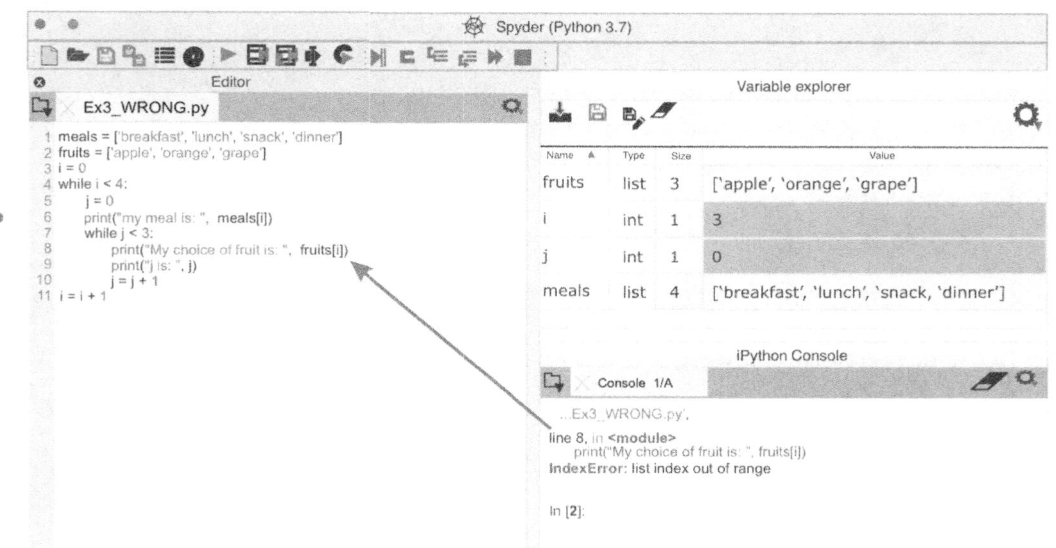

2. In the **Console**, I type **fruits[i]**, which returns the same IndexError.

   Variable Explorer shows "**i**" has a value of 3. The **fruits** list has three items, and the indices are 0-2. Now I realize I should have used the "**j**" variable as a counter for the **fruits** list.

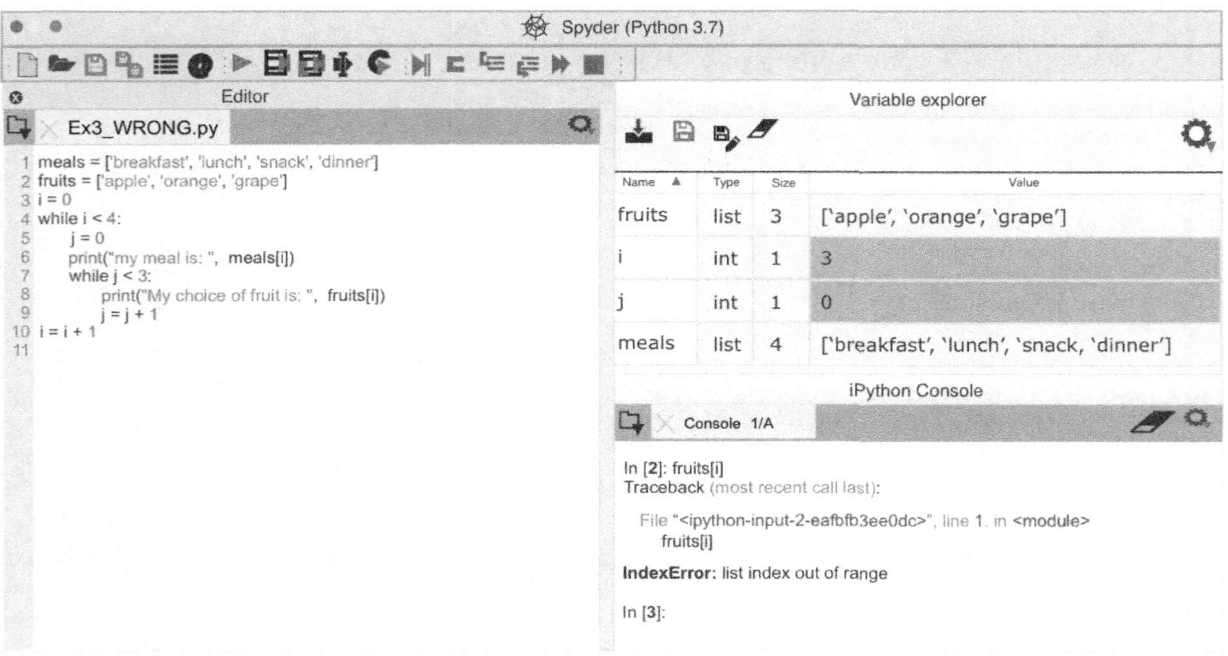

At this point, I just typed a statement in the **Console**, and I didn't use **Debug Mode**. Instead, I'll update my script in the **Editor** pane to resolve the issue.

How to Resolve the Issue

In the print statement I change the variable to "j" on line 8.

```
print("My choice of fruit is:", fruits[j])
```

Good Code

```
meals = ['breakfast', 'lunch', 'snack', 'dinner']
fruits = ['apple', 'orange', 'grape']
i = 0
while i < 4:
    j = 0
    print("my meal is: ", meals[i])
    while j < 3:
        print("My choice of fruit is: ", fruits[j])
        print("j is: ", j)
        j = j + 1
    i = i + 1
```

Reference

These topics from previous chapters are a good reference for this example.

Chapter 3 - Indexing
Chapter 3 - IndentationError
Chapter 3 - Iterate through Items in a List
Chapter 4 - Debug Mode
Chapter 4 - Debug Mode Variable Explorer
Chapter 6 - Check Object Type

7.4 Invalid Assignment

Description: The assignment statement is invalid. This kind of runtime error is uncovered when you run the program.

Intended Outcome

This program should print "mylist" items to the **Console**.

Actual Result

The **Console** output shows the print statement on line 4 repeats with the first item in the List.

Incorrect Code

This is the Example 7.4 code before any changes.

```
1   mylist = [‘soda’, ‘water’, ‘coffee’]
2   i = 0
3   while i < 3:
4           print(mylist[i])
5           i =+ 1
```

Debugging Steps

1. Run the program. The program runs endlessly. The program is caught in an infinite loop. In the **Console**, the Python Interpreter repeatedly outputs the print statement from line 4.

2. To stop the program, in the **Consoles** menu, I select "Restart kernel."

   Double click twice on line 4 to add a breakpoint. Select "Debug File" on the menu.

3. The **Console** prompt changes to **ipdb>** to indicate you are in **Debug Mode.** In the **Console**, type "**s**" to step through the program. The Python Interpreter moves to the next line.

   Type "**s**" a few times, and you'll notice the program loops back to line 3. Variable Explorer shows the value of "**i**" is 0 and is not changing as the program runs.

How to Resolve the Issue

The counter is not incremented on line 5 because I reversed the syntax. The statements "i = i + 1" and "i **+=** 1" both increment the "i" counter. I update line 5 with the correct syntax.

Good Code

```
1   mylist = [‘soda’, ‘water’, ‘coffee’]
2   i = 0
3   while i < 3:
4           print(mylist[i])
5           i += 1
```

Reference

These topics from previous chapters are a good reference for this example.

Chapter 3 - Arithmetic Operators

Chapter 4 - Debug Mode
Chapter 4 - Debug Mode - Variable Explorer
Chapter 4 - Infinite Loop

7.5 While Indentation Error

Description: The "while" statement is not indented properly. The **Console** displays an **IndentationError**.

Intended Outcome

Print a list of numbers.

Actual Result

When I run the program, it halts with an error. In the **Console**, there is an arrow pointing to "t" in the word "print" on line 5.

IndentationError: expected an indented block

Incorrect Code

This is the Example 7.5 code before any changes.

```
1  wadofcash = [111, 222, 333, 444]
2  i = 0
3  x = 3
4  while i <= x:
5  print(wadofcash[i])
6      i = i + 1
```

Debugging Steps

Spyder displays a yellow warning triangle next to the print statement on line 5. When I hover my mouse over the triangle, a pop-up message is displayed, as shown below.

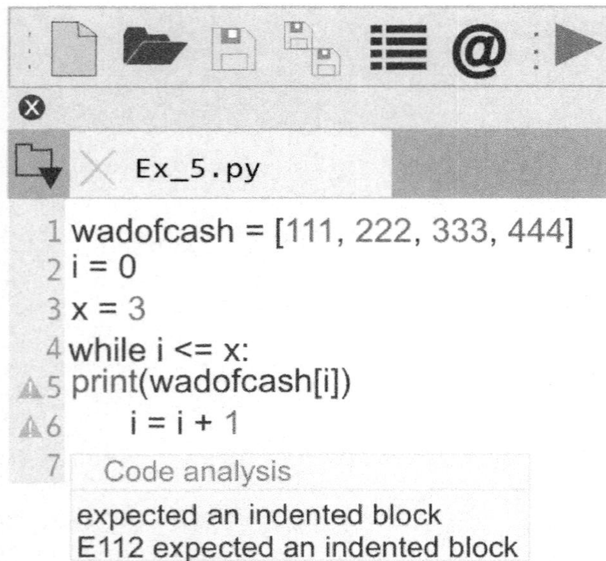

Figure 7.1 Indentation Warning

On the **View**, Panes menu, select "Outline" to see your code grouped in "suites." Because line 5 is not indented, it is not part of the suite of code that begins with the control statment on line 4. The Chapter 3 topic, "Indented Code," looks at suites.

How to Resolve the Issue

Indent the print statement on line 5.

Good Code

```
1  wadofcash = [111, 222, 333, 444]
2  i = 0
3  x = 3
4  while i <= x:
5      print(wadofcash[i])
6      i = i + 1
```

Reference

These topics from previous chapters are a good reference for this example.

Chapter 3 - Indented Code (a Suite)

Chapter 3 - Control Statements
Chapter 4 - Help()
Chapter 5 - Traceback
Chapter 5 - IndentationError

7.6 Incorrect Method Arguments

Description: The openpyxl "cell" method has incorrect attributes. The **Console** displays an **AttributeError**.

Intended Outcome

My intention was for the code to open an Excel file and print each column 2 value as the program iterates through the rows.

Actual Result

The program halted with an "AttributeError" exception when run with the Python 2.7 Interpreter. The program runs fine on my Python 3 environment. This **AttributeError** indicates the Python Interpreter doesn't recognize the line 8 syntax.

AttributeError: 'int' object has no attribute 'upper'

Line 8 is calling the "**.cell()**" method. In the discussion of Classes in Chapter 3, we created an instance of a class. Valid attribute names of a class include both "**data attributes**" and "**methods**." Python objects have attributes that are referenced with the dot notation.

Incorrect Code

This is the Example 7.6 code before any changes.

```
1   # Ex_6_WRONG.py
2   #
3   from openpyxl import load_workbook
4   wb1 = load_workbook('Before.xlsx', data_only=True)
5   ws1 = wb1["ExportedData"]
6   bfr = 2
7   while bfr <= ws1.max_row:
8       bfritem = ws1.cell(bfr, 2).value
9       print(bfritem)
10      bfr = bfr + 1
```

Debugging Experiment

In this example, when I run the program, the Python Interpreter prints an "AttributeError" to the **Console**. I use Help to research what is happening.

1. Run the program. The Python Interpreter halts because of an exception and displays an **AttrbuteError** in the **Console**.

   In the **Console**, the Python Interpreter displays a Traceback message telling me the error is in Line 8. If I click on "line 8" in the **Console**, it is a hyperlink to that location in my code **Ex_6_WRONG.py** in the **Editor** pane.

2. The issue seems related to the object on line 8, and I suspect there is something wrong with the syntax for the atttributes "cell" or "value." I'm curious about what syntax I should use with the cell method. In the **Console**, I can type **help(ws1.cell())** or **dir(ws1.cell())** for more information on the "**.cell()**" method.

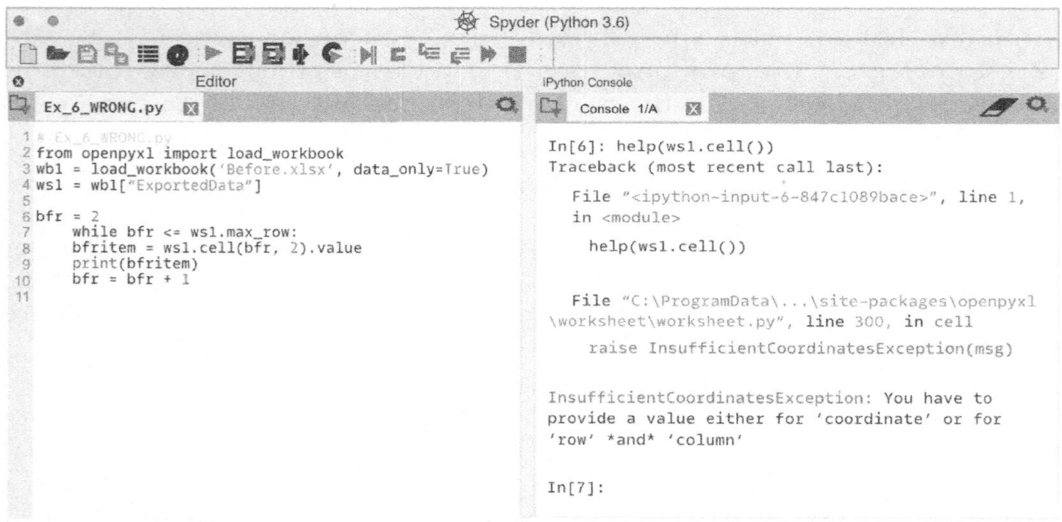

Spyder (Python 3.6)
Editor
Ex_6_WRONG.py
1 # Ex_6_WRONG.py
2 from openpyxl import load_workbook
3 wb1 = load_workbook('Before.xlsx', data_only=True)
4 ws1 = wb1["ExportedData"]
5
6 bfr = 2
7 while bfr <= ws1.max_row:
8 bfritem = ws1.cell(bfr, 2).value
9 print(bfritem)
10 bfr = bfr + 1
11
IPython Console
Console 1/A
In[6]: help(ws1.cell())
Traceback (most recent call last):
File "<ipython-input-6-847c1089bace>", line 1, in <module>
help(ws1.cell())
File "C:\ProgramData\...\site-packages\openpyxl\worksheet\worksheet.py", line 300, in cell
raise InsufficientCoordinatesException(msg)
InsufficientCoordinatesException: You have to provide a value either for 'coordinate' or for 'row' *and* 'column'
In[7]:

3. Help indicates the Python Interpreter could not use the values for row and column when calling the function "cell." In line 8, I need to add the argument keywords.

How to Resolve the Issue

In the **Editor** pane, I update line 8 of **Ex_6_WRONG.py** to use the keywords, as shown below. This change ensures the program runs with Python 2.7 or 3.7.

bfritem = ws1.cell(row=bfr, column=2).value

Good Code

```
# Ex_6_WRONG.py
#
from openpyxl import load_workbook
wb1 = load_workbook('Before.xlsx', data_only=True)
ws1 = wb1["ExportedData"]
bfr = 2
while bfr <= ws1.max_row:
    bfritem = ws1.cell(row=bfr, column=2).value
    print(bfritem)
    bfr = bfr + 1
```

Reference

These topics from previous chapters are a good reference for this example.

Chapter 3 - Attributes
Chapter 3 - keyword arguments
Chapter 3 - Iterate through Items in a List
Chapter 3 - Class Variables and Attributes
Chapter 3 - Methods
Chapter 4 - Help()
Chapter 4 - Interactive Mode
Chapter 5 - Traceback
Chapter 5 - AttributeError
Chapter 6 - Check Arguments

7.7 Empty Block of Code

Description: An empty block of code is illegal. When you have an empty block of code the **Console** displays an **IndentationError**.

Intended Outcome

While writing a program, I want a block of code that does nothing. At some point, I intend to add logic.

Actual Result

The Python Interpreter raises an IndentationError exception.

IndentationError: expected an indented block

Incorrect Code

This is the Example 7.7 code before any changes.

```
1  for mynum in [157, 19, 56]:
2          if mynum == 157:
3          else:
4                  print('Happy birthday, you are', mynum)
```

Debugging Steps

The **Console** shows an **IndentationError** on line 3. As is often the case, the actual error is the line above.

How to Resolve the Issue

In keeping with my design goal, I want the code to do nothing. On line 3 I add a pass() statement.

Good Code

```
1  for mynum in [157, 19, 56]:
2          if mynum == 157:
3                  pass
4          else:
5                  print('Happy birthday, you are', mynum)
```

Reference

These topics from previous chapters are a good reference for this example.

Chapter 3 - Suite
Chapter 4 - Help()
Chapter 5 - Traceback
Chapter 5 - RuntimeError
Chapter 5 - SyntaxError

7.8 Parentheses Not Matched

Description: Parentheses are not matched. The **Console** displays a **SyntaxError**.

Intended Outcome

On line 3, I want to calculate projected sales.

Actual Result

When I run the program, the **Console** displays a SyntaxError in line 3. There is an arrow highlighting the location where the parentheses is missing.

SyntaxError: invalid syntax

Incorrect Code

This is the Example 7.8 code before any changes.

```
1  sales = 150.00
2  days = 31
3  projectedsales = (sales/days)*31)
```

Debugging Steps

The **Editor** displays a red circle with an "x" to the right of line 3, indicating the parser identified invalid syntax. When I hover my mouse over the parentheses on that line, the paired parentheses are highlighted in green.

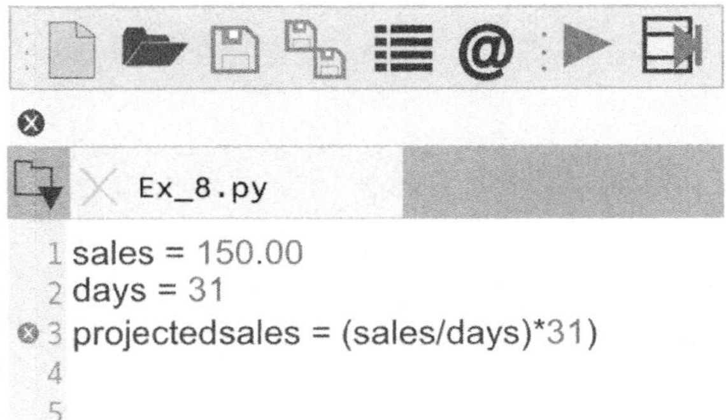

When I move my mouse to the end of the line, the last parenthesis is highlighted in orange, indicating there is no corresponding parenthesis.

How to Resolve the Issue

On line 3, I add an open parenthesis in front of "sales," as shown below.

Good Code

```
1   sales = 150.00
2   days = 31
3   projectedsales = ((sales/days)*31)
```

Reference

These topics from previous chapters are a good reference for this example.

Chapter 4 - Help()
Chapter 4 - The Editor
Chapter 5 - SyntaxError

7.9 Missing Colon

Description: The colon is missing. The **Console** displays a **SyntaxError**.

Intended Outcome

This code should print "mylist" items to the **Console**.

Actual Result

When I run the program, there is a SyntaxError. An arrow points to the location of the error on line 2.

SyntaxError: invalid syntax

Incorrect Code

This is the Example 7.9 code before any changes.

```
1   mylist = ['soda', 'water', 'coffee']
2   for i in range(3)
3   print(mylist[i])
```

Debugging Steps

The **Editor** has a **red** circle with an "x" by line 2 and a **yellow triangle** to the left of line 3. When I hover over the yellow triangle, a pop-up message is displayed, "unexpected indentation."

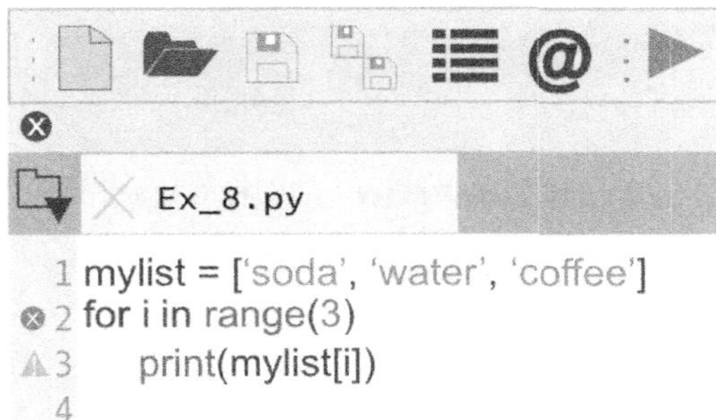
Ex_8.py
1 mylist = ['soda', 'water', 'coffee']
2 for i in range(3)
3 print(mylist[i])
4

How to Resolve the Issue

Line 2 is a "for" control statement, so I must add a colon at the end of the line.

Good Code

```
1    mylist = ['soda', 'water', 'coffee']
2    for i in range(3):
3          print(mylist[i])
```

Reference

These topics from previous chapters are a good reference for this example.

Chapter 3 - Control Statements
Chapter 4 - The Editor
Chapter 4 - Help()
Chapter 5 - SyntaxError

7.10 Case Sensitive

Description: Python is case sensitive. Variables with the wrong case are interpreted as misspelled by the Python Interpreter and cause a NameError.

Intended Outcome

This code should print "mylist" items to the **Console**.

Actual Result

When I run the program, the **Console** displays a NameError on line 3.

NameError: name 'mylist' is not defined

Incorrect Code

In this example, I changed the case of the variable "myList" on line 1, to demonstrate a NameError.

If you previously ran Example 7.9, "mylist" is still in memory, and you won't see a NameError. I wanted to demonstrate that sometimes you need to update the "namespace" to be certain you're looking at values from this program.

This is the Example 7.10 code before any changes.

```
1 myList = ['soda', 'water', 'coffee']
2 for i in range(3):
3     print(mylist[i])
```

Debugging Steps

1. To clear memory (the namespace), in the **Consoles** menu select "Restart kernel." You could also type %reset in the **Console**.
2. When I run the program, the **Console** raises a **NameError** from line 3.

How to Resolve the Issue

On the first line, I change "mylist" to all lowercase.

Good Code

```
mylist = ['soda', 'water', 'coffee']
for i in range(3):
    print(mylist[i])
```

Reference

These topics from previous chapters are a good reference for this example.

Chapter 3 - Keyword Arguments
Chapter 4 - Help()
Chapter 5 - NameError

7.11 Missing Keyword

Description: A keyword is missing when defining a function causing a SyntaxError.

Intended Outcome

This code creates a new function that adds two numbers together.

Actual Result

The **Editor** displays a red circle with an "x" to the left of line 1. When I run the program, the **Console** traceback says there is a SyntaxError on line 1.

SyntaxError: invalid syntax

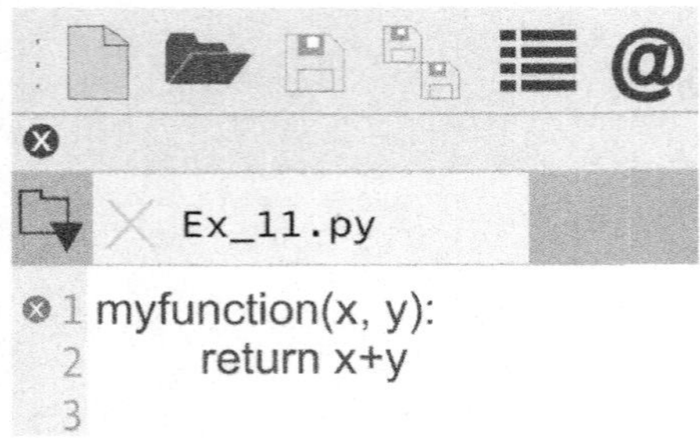

Figure 7.2 Function with Error

Incorrect Code

This is the Example 7.11 code before any changes.

```
1   myfunction(x, y):
2       return x+y
```

Debugging Steps

When looking at line 1, I see that I left off the keyword "def." I could also search online for the Python documentation on defining a function.

How to Resolve the Issue

Add "**def**" to the beginning of line 1.

Good Code

```
1   def myfunction(x, y):
2       return x+y
```

Reference

These topics from previous chapters are a good reference for this example.

Chapter 3 - Define Functions
Chapter 4 - The Editor
Chapter 5 - Traceback
Chapter 5 - SyntaxError

7.12 Illegal Character

Description: Illegal character in identifier name causes a SyntaxError.

Intended Outcome

This code creates a string variable.

Actual Result

The program halts with a SyntaxError. When I run the program, the **Console** displays an arrow pointing to the invalid character in “my$str.”

```
Ex_12.py", line 1
    my$str = ‘hello’
      ^
SyntaxError: invalid syntax

In [2]:
```

Incorrect Code

This is the Example 7.12 code before any changes.

```
1   my$str = ‘hello’
2   print(my$str)
```

Debugging Steps

The **Editor** has a red circle with an “x” to the left of line 1, indicating there is a syntax error in my assignment statement. On my computer, the **Editor** normally displays functions and methods in purple, and variables are black. The color formatting is different because the **Editor** is unable to interpret my code.

How to Resolve the Issue

Special characters like $, #, and @ are not allowed for variable names. I rename my variable to “mystr” and the SyntaxError is resolved.

Good Code

```
mystr = 'hello'
print(mystr)
```

Reference

These topics from previous chapters are a good reference for this example.

Chapter 3 - Variables
Chapter 4 - The Editor
Chapter 4 - Help()
Chapter 4 - Debug Mode
Chapter 4 - Interactive Mode
Chapter 5 - NameError
Chapter 5 - SyntaxError

7.13 Undefined Name

Description: There is an undefined name when a variable name is misspelled. The traceback shows a NameError.

Intended Outcome

Line 2 calculates profit using the "royalties" variable.

Actual Result

The **Editor** has a yellow triangle to the left of line 2 warning me there is an error. When I run the program the Traceback shows a NameError.

NameError: name 'royaltie' is not defined

Incorrect Code

This is the Example 7.13 code before any changes.

```
1   royalties = 300
2   profit = royaltie - 25
```

Debugging Steps

In the **Editor**, if I click on the variable name "royaltie" on line 2, the **Editor** highlights all instances of the variable throughout the code. I assign 300 to the "royalties" variable in line 1. The variable name is misspelled on line 2.

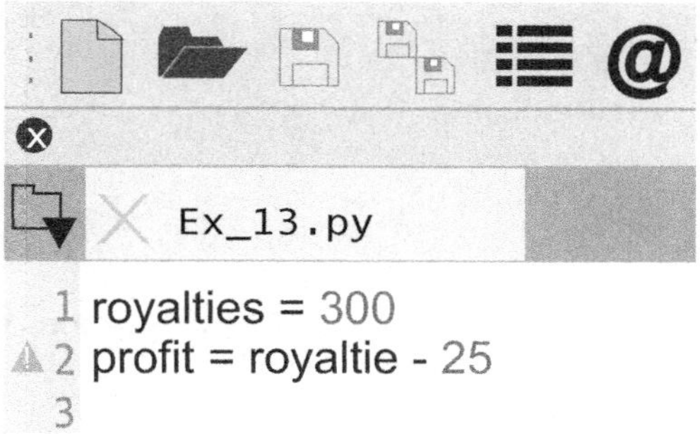

Ex_13.py

```
1 royalties = 300
2 profit = royaltie - 25
3
```

How to Resolve the Issue

On line 2 I correct the variable name. The **Editor** pane highlights all instances of the variable name in yellow, so I know I am using the same variable from line 2.

Good Code

```
1   royalties = 300
2   profit = royalties - 25
```

Reference

These topics from previous chapters are a good reference for this example.

Chapter 5 - Traceback
Chapter 4 - The Editor
Chapter 5 - NameError

7.14 FileNotFound

Description: While reading a file, the **Console** halts with an error "FileNotFoundError." In this example, factors outside my program impact my program.

Intended Outcome

This program opens a text file and prints the contents in the **Console**.

Actual Result

The **Console** displays a "FileNotFoundError."

FileNotFoundError: [Errno 2] No such file or directory: 'file.txt'

Incorrect Code

This is the Example 7.14 code before any changes. Note that this syntax to open a file would work for a .txt or .csv file.

```
file = open('file.txt', 'r')
print(file.read())
```

Debugging Steps

The "FileNotFoundError" has a base class of "IOError." I want to check the filename in my OS directory.

1. Import the "**os**" library to work with the OS commands. In the **Console**, type "import os" and then type the list command, as shown below.

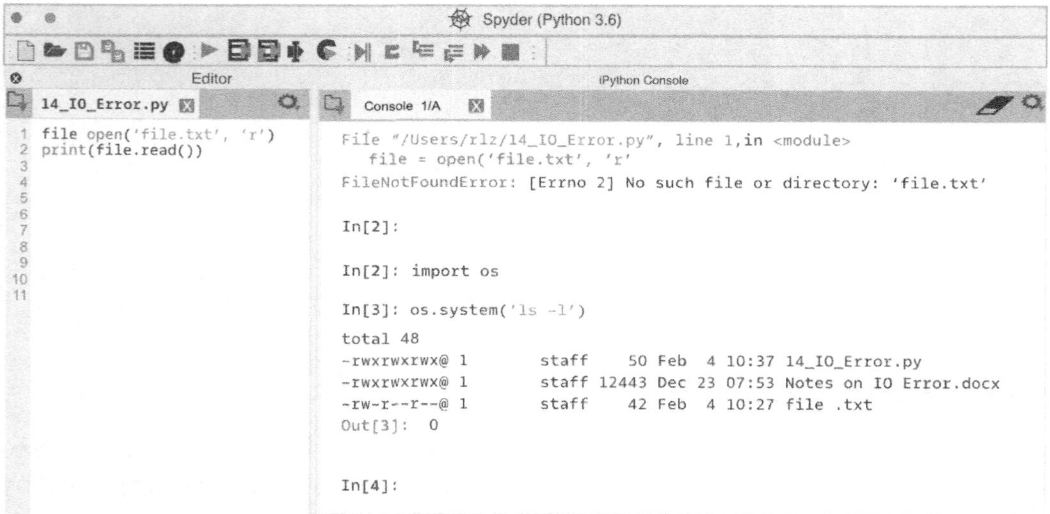

```
Spyder (Python 3.6)
Editor                         IPython Console
14_IO_Error.py                 Console 1/A

file open('file.txt', 'r')
print(file.read())

File "/Users/rlz/14_IO_Error.py", line 1,in <module>
   file = open('file.txt', 'r'
FileNotFoundError: [Errno 2] No such file or directory: 'file.txt'

In[2]:

In[2]: import os

In[3]: os.system('ls -l')
total 48
-rwxrwxrwx@ 1       staff    50 Feb  4 10:37 14_IO_Error.py
-rwxrwxrwx@ 1       staff 12443 Dec 23 07:53 Notes on IO Error.docx
-rw-r--r--@ 1       staff    42 Feb  4 10:27 file .txt
Out[3]:  0


In[4]:
```

2. Type **os.system('ls -l')** to see a list of files in the current directory. The filename has a space in the name. I can rename the file or update my program.

How to Resolve the Issue

I decided to rename the file. I did not need to change my code. I could also add "try" and "except" logic to handle this type of error as shown in the next example.

Good Code

```
file = open('file.txt', 'r')
print(file.read())
```

Reference

These topics from previous chapters are a good reference for this example.

Chapter 4 - Interactive Mode
Chapter 5 - Traceback
Chapter 5 - RuntimeError
Chapter 5 - OSError (IOError)

7.15 Error Adding Numbers

Description: TypeError when adding numbers.

Intended Outcome

Print the total when adding two numbers.

Actual Result

When I run the program, the **Console** Traceback message is a TypeError. The code uses "try" and "except" to provide exception details in the Traceback message.

In this example, the code prints a custom message when there is a TypeError. The last line prints my custom error message if there is another type of Exception besides a TypeError. Chapter 4 has more information on "try" and "except."

```
Type error when adding; eur euro ; usd 3.45
```

Incorrect Code

This is the Example 7.15 code before any changes.

```
1   eur = 'euro'
2   gbp = 8
3   usd = 3.45
4   try:
5       mymoney = eur + usd
6       print(mymoney)
7   except TypeError:
8       print('Type error when adding', eur, '; usd', usd)
9   except Exception as strmsg:
10      print(strmsg)
```

Debugging Steps

This code has a print statement on line 8 to show the values.

```
print('Type error when adding', eur, '; usd', usd)
```

The **Console** Traceback shows the variable values. After reviewing my code, I realize I used the "eur" variable which is a string, and I meant to use the "gbp" variable.

Note: I could also have used the "**type()**" function to identify the type of variable.

How to Resolve the Issue

On line 5, I update the assignment statement to use the variables **gbp + usd**.

Good Code

```
eur = ‘euro’
gbp = 8
usd = 3.45
try:
    mymoney = gbp + usd
    print(mymoney)
except TypeError:
    print(‘Type error when adding; gbp’, gbp, ‘; usd’, usd)
except Exception as strmsg:
    print(strmsg)
```

Reference

These topics from previous chapters are a good reference for this example.

Chapter 4 - Print Statements
Chapter 4 - Type()
Chapter 5 - Traceback
Chapter 5 - Try and Except
Chapter 5 - TypeError

7.16 Misspelled Keyword

Description: A misspelled keyword causes a SyntaxError. This is similar to Example 7.13 where a variable name was misspelled causing a NameError.

Intended Outcome

An if-else statement prints a message to the **Console**.

Actual Result

The **Editor** has a red circle with an “x” next to line 3. When I run the program it halts with a “SyntaxError.” There is an arrow pointing to the end of line 3.

SyntaxError: invalid syntax

Incorrect Code

This is the Example 7.16 code before any changes.

```
1 if 4 < 5:
2     pass
3 esle:
4     print(“Python rocks”)
```

Debugging Steps

There is a typographical error on line 3 where “else” is misspelled.

How to Resolve the Issue

Update line 3 with the correct spelling of the keyword.

Good Code

```
1 if 4 < 5:
2     pass
3 else:
4     print(“Python rocks”)
```

Reference

These topics from previous chapters are a good reference for this example.

Chapter 3 - Reserved Keywords
Chapter 3 - Keyword Arguments
Chapter 4 - Help()
Chapter 4 - The Editor
Chapter 5 - Traceback
Chapter 5 - NameError
Chapter 5 - SyntaxError

7.17 Value is None

Description: The function return value is “None”.

Intended Outcome

My calculation using the “mymath” function’s **return value** prints the result to the **Console**.

Actual Result

When "i" is 3, the Traceback in the **Console** displays a **TypeError**.

TypeError: unsupported operand type(s) for /: 'NoneType' and 'int'

Incorrect Code

This is the Example 7.17 code before any changes.

```
def mymath(i=5, j=200):
    if i > 3:
        return i * j
    if i < 3:
        return j / i
    #
    #
result = mymath(3, 100)
print(result/10)
```

Debugging Steps

This program works as expected when "i" is any number except 3.

1. To identify what object type the function returns, I use the **type()** function in the **Console**.

```
In [2]: type(mymath(3,100))
Out[2]: NoneType
```

The function returns "None" when "i" is 3.

2. In the **Console**, I call the "mymath" function again where "i" is 4. Now the type is "int." This means that there is a path through the "mymath()" function without a return value.

   In Chapter 3, we looked at a function that did not have a return value for all paths. For this example, I'm not going to change the "mymath()" function. Instead, I add logic to my program to handle a "None" value.

How to Resolve the Issue

Ideally, I would insure all paths through my code have a return statement. For this demonstration I add an "if" statement to test for a "None" value.

Good Code

```
def mymath(i=5, j=200):
    if i > 3:
        return i j
    if i < 3:
        return j / i


result = mymath(3, 100)
if result is not None:
    print(result/10)
else:
    print("result is None")
```

Reference

These topics from previous chapters are a good reference for this example.

Chapter 3 - Function Returns None
Chapter 3 - All Paths Do Not Have a Return Object
Chapter 3 - NoneType
Chapter 4 - Interactive Mode
Chapter 4 - The Editor
Chapter 5 - Traceback
Chapter 5 - Try and Except
Chapter 6 - Does the Object have a Value of NoneType or Whitespace?
Chapter 6 - Check Object Type
Chapter 6 - Value is None

7.18 Method Not Found

Description: This code has an AttributeError when a method is not found.

Intended Outcome

Using the math library, I would like to use a cube method.

Actual Result

When I run the code the **Console** displays this message.

AttributeError: module 'math' has no attribute 'cube'.

Incorrect Code

This is the Example 7.18 code before any changes.

```
import math
mynum = (.3, .7)
mytotal = math.fsum(mynum)
mycube = math.cube(3)
print(mytotal)
```

Debugging Steps

I need to see what functions or methods are available for the "**math**" library. In the **Editor**, after I type "math." I pause for a moment, until a pop-up opens with available functions, as shown below.

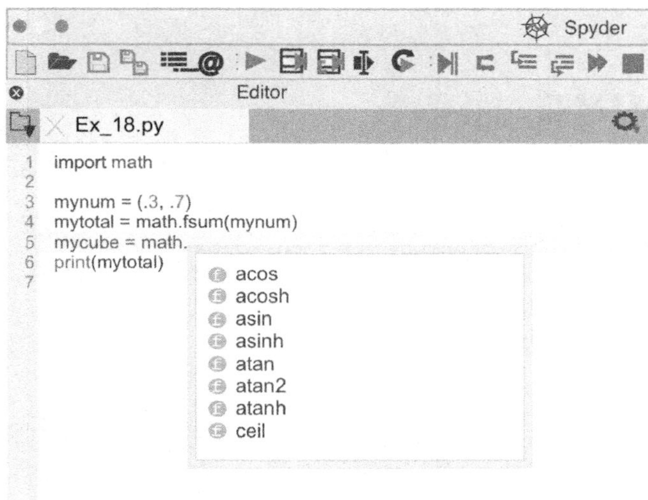

In the **Console**, I could also type dir(math) to see a list of functions/methods in the math library.

How to Resolve the Issue

After scanning the list I see there is no "cube" method available. I update the code to manually calculate the cube of "3" on f.

Good Code

```
import math
mynum = (.3, .7)
mytotal = math.fsum(mynum)
mycube = 3 * 3 * 3
print(mytotal)
```

Reference

These topics from previous chapters are a good reference for this example.
Chapter 3 - Tuple
Chapter 4 - Debug Mode
Chapter 4 - Interactive Mode
Chapter 5 - Traceback
Chapter 5 - NameError

7.19 Module Not Found

Description: This code has a ModuleNotFoundError because the Python Interpreter can't find a method.

Intended Outcome

Using the "matplotlib" library I want to plot a chart.

Actual Result

When I run the code, the Console displays:

NameError: name 'plt' is not defined

Incorrect Code

This is the Example 7.19 code before any changes.

```
import matplotlib pyplot as plot
plt.plot([1, 2, 3, 4], [25, 30, 29, 31])
plt.ylabel('age')
plt.xlabel('participants')
plt.show()
```

Debugging Steps

I am trying to use the "matplotlib" library's "pyplot" function using the alias "plot," but am unsure how to import the library. When I search the Internet for "import matplotlib" I find the correct syntax. In the Help pane, I could search for "mathplotlib.pyplot" for additional details.

How to Resolve the Issue

The first line of my program needs updated to import the correct module. There is a missing period. After I run the updated program, in the **Console** I can type **help(plot.figure(1))** to see additional information on my new object.

```
import matplotlib.pyplot as plot
```

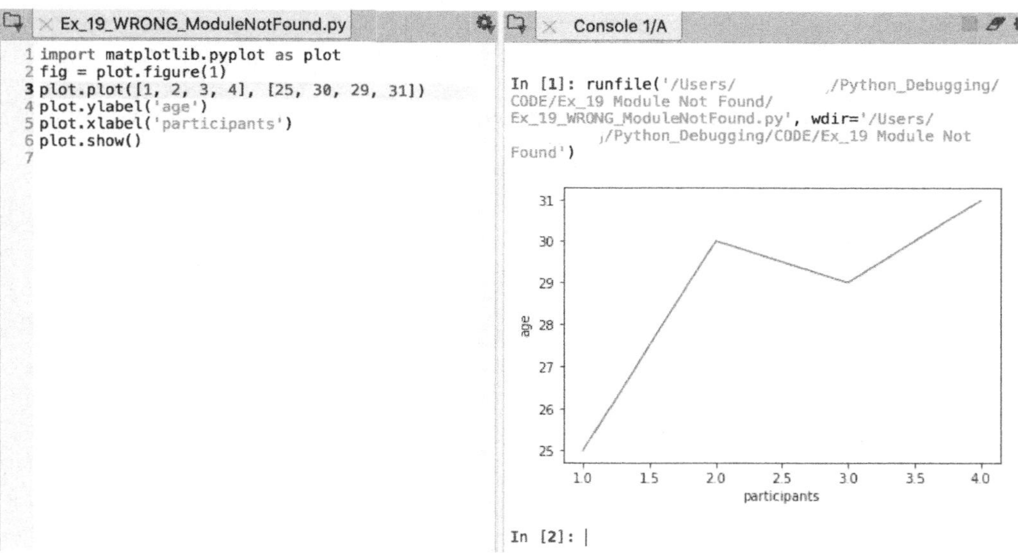

Good Code

```
import matplotlib.pyplot as plot
plot.plot([1, 2, 3, 4], [25, 30, 29, 31])
plot.ylabel('age')
plot.xlabel('participants')
plot.show()
```

Reference

These topics from previous chapters are a good reference for this example.

Chapter 3 - Import Library
Chapter 4 - Help()
Chapter 5 - Traceback
Chapter 5 - ModuleNotFound

7.20 Key Not in Dictionary

Description: This code has a KeyError. The key is not in the "**wb**" Dictionary.

Intended Outcome

This program works with an Excel file and formats cells. Line 11 loops through the rows, and line 12 loops through the cells of each row.

Actual Result

The program halts and the **Traceback** in the **Console,** displays this error:

KeyError: 'Worksheet Sheet1 does not exist.':

Incorrect Code

This is the Example 7.20 code before any changes.

```
1   # 20_KeyError.py
2   from openpyxl import load_workbook, styles
3   wb = load_workbook('before.xlsx', data_only=True)
4   ws = wb["Sheet1"]
5   #
6   ft = styles.Fontt(color='4F81BD', bold=True)
7   ws['A1'].font = ft
8   ws.cell(row=1, column=1).value = 'Heading 1'
9   ws.column_dimensions['A'].width = 12
10  #
11  for row in ws.iter_rows():
12      for cell in row:
13          print("Looping through data")
```

Debugging Experiment

In this example, when I run the program the program halts with a KeyError, which points to a dictionary. I use Debug Mode to research what is happening.

1. Run the program. The Python Interpreter halts because of an exception.

2. In the **Console**, pane the **Traceback** displays an error, as shown below.

   KeyError: 'Worksheet Sheet1 does not exist.':

3. Type **%debug** in the **Console** pane to start Debug Mode. The **Console** prompt changes to **ipdb>**.

4. While in Debug Mode, in the **Console**, type "**u**" to step backward through the program. The Python Interpreter moves back to the previous call. Now an arrow indicates the last line of code was line 4 in my 20_KeyError.py script.

```
ipdb> u
      1 20_KeyError.py(4)<module>()
      2 from openpyxl import load_workbook, styles
      3 wb = load_workbook('before.xlsx', data_only=True)
----> 4 ws = wb["Sheet1"]
      5
      6 ft = styles.Fontt(color='4F81BD', bold=True)
```

   Line 4 references "Sheet1." A **KeyError** indicates this is a dictionary key. In the **Console** pane, type "**q**" to quit Debug Mode.

5. Now I need a method to find the **sheetnames** for the "**wb**" object. In the **Console**, I use the **help** command, as shown below.

```
In [2]:  myStr

Out [1]: 'hello'
```

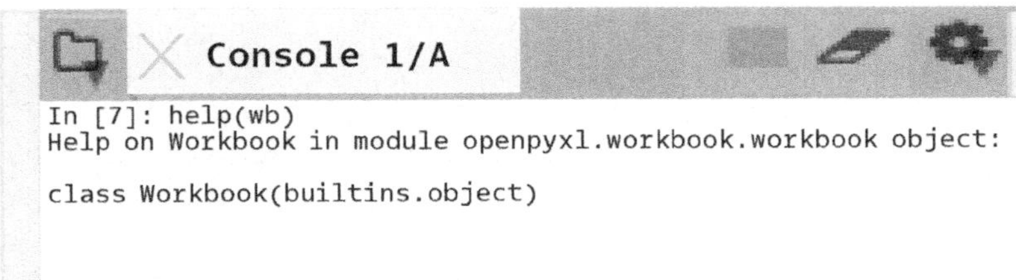

Figure 7.3 Help In the **Console**, *Pane*

When I scroll down in the **Console** pane, I see the methods for the "**wb**" object. A small sample of the output is shown below. I am interested in the "sheetnames" method.

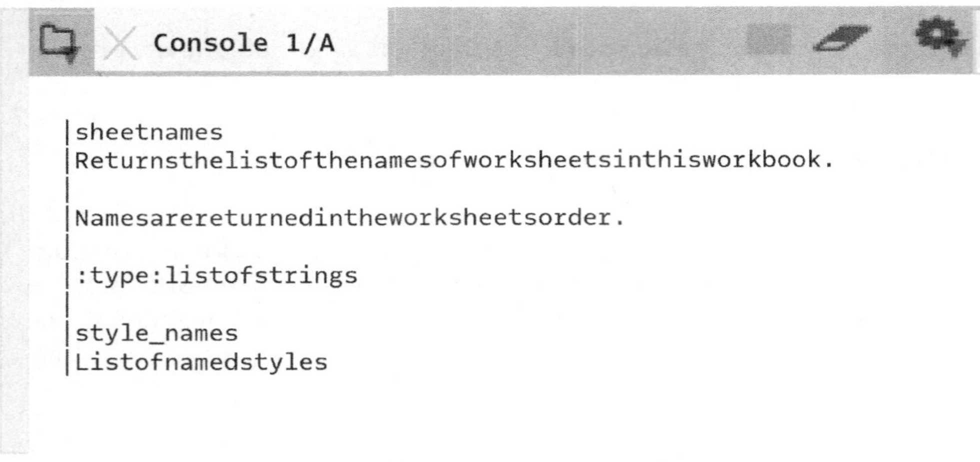

Figure 7.4 Details on "wb" Object Methods and Functions

To see the sheetnames for the "**wb**" object type "**ws.sheetnames**" in the **Console** pane, as shown below.

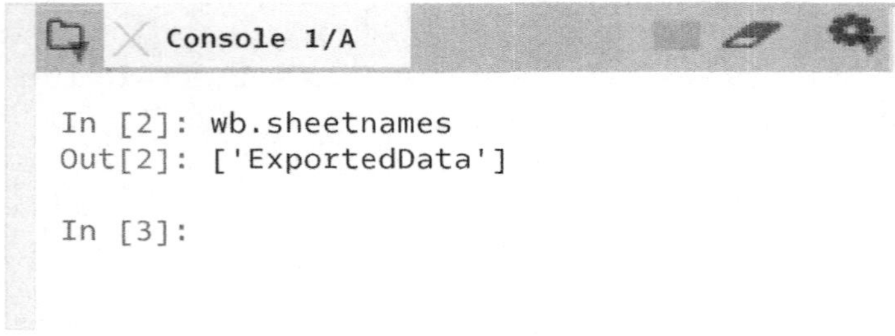

Figure 7.5 The sheetnames Method

The output indicates there is only one worksheet named "**ExportedData**".

How to Resolve the Issue

When you create your own dictionary named "mydictionary," it's easier to recognize a dictionary KeyError. Because the openpyxl library created the "**ws**" object it's not as obvious that this was a dictionary KeyError. For additional information, search the Intranet for help on openpyxl worksheet objects.

To resolve the error, I update my code to the correct worksheet name, as shown below.

Good Code

In the **Editor**, I updated line 4 with the sheetname "ExportedData," as shown below.

```
1  # 20_CORRECT_KeyError.py
2  from openpyxl import load_workbook, styles
3  wb = load_workbook('before.xlsx', data_only=True)
4  ws = wb["ExportedData"]
5  #
6  ft = styles.Fontt(color='4F81BD', bold=True)
7  ws['A1'].font = ft
8  ws.cell(row=1, column=1).value = 'Heading 1'
9  ws.column_dimensions['A'].width = 12
10 #
11 for row in ws.iter_rows():
12         for cell in row:
13                 print("Looping through data")
```

Additional Troubleshooting

In step 4, I wanted more information on "**load_workbook**." The signature function from the Chapter 6 topic, "The Function Call Signature" would be perfect for this purpose. With Python v3.x the "signature" lists each parameter accepted by a function. In the **Console**, import the module and print the signature for the object, as shown below.

```
In [3]: from inspect import signature
In [4]: print(str(signature(load_workbook)))
(filename, read_only=False, keep_vba=False, data_only=False, keep_links=True)
```

Reference

These topics from previous chapters are a good reference for this example.

Chapter 3 - Dictionary
Chapter 3 - Search for Key Name
Chapter 3 - Tuple
Chapter 4 - Debug Mode
Chapter 4 - Help()
Chapter 5 - Traceback
Chapter 5 - KeyError

7.21 Incorrect Argument Type

Description: A Function Argument is an incorrect type causing a ValueError.

Intended Outcome

The program asks for a month as user input. The int() function converts the data to an integer so I can use it in a calculation. The print() function outputs the value to the Console.

Actual Result

When the program runs, on line 1 it prompts for user input. If I enter the string "July" for the input, a ValueError is displayed in the Console. A ValueError is raised when a function gets an argument of correct type but improper value.

ValueError: invalid literal for int() with base 10: 'July'

Incorrect Code

This is the Example 7.21 code before any changes.

```
1   birthmo = int(input('what month were you born?'))
2   monthstogo = 12 - birthmo
3   print(monthstogo, "months until your birthday")
```

Debugging Steps

The Traceback shows the program fails on line 1, which means the variable "birthmo" is not created in memory, and is not shown in Variable Explorer.

The Traceback message shows ValueError: invalid literal for int() with base 10: 'June.' The string input 'June' causes a ValueError when the int() function tries to convert the string to an integer.

How to Resolve the Issue

I am going to add "try" and "except" logic to handle the ValueError exception. On line 6 I print a message for the user to enter a number.

Good Code

```
1   try:
2       birthmo = int(input('what month were you born?'))
3       monthstogo = 12 - birthmo
4       print(monthstogo, "months until your birthday")
5   except ValueError:
6       print('enter a number, no letters')
```

Reference

These topics from previous chapters are a good reference for this example.

Chapter 3 - Function Arguments
Chapter 3 - Types of Data
Chapter 5 - Traceback
Chapter 5 - Try and Except
Chapter 5 - ValueError
Chapter 6 - Check Object Type

7.22 Name Error

Description: When I try to use "plot" there is a NameError.

Intended Outcome

Using the "matplotlib" library I want to plot a histogram chart.

Actual Result

When I run the code, the Console displays a NameError and highlights line 4.

```
In [3]: ..Ex_22_WRONG.py", line 4, in <module>
    plt.plot([1, 2, 3, 4], [25, 30, 29, 31])
NameError: name 'plt' is not defined
```

Incorrect Code

This is the Example 7.22 code before any changes.

```
1   import matplotlib.pyplot as plot
2   #
3   #
4   myL = [13.7, 4.1, 14.4, 23.3, 27, 22, 31.99, 36.2]
5   bins = [0, 11, 21, 31, 40]
6   plt.hist(myL, bins, rwidth=0.5)  # histogram graph
7   plt.xticks([10, 20, 30, 40])
8   plt.xlabel('age')
9   plt.ylabel('participants')
10  plt.show()
```

Debugging Steps

The NameError indicates the object can't be found. In the **Editor**, if I hover over the word "plot" on line 1, and I see there are no other instances of "plot" highlighted in my code. When I imported the library on line 1, I used the alias "plot," and on lines 6-10 I used "plt."

How to Resolve the Issue

In the Editor, I update line 1 to use "plt."

Good Code

```
1   import matplotlib.pyplot as plt
2   #
3   #
4   myL = [13.7, 4.1, 14.4, 23.3, 27, 22, 31.99, 36.2]
5   bins = [0, 11, 21, 31, 40]
6   plt.hist(myL, bins, rwidth=0.5)  # histogram graph
7   plt.xticks([10, 20, 30, 40])
8   plt.xlabel('age')
9   plt.ylabel('participants')
10  plt.show()
```

Reference

These topics from previous chapters are a good reference for this example.

Chapter 5 - NameError

7.23 Value Error

Description: There is invalid data passed to a method that is causing a ValueError.

Intended Outcome

I want to remove one item from my list.

Actual Result

When the program runs it halts with a ValueError on line 3. A ValueError is raised when a function or method gets an argument of correct type but improper value.

ValueError: list.remove(x): x not in list

Incorrect Code

This is the Example 7.23 code before any changes.

```
1   fruits = ['apple', 'orange', 'grape']
2   myfruit = 2
3   fruits.remove(myfruit)
```

Debugging Steps

Line 3 uses the "remove" method. I would like to inspect the list object to see what methods are available.

1. In the **Console**, type **help(fruits)**. The interpreter returns a list of methods available, showing "remove" uses the value of a list item.

2. In the **Editor**, I could position my cursor in front of "remove" and press **Cntrl + I**. The Help pane displays the same information on the remove method.

How to Resolve the Issue

Instead of using the value "2", I update the assignment statement on line 2 to assign the value "orange" to "myfruit." When I rerun the program there is no error, and Variable Explorer shows the value "orange" was removed from my list.

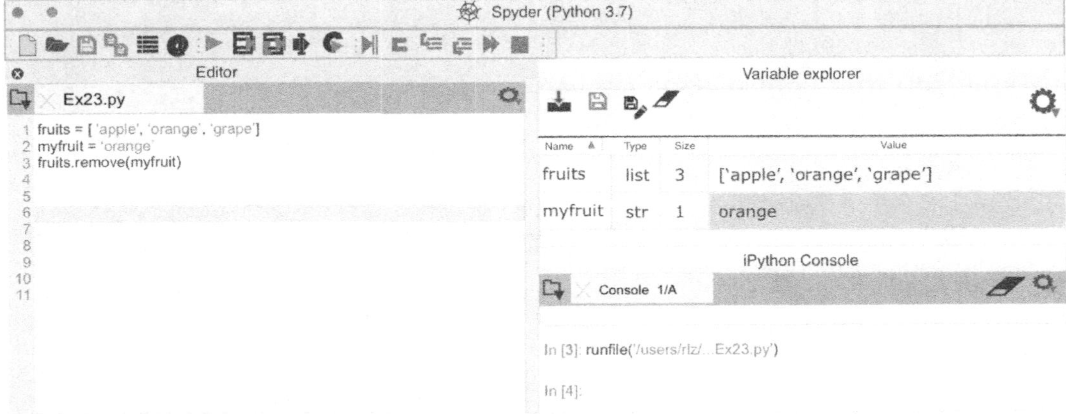

Good Code

```
fruits = ['apple', 'orange', 'grape']
myfruit = 'orange'
fruits.remove(myfruit)
```

Reference

These topics from previous chapters are a good reference for this example.

Chapter 3 - Lists
Chapter 3 - remove
Chapter 4 - Interactive Mode
Chapter 4 - Help()
Chapter 5 - ValueError
Chapter 5 - RuntimeError

7.24 Divide by Zero Error

Description: The calculation in this code causes a ZeroDivisionError.

Intended Outcome

The program retrieves the current GBP exchange rate, and then converts "gbp" to the equivalent USD value.

Actual Result

When the program runs, a **ZeroDivisionError** from line 7 is displayed in the Console.

ZeroDivisionError: float divison by zero

Incorrect Code

This is the Example 7.24 code before any changes.

```
from bs4 import BeautifulSoup
from urllib.request import urlopen
usd, gbp, gbpex = 10.0, 20.0, 0.00
html2 = urlopen(‘https://usd.fxexchangerate.com’)
soup2 = BeautifulSoup(html2, ‘lxml’)
tables2 = soup2.findChildren(‘td’)
gbp = gbp/gbpex
print(“gbp converted to USD is:”, gbp)
```

Debugging Steps

Variable Explorer shows the value of “gbpex” is zero. In this example, I omitted the line to retrieve the GBP exchange rate.

How to Resolve the Issue

In addition to adding the line of code to retrieve the GBP exchange rate from a web page, I added try and except code to handle when “gbpex” causes an exception. In Chapter 4, I also added logging to handle this type of error.

Good Code

```
from bs4 import BeautifulSoup
from urllib.request import urlopen
usd, gbp, gbpex = 10.0, 20.0, 0.00
html2 = urlopen(‘https://usd.fxexchangerate.com’)
soup2 = BeautifulSoup(html2, ‘lxml’)
tables2 = soup2.findChildren(‘td’)
try:
    gbpex = float(tables2[3].string[:6])
    gbp = gbp/gbpex
    print(“gbp converted to USD is:”, gbp)
except ZeroDivisionError:
    print(‘ZeroDivisionError where gbpex is:’, gbpex)
```

Reference

These topics from previous chapters are a good reference for this example.

Chapter 4 - Interactive Mode
Chapter 4 - Debug Mode - Variable Explorer
Chapter 4 - Logging
Chapter 5 - Traceback
Chapter 5 - Try and Except
Chapter 5 - ZeroDivisionError

7.25 Math Logic Error

Description: There is a logic error in the math calculation.

Intended Outcome

The math calculation should return 10.

Actual Result

The calculation returns 40 instead of 10.

Incorrect Code

This is the Example 7.25 code before any changes.

```
myval = 60.0/3.0 * 2
print("myval is:", myval)
```

Debugging Steps

To ensure multiplication occurs before the division, I add parentheses to my code.

How to Resolve the Issue

Add parentheses to change the operator precedence.

Good Code

```
myval = 60.0/(3.0 * 2)
print("myval is:", myval)
```

7.26 ValueError Assigning Date

Description: This is an example of an operation on incompatible types. There is a ValueError when assigning a datetime object.

Intended Outcome

After creating a datetime object with a date of 12/31/1999, I want to print the value to the **Console**.

Actual Result

The program halts with a **ValueError** exception, as shown below. The Traceback indicates the error is on line 3.

ValueError: month must be in 1..12

Incorrect Code

This is the Example 7.26 code before any changes.

```
1  from datetime import datetime
2  d1 = datetime.strftime(datetime(1999, 13, 31), '%Y-%m-%d')
```

Debugging Steps

At a glance I can see that while my intentions were good, I made a mistake on line 2. It's obvious there is no month "13" and the statement on line 2 is invalid.

When the cause of the ValueError is not obvious, you could use the Help pane, or search the Internet, to find correct arguments for a function or method.

How to Resolve the Issue

Line 2 needs updated to use "12" for the month instead of "13."

Good Code

```
1  from datetime import datetime
2  d1 = datetime.strftime(datetime(1999, 12, 31), '%Y-%m-%d')
```

Reference

These topics from previous chapters are a good reference for this example.

Chapter 4 - Interactive Mode

Chapter 5 - Traceback
Chapter 5 - ValueError
Chapter 6 - Check Arguments
Chapter 6 - Check Function Return Objects

7.27 Matching Strings NoneType Error

Description: This is the first example looking at a comparison expression. I am comparing two strings inside two list objects.

I have to account for object types and case.

Intended Outcome

The expression comparing two string objects should evaluate to "True" and print the message on line 9 when there is a match.

Actual Result

When the program runs, it prints "no match" three times.

Incorrect Code

This is the Example 7.27 code before any changes.

```
1   s1 = [[‘history’], [‘math’], [‘social studies’]]
2   s2 = [‘Math’, None, ‘Social Studies’]
3   #
4   for c in range(0, 3):
5       course1, course2 = ‘’, ‘’
6       course1 = s1[c]
7       course2 = s2[c]
8       if course1 == course2:
9           print(‘Repeating class: ’ , course2)
10      else:
11          print(“no match”)
```

Debugging Steps

1. In the **Console** type the following comparison statement to see if the Python Interpreter returns 'True' or 'False.'

   When you type s2[2] and s1[2] the Python Interpreter outputs a "string" in quotes and a "list" in brackets, as shown below.

```
In [2]: s1[2] == s2[2]
Out[2]: False

In [3]: s2[2]
Out[3]: 'Social Studies'

In [4]: s1[2]
Out[4]: ['social studies']
```

2. In Variable Explorer, notice the values for the third element in S1 and S2 are different. The type of object is also shown.

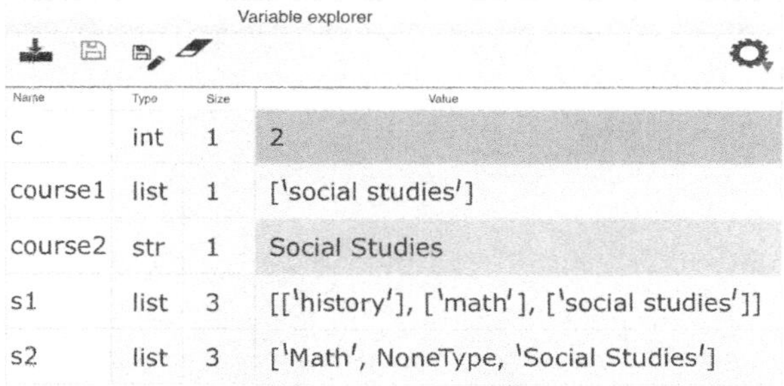

Variable explorer

Name	Type	Size	Value
c	int	1	2
course1	list	1	['social studies']
course2	str	1	Social Studies
s1	list	3	[['history'], ['math'], ['social studies']]
s2	list	3	['Math', NoneType, 'Social Studies']

How to Resolve the Issue

On line 6 I added try and except logic. I convert the variable to a string, and use the **.upper()** method to change the case. I use slicing **[2:-2]** to remove the square brackets and apostrophes on line 6 after I convert the list to a string.

Good Code

```
s1 = [[‘history’], [‘math’], [‘social studies’]]
s2 = [‘Math’, None, ‘Social Studies’]
for c in range(0, 3):
    course1, course2 = ‘’, ‘’
    try:
        course1 = str(s1[c])[2:-2].upper()
    except Exception:
        course1 = ‘’
    try:
        course2 = s2[c].upper
    except Exception:
        course1 = ‘’
    if course1 == course2:
        print(‘Repeating class: ’, course2)
```

Reference

These topics from previous chapters are a good reference for this example.

Chapter 3 - NoneType
Chapter 3 - Slicing
Chapter 3 - Strings
Chapter 3 - Types of Data
Chapter 4 - Debug Mode - Variable Explorer
Chapter 4 - Interactive Mode
Chapter 5 - Traceback
Chapter 6 - Check Object Type
Chapter 6 - Value is None
Chapter 6 - Does the Object have a Value of NoneType or Whitespace?
Chapter 6 - Object Value

7.28 Matching Strings Fails

Description: Let’s continue with Example 7.27. While I have accounted for object types and case, this code has another problem that may not be obvious. When iterating through container objects, sometimes you are not sure what values are stored in each item. Take for example a large XML file that contains a series of nodes. If you write code to iterate through the XML nodes, you may encounter a node without a value. Python assigns this type of object to ‘NoneType.’ NoneType is the special Python type that indicates there is no value.

Intended Outcome

The expression comparing two string objects should evaluate to “true.”

Actual Result

When the program runs, now it halts with a traceback message.

AttributeError: ‘NoneType’ object has no attribute ‘upper’.

Incorrect Code

This is the Example 7.28 code before any changes.

```
1  s1 = [[‘history’], [‘math’], [‘social studies’]]
2  s2 = [‘Math’, None, ‘Social Studies’]
3  for c in range(0, 3):
4      course1 = str(s1[c])[2:-2].upper()
5      course2 = s2[c].upper
6      if course1 == course2:
7          print(‘Repeating class: ’, course2)
```

Debugging Steps

The Traceback shows and error on line 5 where I am converting the s2 element to uppercase.

1. In Variable Explorer, check the values of the second element are the same. The second element in list “s2” has a value of “None.” In the **Console**, I check the type of s2[1].

```
In [5]: type(s2[1])
Out[5]: NoneType
```

How to Resolve the Issue

Since “NoneType” isn’t a string, the **.upper()** method raises an error. I’ll add try and except logic beginning on line 5. When an exception occurs, the variable is assigned a value of ‘’ which is an empty string.

Good Code

```
s1 = [[‘history’], [‘math’], [‘social studies’]]
s2 = [‘Math’, None, ‘Social Studies’]
for c in range(0, 3):
    course1, course2 = ‘’, ‘’
    try:
        course1 = str(s1[c])[2:-2].upper()
    except Exception:
        course1 = ‘’
    try:
        course2 = s2[c].upper
    except Exception:
        course1 = ‘’
    if course1 == course2:
        print(‘Repeating class: ’, course2)
```

Reference

These topics from previous chapters are a good reference for this example.

Chapter 3 - Iterate through Items in a List
Chapter 3 - NoneType
Chapter 3 - Strings
Chapter 3 - Types of Data
Chapter 4 - Debug Mode - Variable Explorer
Chapter 4 - Interactive Mode
Chapter 5 - Traceback
Chapter 6 - Check Object Type
Chapter 6 - Object Value

7.29 Whitespace or Special Characters

Description: This example demonstrates a whitespace line feed character. When comparing strings, you may have to remove unseen whitespace characters. This is not a real world example but does show the ‘repr’ function that prints hidden whitespace characters.

Intended Outcome

This example should print ‘hello world’ in the **Console**.

Actual Result

When the program runs, the Python Interpreter prints ‘hello world\n.’

Incorrect Code

This is the Example 7.29 code before any changes.

```
In [4]: mystr = 'hello world\n'
In [5]: print(repr(mystr))
Out[5]: 'hello world\n'
```

Debugging Steps

It's not obvious in Variable Explorer that there is a paragraph return at the end of "mystr." However, the **Console** displays "\n" at the end of the string in the Incorrect Code example above.

How to Resolve the Issue

The .rstrip() function removes the whitespace character from the right side of the string.

Good Code

```
In [4]: mystr = 'hello world\n'
In [5]: mystr = mystr.rstrip()
In [6]: print(repr(mystr))
Out[6]: 'hello world'
```

Reference

These topics from previous chapters are a good reference for this example.

Chapter 3 - NoneType
Chapter 4 - Debug Mode - Variable Explorer
Chapter 4 - Interactive Mode
Chapter 5 - Traceback
Chapter 6 - Check Object Type
Chapter 6 - Object Value
Chapter 7 - Does the Object have a Value of NoneType or Whitespace?

7.30 Debug: Step Through Your Function

Description: The program halts and the exception is an AttributeError. I want to step through the program in debug mode and look at variable values inside my function. I start debug mode and click on "Run current line." The program runs and evaluates the function definition that starts on line 4 and runs through line 15. Then the program runs line 18, followed by line 19, and finally line 20.

Intended Outcome

My function takes a birth date and name and prints out 'Happy Birthday" if today is the birthday.

Actual Result

When the program runs it halts with an exception, and the Traceback message is an AttributeError.

AttributeError: 'builtin_function_or_method' object has no attribute 'month'

Incorrect Code

This is the Example 7.30 code before any changes.

```
1   import datetime
2   #
3   #
4   def happybirthday(dob, name):
5       thetype = type(dob)
6       thedate = datetime.datetime.now
7       month = thedate.month
8       day = thedate.day
9       if thetype == datetime.datetime:
10          dobmonth = dob.month
11          dobday = dob.day
12          if dobmonth == month and dobday == day:
13              print('Happy Birthday', name)
14          else:
15              print('Please enter a birthday')
16  #
17  #
18  name = 'Mary Lee'
19  dob = datetime.datetime(1976, 6, 15)
20  happybirthday(dob, name)
```

Debugging Steps

The Traceback shows and error on line 6. When I start debug mode, I choose "Run current line" until line 20 is highlighted. At this point, I use "Step into current function or method of current line" to **step into** my function code.

Now the debugger moves to the function on line 4, and I continue to click on "run current line" until line 6 when the AttributeError occurs. In the **Console** window I type "**type(thedate)**" to see the object type for "thedate."

ipdb> **type(thedate)**

How to Resolve the Issue

Although I was expecting a **datetime.datetime** type, the **Console** returns builtin_function_or_method. When I search the internet for help on this datetime "now" method I find the statement should end in **.now()**, as shown below.

```
thedate = datetime.datetime.now()
```

Good Code

```
import datetime
#
#
def happybirthday(dob, name):
      thetype = type(dob)
      thedate = datetime.datetime.now()
      month = thedate.month
      day = thedate.day
      if thetype == datetime.datetime:
            dobmonth = dob.month
            dobday = dob.day
            if dobmonth == month and dobday == day:
                print('Happy Birthday', name)
            else:
                print('Please enter a birthday')
#
#
name = 'Mary Lee'
dob = datetime.datetime(1976, 6, 15)
happybirthday(dob, name)
```

Reference

These topics from previous chapters are a good reference for this example.

Chapter 3 - NoneType
Chapter 3 - Invoke a Function
Chapter 4 - Interactive Mode
Chapter 5 - Traceback
Chapter 6 - Check Object Type
Chapter 6 - Object Value

7.31 Key Not in Dictionary

Description: When I try to retrieve a key value there is a key error.

Intended Outcome

Line 3 prints the value of key '4.'

Actual Result

The program raises a KeyError, pointing to line 2. This error message means there is no key '4' in myDict.

KeyError: 4

Incorrect Code

This is the Example 7.31 code before any changes.

```
1   myDict = {1: 'A', 2: 'B', 3: 'C'}
2   if myDict[4] == 'D':
3       print('4 is:', myDict[4])
```

Debugging Steps

Open Variable Explorer and double click on "myDict." The popup window shows there is no key '4.'

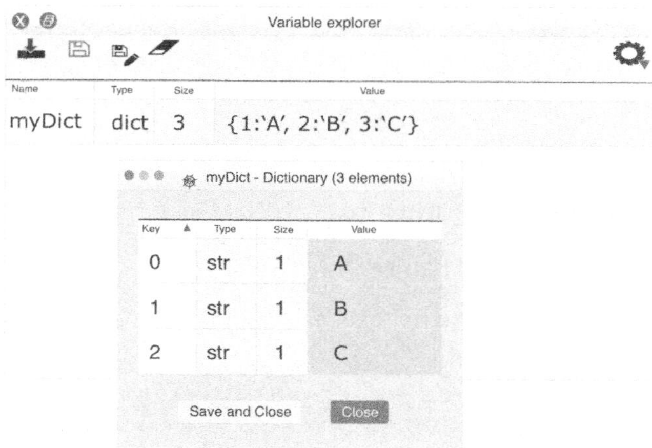

How to Resolve the Issue

Instead of directly referencing the key in myDict, I change the code on line 2 to use the .get method. The get() method returns 0 by default and does not raise an error.

Good Code

```
1   myDict = {1: 'A', 2: 'B', 3: 'C'}
2   if myDict.get(4, 0) == 0:
3       print('4 is not in the dictionary')
```

Reference

These topics from previous chapters are a good reference for this example.

Chapter 3 - Dictionary
Chapter 3 - Search for Key Name
Chapter 4 - Debug Mode - Variable Explorer
Chapter 5 - Traceback

7.32 Error Combining Strings

Description: This code cocatenates two strings.

Intended Outcome

myvar3 should equal 23.

Actual Result

When the program runs, this error is raised pointing to line 3.

TypeError: can only concatenate str (not "int") to str

Incorrect Code

This is the Example 7.32 code before any changes.

```
1 myvar1 = ‘2’
2 myvar2 = 3
3 myvar3 = myvar1 + myvar2
```

Debugging Steps

Variable Explorer shows the type for all variables. **myvar1** is a ‘str’, but myvar2 is an "int."

How to Resolve the Issue

On line 3, I use the str() function to change the value of myvar2 to a "str." You can only concatenate a "str" value with another "str" value.

Good Code

```
1 myvar1 = ‘2’
2 myvar2 = 3
3 myvar3 = myvar1 + str(myvar2)
```

Reference

These topics from previous chapters are a good reference for this example.

Chapter 3 - Types of Data
Chapter 3 - Concatenation
Chapter 3 - Strings
Chapter 5 - Traceback

Chapter 6 - Check Object Type

7.33 Function Returns 2 Values

Description: Example 7.33 prints the result from a function. The function returns a tuple of two elements, and the code should use the first element.

Intended Outcome

The function should calculate and print the birth year.

Actual Result

The program prints two tuple values.

(33, 'John') was born in 1987

Incorrect Code

This is the Example 7.33 code before any changes.

```
1   from datetime import date
2   #
3   #
4   def myfunction():
5       return 33, 'John'
6   #
7   #
8   year = date.today().year
9   name = myfunction()
10  birthyr = year - myfunction()[0]
11  print(name, 'was born in', birthyr)
```

Debugging Steps

The **Console** printout of "name" is a tuple as indicated by the parentheses, which is also shown in Variable Explorer.

How to Resolve the Issue

On line 9, I add indexing to select the second element.

Good Code

```
from datetime import date
#
#
def myfunction():
        return 33, 'John'
#
#
year = date.today().year
name = myfunction() [1]
birthyr = year - myfunction()[1]
print(name, 'was born in', birthyr)
```

Reference

These topics from previous chapters are a good reference for this example.

Chapter 3 - Indexing
Chapter 3 - Types of Data
Chapter 3 - Tuple and Function Return Objects
Chapter 4 - Debug Mode - Variable Explorer
Chapter 4 - Interactive Mode
Chapter 5 - Traceback

7.34 Unsupported Operand

Description: Trying to concatenate two strings raises an error. This is a simple syntax error.

Intended Outcome

The variable "mystr" is assigned to "greenapples."

Actual Result

When the program runs an error is raised.

TypeError: bad operand type for unary +: 'str'

Incorrect Code

This is the Example 7.34 code before any changes.

```
mystr = 'green' ++ 'apples'
```

Debugging Steps

There is no ++ operand in Python.

How to Resolve the Issue

Update the code to use "+."

Good Code

```
mystr = 'green' + 'apples'
```

7.35 Code Goes Beyond Last Yield Statement

Description: Example 7.35 prints the results from a function. The code halts and raises a StopIteration error because the code goes beyond the last yield statement in a generator.

Intended Outcome

The code should print a series of numbers.

Actual Result

When the program runs, the **Console** shows a StopIteration error pointing to line 9.

Incorrect Code

This is the Example 7.35 code before any changes.

```
1 def genTest():
2       yield 1
3       yield 2
4       print('inside genTest, i is', i)
5 #
6 #
7 foo = genTest()
8 for i in range(3):
9       print('item', foo.__next__())
```

Debugging Steps

The Traceback shows an error on line 9. Variable Explorer only shows the value of i. The print statement on line 4 within the function shows where the error is occurring. As I run the program in Debug Mode, when it prints line 4 "i" has a value of 2. This means there are two elements, and valid indexes are [0] and [1].

How to Resolve the Issue

On line 8 update the range(2) function.

Good Code

```
1 def genTest():
2       yield 1
3       yield 2
4       print('inside genTest, i is', i)
5 #
6 #
7 foo = genTest()
8 for i in range(2):
9       print('item', foo.__next__())
```

Reference

These topics from previous chapters are a good reference for this example.

Chapter 3 - Iteration
Chapter 3 - Yield
Chapter 4 - Debug Mode - Variable Explorer
Chapter 4 - Interactive Mode
Chapter 5 - Traceback

7.36 Missing positional argument

Description: Instead of printing to the **Console**, the sing() function raises a TypeError.

Intended Outcome

The sing() function should print, "Happy Birthday dear John."

Actual Result

When the program runs, the **Console** shows:

TypeError: sing() missing 1 required positional argument: 'person'

Incorrect Code

This is the Example 7.36 code before any changes.

```
1  def sing(words, person):
2      print(words, person)
3  #
4  #
5  sing('John')
```

Debugging Steps

The Traceback shows the error is on line 5 that the second positional argument 'person' is missing. The Python Interpeter uses the value "John" as the first positional argument. The function definition on line 1 shows two Positional Arguments, and the function call on line 5 has only one argument.

How to Resolve the Issue

My function call on line 5 needs updated with the two arguments.

Good Code

```
1  def sing(words, person):
2      print(words, person)
3  #
4  #
5  sing('Happy Birthday dear', 'John')
```

Reference

These topics from previous chapters are a good reference for this example.

Chapter 3 - Positional Arguments
Chapter 5 - Traceback

7.37 Reserved Keyword

Description: This example combines two strings and prints the result to the **Console**. The print statement raises an error.

Intended Outcome

The **Console** prints, "Hello John."

Actual Result

When the program runs the **Console** shows:

TypeError: 'str' object is not callable

Incorrect Code

This is the Example 7.37 code before any changes.

```
1   str = ‘hello’
2   str2 = ‘John’
3   print(str(str + ‘ ’+ str2))
```

Debugging Steps

The Traceback shows and error on line 3.

How to Resolve the Issue

The keyword "str" is reserved and can't be used as a variable name. I'll update lines 1 and 3 with a new variable name.

Good Code

```
str1 = ‘hello’
str2 = ‘John’
print(str(str1 + ‘ ‘ + str2))
```

Reference

These topics from previous chapters are a good reference for this example.

Chapter 3 - Reserved Keywords
Chapter 5 - Traceback

7.38 Dot Instead of Underscore

Description: Calling a class method raises an AttributeError.

Intended Outcome

After creating a new instance of the “Car” class, in line 6 I want to invoke the parallelpark() method. This is the same “Car” class we created in Chapter 3 when we looked at Classes.

Actual Result

When the program runs, an AttributeError is raised pointing to line 7. The AttributeError refers to the “Car” class.

In [2]: runfile..Ex_38_Wrong.py”, line 7, in <module>

myCar.parallel_park()

AttributeError: ‘Car’ object has no attribute ‘parallel_park’

In [3]:

Incorrect Code

This is the Example 7.38 code before any changes.

```
1 # Ex_38_Wrong.py
2 from car import Car
3 #
4 #
5 myCar = Car('Subaru', 'Crosstrek', 2019)
6 myCar.parallel_park()
```

Debugging Steps

An AttributeError is raised when you try to access an object's attribute that doesn't exist. The Traceback message pointed to line 6 where I attempted to use the "parallel_park()" method for the object "myCar." In the **Console**, I type "**help(myCar)**" to view a list of attributes and methods for the "myCar" object.

```
In [2]: help(myCar)

class Car(builtins.object)
 | Car(model, make, year)
 |
 | Class represents a car
 | Data properties:
 |   .model
 |   .make
 |   .year
 | Behavirors/Operations:
 |   .drive
 |   .parallelpark
```

The "Car" class has a docstring that lists the data properties and behaviors for the class. After reviewing the docstring help, I realize I misspelled the name of the "parrallel_park" method.

Note: I could also have typed one of these commands to see information about the class instance "myCar."

```
In [3]: dir(myCar)

In [4]: ?myCar
```

How to Resolve the Issue

Since I know the method name is wrong, I update line 6 with the correct name.

Good Code

```
# Ex_38_Wrong.py
from car import Car
#
#
myCar = Car('Subaru', 'Crosstrek', 2019)
myCar.parallelpark()
```

Reference

These topics from previous chapters are a good reference for this example.

Chapter 3 - Class
Chapter 4 - Interactive Mode
Chapter 5 - Traceback

7.39 Key error in new dictionary key:pair

Description: A TypeError is raised when I try to create a new dictionary key:pair.

Intended Outcome

This example should create a new dictionary object with a list value.

Actual Result

When the program runs the **Console** shows:

```
In [2]: ..Ex_39_wrong.py", line 2, in <module>
mydict1 = {[2019, 2020]: ['great yr', 'bad yr']}

TypeError: unhashable type: 'list'
```

Incorrect Code

This is the Example 7.39 code before any changes.

```
1   mydict1 = {}
2   mydict1 = {[2019, 2020]: ['great yr', 'bad yr']}
```

Debugging Steps

The Traceback shows and error on line 2. Dictionary keys must be a hashable, immutable object. In this example, I tried to use a "list" as my dictionary key, and a list is mutable and not hashable.

How to Resolve the Issue

On line 4, I change the code to use a string for the key name.

Good Code

```
1   mydict1 = {}
2   mydict1 = {['2019']: ['great yr', 'bad yr']}
```

Reference

These topics from previous chapters are a good reference for this example.

Chapter 3 - Dictionary
Chapter 3 - immutable
Chapter 5 - Traceback

7.40 Assign a dictionary key:value

Description: When I try to create a new key:value pair, the Python interpreter raises an error.

Intended Outcome

The code should create a new key:value pair.

Actual Result

When the program runs the **Console** shows:

In [2]: SyntaxError: can't assign to a functional

Out [1]: 'hello'

Incorrect Code

This is the Example 7.40 code before any changes.

```
1 myDict = {}
2 myDict('a') = 3
```

Debugging Steps

The Traceback says the SyntaxError is on Line 2.

How to Resolve the Issue

Because I used parentheses the Python Interpreter processes **myDict('a')** as a function call instead of a dictionary key. The key name should be enclosed in square brackets instead of parantheses.

Good Code

```
myDict = {}
myDict['a'] = 3
```

Reference

These topics from previous chapters are a good reference for this example.

Chapter 3 - Dictionary
Chapter 5 - Traceback

7.41 Too many values to unpack

Description: Too many values to unpack when assigning values to three variables.

Intended Outcome

The assignment statement on line 1 should create three new variables.

Actual Result

The program halts and the Traceback shows an error.

```
In [2]: ..Ex_41_Wrong.py", line 2, in <module>
var1, var2, var3 = 0, 1, 0, 0

ValueError: too many values to unpack (expected 3)
```

Incorrect Code

This is the Example 7.41 code before any changes.

```
1 var1, var2, var3 = 0, 1, 0, 0
```

Debugging Steps

The Traceback shows an error on line 1. While it is legal to assign values to multiple variables on the same line, you must have an equal number of variables and values on the left and right side of the expression.

How to Resolve the Issue

On line 1, I remove the last "0" value.

Good Code

```
1 var1, var2, var3 = 0, 1, 0
```

Reference

These topics from previous chapters are a good reference for this example.

Chapter 3 - Assignment Statement
Chapter 5 - Traceback

7.42 Tuple Assignment Error

Description: Trying to change tuple element [0] raises an error.

Intended Outcome

I want to change the first element in the tuple.

Actual Result

When the program runs it halts with a TypeError.

```
In [2]:  ..Ex_42_wrong.py", line 3, in <module>
mytuple[0] = 1

TypeError: 'tuple' object does not support item assignment
```

Incorrect Code

This is the Example 7.42 code before any changes.

```
1    mytuple = (2, 3, 4)
2    mytuple[0] = 1
```

Debugging Steps

The Traceback shows and error on line 2. Tuples are immutable and can not be changed.

How to Resolve the Issue

Since I can't change an element in a tuple, I have to rethink the code. I can replace the entire tuple with a new tuple with three elements, or use a list object instead of a tuple. In this example, I switch to a list which is mutable and can be changed.

Good Code

```
myList = [2, 3, 4]
myList[0] = 1
```

Reference

These topics from previous chapters are a good reference for this example.

Chapter 3 - Immutable
Chapter 3 - Tuples
Chapter 4 - Debug Mode - Variable Explorer

7.43 str object is not callable

Description: When I try to concatenate two strings and print the result, a TypeError 'str' object is not callable is raised.

Intended Outcome

In this code, I try to concatenate two strings and print the result.

Actual Result

When the program runs the **Console** shows:

In [2]: ..Ex_43_Wrong.py", line 5, in <module>
print(str(str + mystr))

TypeError: 'str' object is not callable

Incorrect Code

This is the Example 7.43 code before any changes.

```
1   str = 'hello'
2   mystr2 =  'world'
3   print(str(str + mystr2))
```

Debugging Steps

The Traceback shows and error on line 3. In the **Editor**, I notice that both instances of "str" are purple on line 3, indicating "str" is a reserved keyword or function. The problem started on line 1 when I used a reserved keyword as a variable name.

How to Resolve the Issue

On line 1 I need to change my variable name, and then I also need to update line 3 to reflect the new variable name.

Good Code

```
1   str = 'hello'
2   mystr2 = 'world'
3   print(str(mystr1 + mystr2))
```

Reference

These topics from previous chapters are a good reference for this example.

Chapter 3 - Reserved Keywords
Chapter 3 - Keyword Arguments
Chapter 5 - Traceback

7.44 Can only Concatenate Tuple

Description: While trying to concatenate a tuple, the Python interpreter raises a TypeError.

Intended Outcome

The code should combine two tuples.

Actual Result

When the program runs the **Console** shows:

```
In [2]: ..Ex_44_Concatenate_Tuple_wrong.py", line 5, in <module>
myTuple3 = myTuple1 + myTuple2[0]
TypeError: can only concatenate tuple (not "int") to tuple
```

Incorrect Code

This is the Example 7.44 code before any changes.

```
1 # Ex_44_Concatenate_Tuple_Wrong.py
2 #
3 myTuple1 = (1, ‘a’, 2, ‘b’)
4 myTuple2 = (3, ‘c’)
5 myTuple3 = myTuple1 + myTuple2[0]
```

Debugging Steps

The Traceback shows an error on line 5, and mentions an "int". In the **Console**, I type "myTuple2[0]" and type(myTuple2[0]). The first object in myTuple2 is an "int" with a value of 3.

```
In [2]: myTuple2[0]
Out [2]: 3

In [3]: type(myTuple2[0])
Out [3]: int
```

How to Resolve the Issue

Because I can't concatenate a "tuple" and an "int," I remove the index notation on line 5.

Good Code

```
1 # Ex_44_Concatenate_Tuple_Correct.py
2 #
3 myTuple1 = (1, ‘a’, 2, ‘b’)
4 myTuple2 = (3, ‘c’)
5 myTuple3 = myTuple1 + myTuple2
```

Reference

These topics from previous chapters are a good reference for this example.

Chapter 3 - Tuple Concatenation
Chapter 4 - Interactive Mode
Chapter 5 - Traceback

7.45 Float Comparison

Description: Comparing two float values fails.

Intended Outcome

The two float values are the same and should print the statement on line 6.

Actual Result

When the program runs the comparison on line 5 is False and the print statement is not executed.

Incorrect Code

You'll have to use your imagination that my computer stored these float values differently. Although the float values look the same to me, internally the computer can store them differently.

```
1   myfloat1 = .017
2   myfloat2 = .017
3   if myfloat1 == myfloat2:
4       print('they are the same')
```

Debugging Steps

When two float values don't match and you know they should, use the abs() function.

How to Resolve the Issue

Rewrite the code to use the abs() function in the comparison on line 3.

Good Code

```
1   myfloat1 = .017
2   myfloat2 = .017
3   if abs(myfloat1 - myfloat2) < .0001:
4       print('they are the same')
```

Reference

These topics from previous chapters are a good reference for this example.

Chapter 3 - Comparing Floats

7.46 Unhashable type:dict

Description: A TypeError is raised when I try to create a new dictionary key:value pair with an "int" value.

Intended Outcome

This example should create a new dictionary object with an "int" value.

Actual Result

When the program runs the **Console** shows:

In [2]: ..Ex_46/Ex_46_Wrong.py", line 5, in <module>

mydict1[mydict2] = 8

TypeError: unhashable type: "dict"

Incorrect Code

This is the Example 7.46 code before any changes.

```
1   # Ex 46 Wrong.py
2   #
3   mydict1 = {}
4   mydict2 = {2: 'orange'}
5   mydict1[mydict2] = 8
```

Debugging Steps

The Traceback shows and error on line 5 and states unhashable type "dict." Dictionary keys must be a hashable, immutable object. In this example, I tried to use the mutable "mydict2" dictionary as a dictionary key for mydict1.

How to Resolve the Issue

Rather than using the "mydict2" object as the key name, I need to use the individual key name. Key names are always an immutable object. I add a for loop on line 5 to iterate through the dictionary keys in "mydict2." Now I am using the key name from "mydict2" as a new key name for "mydict1."

Good Code

```
# Ex 46 Correct.py
#
mydict1 = {}
mydict2 = {2: 'orange'}
for key in mydict2:
    mydict1[key] = 8
```

Reference

These topics from previous chapters are a good reference for this example.

Chapter 3 - immutable
Chapter 3 - Iteration
Chapter 3 - dictionaries
Chapter 5 - Traceback

7.47 builtin_function_or_method' object is not subscriptable

Description: When printing the error "'builtin_function_or_method' object is not subscriptable" is raised.

Intended Outcome

This expression should print "mystr."

Actual Result

When the program runs, and the **Console** shows:

In [2]: Ex_47_Wrong.py", line 2, in <module>
    print[mystr]

TypeError: 'builtin_function_or_method' object is not subscriptable

Out [**1**]: 'hello'

Incorrect Code

This is the Example 7.47 code before any changes.

```
1   mystr = ‘hello’
2   print[mystr]
```

Debugging Steps

The Traceback shows and error on line 2. After reviewing the code, I realize I used square brackets around "mystr" instead of parenthesis. The Python Interpreter tries to use subscripting with "print" because of the brackets. Since print is a function I should use parenthesis around the argument "mystr."

How to Resolve the Issue

On line 2 I change the square brackets to parentheses.

Good Code

```
1   mystr = ‘hello’
2   print(mystr)
```

Reference

These topics from previous chapters are a good reference for this example.

Chapter 3 - Print Statements
Chapter 3 - Invoke a Function
Chapter 5 - Traceback

7.48 String Comparison Error

Description: The expression to test if a word is in a string raises a TypeError.

Intended Outcome

On line 6, I am testing if a word is in the string "myphrase." I want to print a phrase on line 7 if the expression is true.

Actual Result

When the program runs the **Console** shows:

In [3]: Ex_48_Wrong.py”, line 6, in <module>
if words in myphrase:

TypeError: ‘in <string>’ requires string as left operand, not list

Incorrect Code

This is the Example 7.48 code before any changes.

```
1  # Ex 48 Wrong.py
2  #
3  words = [‘hello’, ‘1999’]
4  myphrase = ‘hello world it is 1999’
5  #
6  if words in myphrase:
7      print(“It’s 1999”)
```

Debugging Steps

The Traceback shows and error on line 6, and says my left operand must be a string instead of a list. In the **Console**, I can use the “type()” function to find the type of “words”.

In [3]: type(words)
Out [**1**]: list

How to Resolve the Issue

On line 6, I add a for loop to iterate over the list “words.” I also change the “if” statement on line 7 to use the iterator “word.” Now the test on line 7 is comparing each individual word in the “words” list.

Good Code

```
1  # Ex 48 Wrong.py
2  #
3  words = [‘hello’, ‘1999’]
4  myphrase = ‘hello world it is 1999’
5  #
6  for word in words:
7      if word in myphrase:
8          print(“It’s 1999”)
```

Reference

These topics from previous chapters are a good reference for this example.

Chapter 3 - In comparison operator
Chapter 3 - Invoke a Function
Chapter 3 - Iterate through Items in a List
Chapter 3 - Data Types
Chapter 4 - Interactive Mode
Chapter 5 - Traceback
Chapter 6 - Check Object Type

7.49 Invalid literal for int() with base 10

Description: This code raises an error when converting a string into an integer.

Intended Outcome

This code converts a string into an integer for an arithmetic operation.

Actual Result

When the program runs, and the **Console** shows:

```
In [2]:  ..Ex_49/Ex_49_Wrong.py", line 4, in <module>
     total = 567 + int(mystr)

ValueError: invalid literal for int() with base 10: '1.25'
```

Incorrect Code

This is the Example 7.49 code before any changes.

```
1   # Ex 49 Wrong.py
2   #
3   mystr = '1.25'
4   total = 567 + int(mystr)
```

Debugging Steps

The Traceback shows and error on line 4 that indicates something is wrong with my **int()** function. I know this expression is valid to convert "4" into the integer four, so something must be wrong with the "value" of the "mystr" variable. In fact, the Traceback showed ValueError.

The int() function is one of the "Built-in Functions" in the Python Standard Library. The online help for int(x) says "x" must be a string that represents an integer literal. While I can't convert the string '1.25' into a whole number int, it is legal to convert a float to an int.

How to Resolve the Issue

Since it is invalid to change "1.25" into an "int," I first change the string into a **float**. As shown below, I updated line 4.

Good Code

```
1   # Ex 49 Correct.py
2   #
3   mystr = '1.25'
4   total = 567 + int(float(mystr))
```

Reference

These topics from previous chapters are a good reference for this example.

Chapter 5 - Traceback
Chapter 6 - Check Object Type
Chapter 6 - Object Value

7.50 Variable Referenced Before Assignment

Description: A variable is referenced before assignment.

Intended Outcome

My function "myfunc()" should increment my "transaction" variable.

Actual Result

When the program runs the **Console** shows an error on line 3.

In [3]: Ex_50_Wrong.py", line 3, in myfunc
transaction += 1

UnboundLocalError: local variable 'transaction' referenced before assignment

Incorrect Code

This is the Example 7.50 code before any changes.

```
1   def myfunc():
2       transaction += 1
3       print(transaction)
4   #
5   #
6   myfunc()
```

Debugging Steps

The Traceback shows and error on line 3. The variable "transaction" is inside the myfunc() definition, which is why the error is an "UnboundLocalError." If this expression was contained in the main program instead of a function definition, the error would be a "NameError" that the variable "transaction" was not defined.

How to Resolve the Issue

The error message says I used "transaction" on line 3 before it was assigned a value, so I insert an assignment statement on line 2.

Good Code

```
1   def myfunc():
2       transaction = 0
3       transaction += 1
4       print(transaction)
5   #
6   #
7   myfunc()
```

Reference

These topics from previous chapters are a good reference for this example.

Chapter 3 - Scope and Namespace
Chapter 3 - Assignment
Chapter 5 - Traceback

7.51 Plot: Shape Mismatch

Description: While creating a bar chart a ValueError is raised.

Intended Outcome

This code draws a bar chart.

Actual Result

When the program runs, the **Console** shows:

```
In [2]: ValueError: shape mismatch: objects cannot be broadcast to a single shape
```

Incorrect Code

This is the Example 7.51 code before any changes.

```
1  import matplotlib.pyplot as plot
2  import statistics
3  #
4  #
5  myL = [1.41, 2.3, 1.99, 1.2]
6  total = str(len(myL))
7  bins = [0, 1, 2, 3, 4]  # change to whole numbers
8  avg = str(round(statistics.mean(myL), 2))
9  xlbl = total + ‘Purchases, Avg: $’ + avg
10 xl = [‘Item1’, ‘item2’, ‘item3’, ‘item4’]
11 fig, ax = plot.subplots()
12 ax.bar(bins, myL, width=.3, color=‘b’)
13 plot.xticks(bins, xl, color=‘cornflowerblue’)
14 plot.yticks(color=‘g’)
15 plot.ylabel(‘cost’, color=‘g’)
16 plot.xlabel(xlbl, color=‘g’, style=‘italic’)
17 ax.set_title(‘Avg Cost Per Purchase’, color=‘r’,
18              fontweight=‘bold’, fontsize=12)
19 ax.spines[‘top’].set_color(‘y’)
20 ax.spines[‘bottom’].set_color(‘y’)
21 ax.spines[‘left’].set_color(‘y”)
22 ax.spines[‘right’].set_color(‘y’)
23 fig.subplots_adjust(top=1.1)  # add space at top
24 #
25 plot.text(3.6, 1.8, ‘2020’, bbox={‘alpha’: 0.1})
26 plot.show()
```

Debugging Steps

The Traceback shows and error on line 12, which is the function call **bar()**.

The error is not immediately obvious. I can search the internet for the exact error message, or I can look at the arguments to see if they are reasonable for this function. I experiment with only one element in both lists, and realize Matplotlib requires the x and y iterators have the *same number of elements*. Line 12 uses the "bins" and "myL" lists created on lines 5 and 7, which do not have the same number of elements.

How to Resolve the Issue

On line 7, I change my "bins" list.

Good Code

```
1   import matplotlib.pyplot as plot
2   import statistics
3   #
4   #
5   myL = [1.41, 2.3, 1.99, 1.2]
6   total = str(len(myL))
7   bins = [1, 2, 3, 4]  # change to whole numbers
8   avg = str(round(statistics.mean(myL), 2))
9   xlbl = total + ‘Purchases, Avg: $’ + avg
10  xl = [‘Item1’, ‘item2’, ‘item3’, ‘item4’]
11  fig, ax = plot.subplots()
12  ax.bar(bins, myL, width=.3, color=‘b’)
13  plot.xticks(bins, xl, color=‘cornflowerblue’)
14  plot.yticks(color=‘g’)
15  plot.ylabel(‘cost’, color=‘g’)
16  plot.xlabel(xlbl, color=‘g’, style=‘italic’)
17  ax.set_title(‘Avg Cost Per Purchase’, color=‘r’,
18               fontweight=‘bold’, fontsize=12)
19  ax.spines[‘top’].set_color(‘y’)
20  ax.spines[‘bottom’].set_color(‘y’)
21  ax.spines[‘left’].set_color(‘y”)
22  ax.spines[‘right’].set_color(‘y’)
23  fig.subplots_adjust(top=1.1)  # add space at top
24  #
25  plot.text(3.6, 1.8, ‘2020’, bbox={‘alpha’: 0.1})
26  plot.show()
```

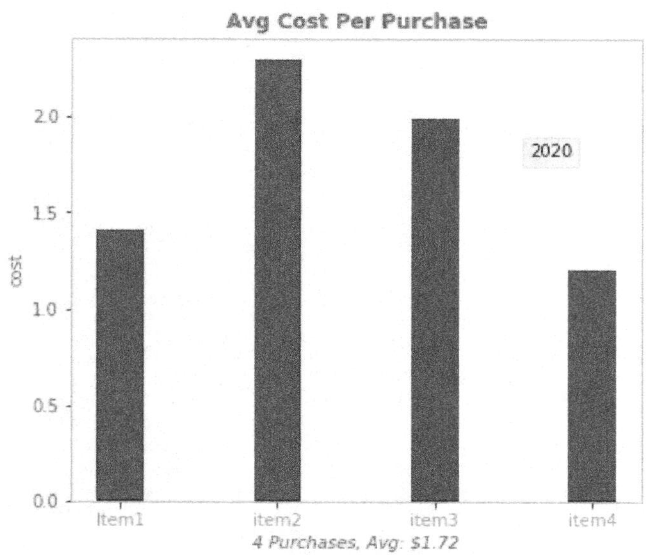

Reference

These topics from previous chapters are a good reference for this example.

Chapter 5 - Traceback

7.52 Unpacking Operator

Description: In a function call, I leave off the * unpacking operator and an IndexError is raised.

Intended Outcome

This code prints tickets for each name from the "name" tuple.

Actual Result

When the program runs, the **Console** shows an error from line 4.

```
In [2]:  .. line 4, in print_tickets
    print(name[i])
```

IndexError: tuple index out of range

Incorrect Code

This is the Example 7.52 code before any changes.

```
1 def print_tickets(number_of_tickets, *name):
2     i = 0
3         while i < number_of_tickets:
4         print(name[i])
5         i += 1
6             #
7             #
8 names = ('John', 'Alice')
9 print_tickets(2, names)
```

Debugging Steps

The Traceback shows and index error on line 4, indicating the tuple indexing I'm using is wrong. Because the program has ended, I need to enter "debug mode" to see the value of the "names" object.

1. In the **Console**, type **%debug** to start "debug mode."

```
In [2]: %debug
      2  i = 0
      3    while i < number_of_tickets:
----> 4  print(name[i])
      5  i += 1
      6
ipdb>
```

2. The **Console** displays an arrow next to line 4, and the prompt changes to ipdb>. In the **Console**, type "names."

```
ipdb> names
```

The Python Interpreter returns a tuple.

```
('John', 'Alice')
```

How to Resolve the Issue

I realize I left the * **unpacking operator** off my function call on line 9.

Good Code

On line 9 I add the unpacking operator *.

```
1  def print_tickets(number_of_tickets, *name):
2      i = 0
3          while i < number_of_tickets:
4          print(name[i])
5          i += 1
6              #
7              #
8  names = ('John', 'Alice')
9  print_tickets(2, *names)
```

Reference

These topics from previous chapters are a good reference for this example.

Chapter 3 - Unpacking Operators
Chapter 3 - Iterate through items in a tuple
Chapter 4 - Debug Mode
Chapter 4 - Interactive Mode
Chapter 5 - Traceback
Chapter 6 - Check Object Type
Chapter 6 - Object Value

7.53 Unpack Non-iterable Bool

Description: In a function call, there are two different types of return statements, causing a TypeError.

Intended Outcome

The code assigns values to variables "i" and "j."

Actual Result

When the program runs, the **Console** shows an error from line 10.

```
In [2]:  ...File "/...Ex53_Wrong.py", line 10, in <module>
    j, k = myfunction(-1)
```

TypeError: cannot unpack non-iterable bool object

Incorrect Code

This is the Example 7.53 code before any changes.

```
1   def myfunction(i):
2       if i > 0:
3           return i, ‘some text’
4       else:
5           return False
6   #
7   #
8   j = 0
9   k = ‘’
10  j, k = myfunction(-1)
```

Debugging Steps

The Traceback shows a TypeError on line 10, pointing to a bool object which is a True or False value. Line 10 assigns the function return values to "j" and "k". When the function returns the "False" bool on line 5 it causes an error.

How to Resolve the Issue

I update the return statement on line 5.

Good Code

On line 5 I update the return statement.

```
1   def myfunction(i):
2       if i > 0:
3           return i, ‘some text’
4       else:
5           return i, ‘some text’
6   #
7   #
8   j = 0
9   k = ‘’
10  j, k = myfunction(-1)
```

Reference

These topics from previous chapters are a good reference for this example.

Chapter 3 - Unpacking Operators
Chapter 3 - Boolean

Chapter 3 - Function Return Objects
Chapter 3 - Tuple Return Object
Chapter 5 - Traceback
Chapter 6 - Check Object Type
Chapter 6 - Object Value

Appendix

URLs

Arguments

The Python design and glossary entries for arguments are shown in this section. Also see Calls, Functions, and Parameters.

The design of keyword only arguments is covered in PEP 3102:

https://www.python.org/dev/peps/pep-3102/

The Python glossary entry for arguments:

https://docs.python.org/3/glossary.html#term-argument

Python terminology on arguments and parameters:

https://docs.python.org/3.3/library/inspect.html#inspect.Parameter

The difference between Arguments and Parameters:

https://docs.python.org/3/faq/programming.html#faq-argument-vs-parameter

Assert

The Python reference for assert statements is available on the **docs.ptyhon.org** website.

https://docs.python.org/3/reference/simple_stmts.html#the-assert-statement

Attributes

The Python glossary entry for "attributes" is available on the **docs.ptyhon.org** website.

https://docs.python.org/3/glossary.html#term-attribute

Built-in Functions

The Python reference for built-in functions is available on the **docs.ptyhon.org** website.

https://docs.python.org/3/library/functions.html

Calls

The Python reference documentation explains "calling" functions and methods, and is available on the **docs.ptyhon.org** website.

https://docs.python.org/3/reference/expressions.html#calls

Classes

Information on Python Classes is available on the **docs.ptyhon.org** website.

9.3.2 Instantiation and Attribute References

9.3.3 Instance Objects, Attributes and Methods

9.3.4 Method Objects

9.9 Container Objects, Elements, and Iterators.

https://docs.python.org/2/tutorial/classes.html

Comparisons

The following link is the Python reference on comparisons.

https://docs.python.org/3/reference/expressions.html#comparisons

Containers

The **docs.ptyhon.org** website explains "containers" in the 9.9 section "Container Objects and Iterators." The section 3.1 topic "Objects, values and types" also explains that objects that contain references to other objects are containers. Examples of containers are tuples, lists and dictionaries.

https://docs.python.org/3.8/reference/datamodel.html#index-3

The 3.1 topic "objects, values, and types" explains that "container" objects contain references to other objects. This "Data Model" reference is available on the **docs.ptyhon.org** website.

https://docs.python.org/3/reference/datamodel.html#index-3

doctest

The **docs.ptyhon.org** website has details on using the doctest module to search and validate examples in docstrings.

https://docs.python.org/3/library/doctest.html?highlight=doctest

Interactive Python examples are also available. These examples include reading in a text file

Functions

The Python reference documentation explains "functions," and is available on the **docs.ptyhon.org** website.

Built-in Functions in the Python Standard Library.

https://docs.python.org/3/reference/compound_stmts.html#function

The Python tutorial for "Defining Functions" is available on the **docs.ptyhon.org** website.

https://docs.python.org/3/tutorial/controlflow.html#defining-functions

https://docs.python.org/3/reference/compound_stmts.html#function-definitions

The difference between function parameters and arguments is explained in the FAQs available on the **docs.ptyhon.org** website.

https://docs.python.org/3/faq/programming.html#faq-argument-vs-parameter

The Python glossary entry for "functions" is available on the **docs.ptyhon.org** website.

https://docs.python.org/3/glossary.html#term-function

Glossary

The official Python glossary is available on the **docs.ptyhon.org** website

https://docs.python.org/3/glossary.html

The if Statement

Information on the **if statement** is available on the **docs.ptyhon.org** website

https://docs.python.org/3/reference/compound_stmts.html#the-if-statement

Immutable

The Python glossary explains the concept of "immutable" objects, and is available on the **docs.ptyhon.org** website.

https://docs.python.org/3/glossary.html#term-immutable

Inspect

The Python reference for the "inspect" library is available on the **docs.ptyhon.org** website.

https://docs.python.org/3/library/inspect.html

Interactive Mode

Interactive Mode in the **Console** is explained on the ipython.readthedocs website.

https://ipython.readthedocs.io/en/stable/interactive/reference.html.

Iterable and Iterations

The Python glossary explains the "iterable" concept, and is available on the **docs.ptyhon.org** website.

https://docs.python.org/3/glossary.html#term-iterable

The **docs.ptyhon.org** website explains Classes in the 9.9 section "Container Objects and Iterators."

https://docs.python.org/2/tutorial/classes.html

Logging

The Python docs for the "logging library" are available on the **docs.ptyhon.org** website.

https://docs.python.org/3/library/logging.html#logging.basicConfig

https://docs.python.org/3.8/howto/logging.html

https://docs.python.org/3/library/logging.html

Magic Functions

Functions that begin with the percent symbol are magic functions or magic commands and are sometimes implemented in a iPython kernel. Read more about magic functions at https://ipython.readthedocs.io/en/stable/interactive/reference.html.

Methods

The Python glossary explains "methods," and is available on the **docs.ptyhon.org** website.

https://docs.python.org/3/glossary.html#term-method

Objects

The Python glossary explains "objects," and is available on the **docs.ptyhon.org** website.

https://docs.python.org/3/glossary.html#term-object

Objects like data attributes have value or "state," and objects like methods have "defined behavior."

The 3.1 topic "objects, values, and types" in the "Data Model" reference is available on the **docs.ptyhon.org** website.

https://docs.python.org/3/reference/datamodel.html#index-3

Parameters

The Python glossary explains "parameters," and is available on the **docs.ptyhon.org** website.

https://docs.python.org/3/glossary.html#term-parameter

There is information on arguments and parameters in the "inspect library."

https://docs.python.org/3.3/library/inspect.html#inspect.Parameter

The difference between Arguments and Parameters is explained in the FAQs.

https://docs.python.org/3/faq/programming.html#faq-argument-vs-parameter

The pass Statement

Information on the **pass statement** is available on the **docs.ptyhon.org** website

https://docs.python.org/3/reference/simple_stmts.html#the-pass-statement

The return Statement

Information on the **return statement** is available on the **docs.ptyhon.org** website

https://docs.python.org/3/reference/simple_stmts.html#the-return-statement

State

The Python glossary explains the "state" of data attributes, or objects with value.

https://docs.python.org/3/glossary.html#term-object

Statements

The Python glossary explains "statements," and is available on the **docs.ptyhon.org** website.

https://docs.python.org/3/glossary.html#term-statement

https://docs.python.org/3/reference/simple_stmts.html

timeit

Information on the timeit() function is available on the **docs.ptyhon.org** website

https://docs.python.org/3/library/timeit.html

The try Statement

Information on the **try statement** is available on the **docs.ptyhon.org** website

https://docs.python.org/3/reference/compound_stmts.html#the-try-statement

Types

The Python glossary explains "types," and is available on the **docs.ptyhon.org** website.

https://docs.python.org/3/glossary.html#term-type

The 3.1 topic "objects, values, and types" in the "Data Model" reference is available on the **docs.ptyhon.org** website.

https://docs.python.org/3/reference/datamodel.html#index-3

Values

The 3.1 topic "objects, values, and types" in the "Data Model" reference is available on the **docs.ptyhon.org** website.

https://docs.python.org/3/reference/datamodel.html#index-3

Chapter 7 Examples

Example	Traceback Error
1	N/A
2	list index out of range
3	list index out of range
4	N/A
5	expected an indented block
6	'int' object has no attribute 'upper
7	expected an indented block
8	invalid syntax
9	invalid syntax
10	name <object> is not defined
11	invalid syntax
12	invalid syntax
13	name <object> is not defined

14	No such file or directory: 'file.txt'
15	Custom error message is raised
16	invalid syntax
17	unsupported operand type(s) for /: 'NoneType' and 'int'
18	module 'math' has no attribute 'cube'
19	name 'plt' is not defined
20	'Worksheet Sheet1 does not exist.'
21	invalid literal for int() with base 10:
22	name 'plt' is not defined
23	list.remove(x): x not in list
24	float divison by zero
25	N/A
26	month must be in 1..12
27	N/A'
28	NoneType object has no attribute 'upper'
29	N/A
30	N/A
31	KeyError: 4
32	can only concatenate str (not "int") to str
33	N/A
34	bad operand type for unary +: 'str'
35	StopIteration
36	missing 1 required positional argument:
37	str object is not callable
38	object has no attribute
39	unhashable type: 'list'
40	can't assign to a functional
41	too many values to unpack
42	'tuple' object does not support item assignment
43	'str' object is not callable
44	can only concatenate tuple (not "int") to tuple
45	N/A
46	unhashable type: 'dict'
47	'builtin_function_or_method' object is not subscriptable
48	'in <string>' requires string as left operand, not list
49	invalid literal for int() with base 10:
50	local variable <variable> referenced before assignment
51	shape mismatch: objects cannot be broadcast to a single shape
52	tuple index out of range
53	unpack non-iterable bool

Chapter 7 Errors

Libraries

This is a list of some common Python libraries.

bs4 - beautiful soup for html

calendar

Collections - container datatypes like defaultdict, Counter, and namedtuple()

copy

csv

datetime

inspect

logging

math

matplotlib - plots and charts

numpy

openpyxl

operator

os

pillow - images

re - regular expression matching

smtplib - email

string

time

timeit

urllib

win32com -Microsoft's COM technology for Windows applications like Outlook or File operations

Conclusion

Einstein said, "If you can't explain it simply, you don't understand it well enough." Learning new things is a passion of mine, and I've found the process of organizing notes, creating illustrations, and pondering how to craft clear examples helps me grasp concepts. Then too, it's nice to go back in a year when I've forgotten something and refer to the examples in this book.

Thank you for reading along with me through the interesting topics and less than thrilling subjects. If the result is you have mastered new features, it was worth it! I'd love to hear the cool things you're doing with Python, so please don't hesitate to leave comments in a review.

Index

Symbols

A

B

C

D

E

F

G

H

I

J

K

L

M

N

O

P

Q

R

S